I0225055

IT'S YOUR TIME
TO *Shine* GIRL

IT'S YOUR TIME TO Shine GIRL

Own Your Brilliance, Step into Your Influence, & LEAD Like a Trailblazer

NATALIE JOBITY

It's Your Time to Shine Girl: Own Your Brilliance, Step into Your Influence, & LEAD Like a Trailblazer

Copyright © 2022 by Natalie Jobity
All rights reserved.

Accept as permitted under the United States Copyright Act of 1976, no part of this publication may be reproduced, distributed, transmitted in any form or by any means, including photocopying, recording, or other electronic or mechanical methods, without the prior written permission of the publisher.

All scripture quotations, unless otherwise indicated, are taken from the Holy Bible, New International Version®, NIV®. Copyright © 1973, 1978, 1984, 2011 by Biblica, Inc.™ Used by permission of Zondervan. All rights reserved worldwide, www.zondervan.com. The "NIV" and "New International Version" are trademarks registered in the United States Patent and Trademark office by Biblica, Inc.™

Published by The Unveiled Way, 8926 Baltimore Street, #14, Savage, MD 20763

In the interest of client confidentiality, names and identifying details in client stories, examples, and anecdotes are changed.

Library of Congress Control Number: 2022913393
Paperback ISBN: 9780982929735
eBook/Kindle ISBN: 9780982929742

Printed in the United States by KDP. Published by The Unveiled Way.

For information about special discounts for bulk purchases, please contact itsyourtimetoshinegirl@gmail.com

Copyediting: Carmen Riot Smith
Proofreader: Nadene Seiters
Interior Book Design & Formatting: Booknookbiz
Cover Design: Immaculate Studios
Photographer: Dale Morrissey

*To all the aspiring and seasoned
game-changers, change-makers, waymakers,
disruptors, and trailblazers.*

*Your light is magnificent,
helping many others find
their way out of darkness.*

Keep shining!

Contents

GLOW

"You are the light of the world. A town built on a hill cannot be hidden. Neither do people light a lamp and put it under a bowl. Instead they put it on its stand, and it gives light to everyone in the house. In the same way, let your light shine before others, that they may see your good deeds and glorify your Father in heaven."

~ Matthew 5:14-16

Praise For *It's Your Time to Shine Girl*

"The best, most helpful books grow out of personal experience, and *It's Your Time to Shine Girl* is no exception. Natalie is a great resource for "overcomer stories," and her book which helps women fully own their brilliance is timely, full of practical insights, and a delight. Highly recommended."

~ **Sally Helgesen**, International Best-Selling Author of *How Women Rise,* and Author of *The Female Vision, The Female Advantage*

"You don't have to be the go-to gal for work that downplays your potential. In this essential guide for professional women, Natalie Jobity shows how to unapologetically unleash your unique brilliance, step into the spotlight, and shine brightly."

~ **Jo Miller,** Women's Leadership Speaker and Author of *Woman of Influence: 9 Steps to Build Your Brand, Establish Your Legacy, and Thrive*

"When asked to read, *It's Your Time to Shine Girl,* I confess I intended to quickly power through it. Life is full, right? However, I was so captivated by Natalie's vulnerable personal stories and wise words that I found myself slowing down, letting the principles speak to my own heart. What a gift Natalie's book has been to me and I know will be to women all over the world. The last few years have resulted in many women, heretofore confident women, surprised to discover themselves shrinking from crippling self-doubt, overthinking and perfectionism. (Or is it that they've finally had a chance to take a good look at what a life of striving and hustling has actually been covering up?) If that's you, friend, let Natalie's words be a balm sent from God to your beautiful soul so we can all bask in the glorious and powerful light He wants to shine through you. And especially for those of you who've immersed yourselves for years in the personal transformation, healing and success achievement spaces and think you've heard it all before, let Natalie's fresh approach allow you to re-engage with familiar concepts. And then let it take you even deeper."

~ **Melissa Williams-Pope**, Performer, Author and Dream Fulfillment Strategist for Creative & Enterprising Women

"Your performance does not speak for itself, you do. If are not confident, it matters little if you are competent. In *It's Your Time to Shine Girl*, Natalie Jobity devotes an entire section on how to showcase your brilliance authentically. She offers practical advice with many down-to-earth stories from her work with clients and other research. Natalie demonstrates how women can use their accomplishments, make their value visible and shine their light in the marketplace. I found this book a beautiful, essential, inspirational and insightful read!"

~ **Beatrice Phillips**, Business & Executive Coach, The Alpha Group

"I'm so happy to see a book that is dedicated to the challenges women face in their careers. If you want to grow in your career, entrepreneurship or in your passion, this is the book for you! In one book, *It's Your Time to Shine Girl*, helps women to identify career-limiting behaviors, gain practical tools and techniques for combatting a negative mindset, and develop the confidence to shine in her area of expertise. This is a book I will come back to!"

~ **Patti Timbers**, MBA, RN/BC, Certified Coach/Speaker, Growing with
Timbers, LLC

"What Natalie has done in this book is to use her story to evoke ours. She gives us permission to reflect on what is beneath what we say and have said, and how we feel and have felt. She brilliantly uses the extensive research she's conducted to bring us concepts that are familiar to us, but now seem much more practical and achievable. At a time when self-awareness seems elusive to many women, this book is a pragmatic resource that enables us to see our present and future self (the vision of the self that we always knew we could be)."

~ **Sackeena Gordon-Jones, PhD, MCC**, Chief Coaching Officer, Transformation
Edge Coaching & Consulting, LLC

"Natalie Jobity will make you get back into the arena of your professional life. Packed with incredible insight on what it means to be an empowered woman, *It's Your Time to Shine Girl* is a GPS for becoming a true trailblazer. She cracks the code on living and leading with bold confidence in your career. True leadership requires us to become who we are. This leadership guide is essential, practical, and powerful."

~ **Carmen Riot Smith**, National Endowment of The Arts Big Reads Speaker

"So many women are afraid to use their voices, gifts, and talents, and Natalie shows us how we can own our brilliance so we can serve and lead with brilliance. *It's Your Time to Shine Girl* inspires women in the midst of a season of uncertainty, doubt and chaos to lead with bold confidence."

~ **Eugina Jordan**, Chief Marketing Officer, TelecomInfra Project

"Jobity offers insight into wisdom in this practical yet powerful masterpiece that inspires readers to become who they are called to be. Her writing, grounded in faith, hope, joy, grace, and perseverance unveils her experiences, and that of her clients, offers diverse and authentic moments for the reader's introspection and evokes a call to action. Abounding with tools and resources, keep this book handy for frequent application!"

~ **Coretta Bennett**, business executive, wife, mother + so much more

Author's Note

*I*T'S THURSDAY, AND I'm hustling to stay on schedule when my phone rings. As I see the name, I'm surprised. It's a client I worked with ten years ago when I was an image consultant.

The last time I worked with Mallory, I helped her dress for a high-end retreat and photoshoot as her personal stylist. It was an incredible styling experience, we worked well together, and I also played the role of communication strategist with her videographer as Mallory recorded the mission video for her new website. We thought about collaborating as a team after that and kept in touch for a couple of years, but I had fallen off the grid, and she'd had a baby.

"Hi, Mallory. How are you?"

"I'm great," she says in her typical upbeat voice. "I need your help. I'm going to Dubai on Saturday, and I need to figure out my wardrobe."

"Mallory, wow, I don't know if you know this, but I'm not an image consultant anymore. I'm a leadership coach now." My brain is spinning, trying to figure out where to take the conversation.

"I know you're a career coach, but I figured you still did the image work too because it would make sense," she replies.

We talk for about twenty minutes as I consider helping her. Since our schedules didn't jive for the next two days, we end our chat simply wishing each other good luck.

That phone call blew my mind because of the timing. *What is God trying to tell me?*

I had been reflecting for some time on my past career as an image consultant, recognizing that it was not the failure I once thought it was. But I still didn't think it had much relevance to my current work as a leadership coach. But lately, that past career kept resurfacing in unexpected ways, so by the time I got Mallory's call, I was paying attention.

I believe there is no such thing as a coincidence. That call was confirmation that my skills and passion for style, fashion, and image work was still relevant to my work now. I just had to figure out how to integrate it.

A week before Mallory's out-of-the-blue call, I found myself in a brainstorming session in a virtual writer's workshop I attended with hopes of bringing ideas together for my new leadership book for women. I had a rough outline, but I struggled to find a clear path to present my distinct and fresh perspective. As the three-minute session timer went off, the idea to explore fun chapter titles that played with fashion and style struck me.

I started reworking my draft titles and found myself getting more and more excited as new titles flowed out of me. I rushed to grab a copy of my book *Frumpy to Fabulous: Flaunting It*[1] from my bookshelf, scanning the table of contents for ideas. A light clicked on.

This makes sense. I could hardly contain myself as furious fingers typed idea after idea. I had not looked at my table of contents for years. In fact, I had never even reread my book.

The workshop timer had long since buzzed, but I continued to ideate until I had a fully revised set of titles. I knew I had to keep going because I was in that creative flow.

Something important was happening. My book was reshaping before my very eyes. I stared in disbelief at the final draft of my new chapter titles.

If I can make this work, I'm going to have another Amazon best-seller in the making. Who else but me could write a book that speaks to how women can be more effective, confident leaders using fashion and style as an overarching metaphor!

I knew deep down that I was designed to write a book like this. All my work styling, coaching, and motivating hundreds of women to transform their lives by changing the way they looked played right into my work coaching, mentoring, inspiring, and challenging women to be influential, impactful leaders in their arenas.

My work as a leadership coach was still relatively new—but at the same time it wasn't. Many of the issues preventing women from bringing their full brilliance to their image were the same ones hindering their career success. Imposter syndrome, perfectionism, low self-esteem, playing small, and fear of failure don't just show up in one facet of our lives, they show up everywhere!

As I contemplated integrating my careers, it became clear that my work as an image consultant focused primarily on the "outer packaging" of a woman, which, while important, was not as game-changing as her *"inner packaging."*

When a woman gets clear on her calling, regains her confidence, knows her superpowers, leverages her authority, owns her voice, and dares to show up brilliantly in her sphere of influence, she is unstoppable. That work, the work that is much of my focus now, is more in-depth than my prior work, but they're incredibly similar.

I knew that if I could get women to see the parallels in how they show up in their style with how they show up in their career, then my book could more profoundly transform their lives.

Because here's the truth: A lot of us are living our lives like dead women walking. We know we're not who we're meant to be, we know we're missing our mark, we know we are operating on an "I just gotta keep going" frequency. Yet we ignore all the warning signs, the unfulfillment, the deep ache in our souls, and we just keep on moving.

It's the same with our clothes. We're in a fashion rut, washing, wearing, and repeating the same boring cycle of ensembles for every occasion, hoping no one notices when we know, *we know*, we're faking it.

There are so many reasons for this, right? Systemic workplace barriers that have been in place for decades haven't changed much, even with all the talk about gender equality and parity. The good old boys' network is still alive and well. Unconscious bias, sexism, racism, otherism, and the glass ceiling still impede women's success at work. That glass ceiling may have moved up, but it's still there.

There are subtle microaggressions in the workplace too. Men using their physicality to intimidate women and men treating women at work as pawns rather than peers. And let's not forget the broken rung on the corporate ladder which limits women's ability to fill senior management roles because they are promoted to manager at a much lower rate than men. As of November 2021, there were only forty-one women at the helm of Fortune 500 companies, which represents just 8.2 percent.

McKinsey and Company's 2021 "Women in the Workplace" report sheds light on many of the burdens women carry—especially women of color—that cause us to be more dissatisfied and stressed out at work. With the COVID-19 pandemic, our lives were upended and things will never be the same. This is most evident at work, where women are more burned out now than ever before. This quote from the report says it all:

"I felt caught in the middle of everyone's emotional response to the pandemic and in between decision-makers who have very, very different outlooks on how to respond. It was the first time I had to solve problems that so directly impacted people's mental and physical health. It was the hardest working year of my life."[2]

Burnout is impacting many of us, which is why I devoted a chapter of this book to work-life balance.

These challenges are burdensome. And they can make us operate on autopilot in our jobs—the place where we spend most of our waking hours.

When you look through your closet, if you find yourself in frumpy land, chances are you're unhappy in your career life as well. This is where the two seemingly unrelated facets of our lives—work and wardrobe—intersect.

Your wardrobe is a symbol of your career fulfillment. "Flaunting It" applies to your style and your life! When you're Flaunting It, you're not only looking good—you're in your element at work and in your personal life. You're firing on all cylinders. You're in your sweet spot. You're mic-dropping it. Do you feel me?

This book is about your leadership and influence as an impact-minded woman. But I am not going to bog you down with jargon and buzzwords. This book will make leadership, influence, and impact accessible to you wherever you work, because these terms are not just reserved for the C-level executives among us. They apply to us all.

"We are all meant to shine… We were born to make manifest the glory of God within us." These famous words from Marianne Williamson graced the inside of my first book and they're just as relevant here.

You, my friend, are uniquely shaped, especially designed, and earmarked to play a specific role with your talents, achievements, gifts, and strengths—your TAGS, as my colleague Nadine Mullings refers to them. Your expertise qualifies you to shine in a lane reserved for you. It's not just some women who are meant to make an impact. It's all of us.

This book is like a fantasy walk-in closet for your career, with many "pegs" to help you unveil your undeniable brilliance, giving you the confidence to step into your fabulousness so you can make your mark in your sphere of influence, blazing your trail down your unique runway.

By the end of this book, you'll be shining all right. But you won't just be looking amazing on the outside. No, you'll be shining from the inside out, knowing what you're meant to do, in the lane meant for you, and unapologetically leading in your arena. You'll be Flaunting It in your career, girl.

To your Brilliance!
Natalie Jobity

Introduction

"There's power in allowing yourself to be known and heard, in owning your unique story, in using your authentic voice."

~ Michelle Obama

*M*Y FIRST BRUSH WITH leadership and self-advocacy happened in kindergarten. At four years old, I was emotionally abused by the principal of the school, a young nun. She would hide my lunch box from me so that I went hungry all day. Then she would reveal it when my mother came to pick me up.

Imagine a four-year-old trying to explain to her mother why her food was still in her lunch kit when she got home. I was in an impossible position, made worse because my mother did not understand why her child, who had loved the prospect of going to school, now screamed and cried every morning when she got dropped off.

I took matters into my own hands and hatched a plan to run away. I planned my getaway one morning, and as the responsible older sister that I was, I picked up my younger sister from her class, took her hand, and walked the fifteen minutes or so to a family friend's home nearby. The cars on the road, the adults passing by, the threat of punishment—nothing fazed me. My singular focus was escaping the torment and confusion that awaited me at school.

When we got to the house, I happily played in their yard, enjoying the food and love around me until my mother (who somehow got wind of where we were) came to pick us up. My mother struggled to understand what would possess me to run away. But our family friend suspected something was off and offered to have her oldest daughter pick me up right after school every day. This was not the solution

I'd hoped for, but it helped. It meant I would spend less time in angst at school.

This memory and others like it were quite painful at one time. But I've done the inner work needed so I can share this story with you to demonstrate one simple truth: we are each designed with special qualities and abilities that set us apart.

My four-year-old self hatching a plan to run away from kindergarten to intervene for herself in a traumatic, abusive situation says a lot about who I was as a young child and who I was destined to be. Leadership, advocacy, and stepping up to fill obvious gaps are part of my DNA. Even though that experience left me so scarred I learned to step back, hide, play small, and not rock the boat, my innate instincts remained. They just needed the right context, healing, experiences, and self-love to reemerge.

This story was the rocky start of my leadership journey, one that has ebbed and flowed and ebbed and flowed again.

Consider your leadership origin story. When did you have that inkling, that sense you were meant for more? When did you first notice that drive to serve your sphere and make a significant impact? Who were you before? Before anyone told you who to be? What would you be doing differently if the things that keep you playing small never happened?

Defining Leadership

Last year I gave a talk at a career symposium. One of the first questions I posed to the women in attendance was what came to their minds when they thought of the word "leader." I was pleasantly surprised when they shared descriptors such as service, empathy, strength, compassionate stewardship, and fortitude because so often women can get hung up on the word itself, thinking it has nothing to do with them. Many women think leadership means they need a specific title or a certain number of people reporting to them or they need permission.

The truth is that none of those things matter.

In her book *Dare to Lead*, author and researcher Brené Brown defines a leader as "anyone who takes the responsibility for finding the potential in people and processes, and who has the courage to develop that potential."[1] So yes, the ladies were on point because leadership demands courage, empathy, insight, and vision.

Increasingly, we hear how important it is for leaders to have "soft skills"—traits like empathy, patience, effective communication, trust, and authenticity. Leadership is no longer merely about our expertise but about our ability to garner trust, respect, and commitment from those we lead. At the end of the day, leadership is about people, so having people skills is foundational to leadership effectiveness.

Those who excel in these areas, while also equipped with the needed expertise for the role, have a better potential to be leaders than qualified high performers with minimal people skills.

As equipped as women may be, we still must fight to get a seat at the table, despite movements, marches, and missions accomplished to get there. There is still a real equity gap in the workplace. Yet women have broken glass ceilings and leaped up ladder rungs, especially in the past few years. Somehow, we rise, despite the many obstacles to our success.

One challenge I've noticed from my own experience and work with clients is when a woman *knows* she's a leader, but no one else seems to notice. She becomes an invisible or unseen leader. This looks like a woman doing the leadership work without the title, pay, or influence. This was my story before I advocated for myself and was promoted to Vice President of Research (more on that story later). Without what I call a Success Squad (your team of championers), it is difficult to move up the ladder and claim our role. It's difficult for us to single-handedly change others' perceptions of our capabilities.

Another challenge is that many women's leadership strengths are hidden in plain sight. Because of this, it is difficult for them to embrace their brilliance so they can confidently assume the leadership role they're already filling. So many women are more of a leader than they're given credit for.

But those external challenges aside, issues like imposter syndrome, perfectionism, fear of failure, and low confidence still rear their ugly heads among women far more than men, even among women who are arguably at the top of their game.

Often the greatest impediment to a woman being the leader she is designed to be is herself. A woman's limiting fears, beliefs, and insecurities are often holding her back. She is her stumbling block.

We've made tangible outward strides toward equality with men but combating the mindsets that continue to hold us hostage will take time. Many of these mindsets have been ingrained into us from the time we were young girls. We were told what we could and couldn't do, who we could and couldn't be. Women from all walks of life—in organizations, corporations, institutions, ministries, and non-profits—are dealing with many of the same challenges.

This is why I'm so passionate about sharing overcomer stories, so we can be inspired by women who have overcome tremendous odds to lead with impact.

Women like Stacey Abrams, who worked tirelessly behind the scenes for years as a voting rights advocate before finally reaching an impactful leading role in 2021, when she led the campaign to turn Georgia blue and won!

Women like Ngozi Okonjo-Iweala, who in 2021 became the first African and the first woman to lead the World Trade Organization, a 164-member group of nations that oversees trade across the world.

Women like Nancy Pelosi, the nation's first woman to become Speaker of the House not once but twice, who most recently used her master negotiating skills to deliver President Joe Biden major legislative victories on the COVID-19 relief package, followed by the $1 trillion infrastructure bill.

Women like Rosalind Brewer, CEO of Walgreens Boots Alliance. With her track record, she's accustomed to being "the first" but remains determined to ensure she is not the last to lead one of the world's largest companies.

Women like Opal Lee, affectionately named the Grandmother of Juneteenth, who has been nominated for the 2022 Nobel Peace Prize. Opal Lee's story is testimony of the transformational power of our voice to make an impact. And how it's never too late to begin your journey.

At eighty-nine years old, Lee began a walking campaign from her home in Fort Worth, Texas to Washington, DC to draw attention to Juneteenth's importance. It took six years, starting in 2016, but her efforts prevailed. On June 17, 2021, President Joe Biden signed the Juneteenth National Independence Day Act into law.

When she decided to start her walking campaign, she had no idea the impact she would have. Yet here we are today as a nation celebrating this holiday one woman felt called to bring to pass.

We're all meant to shine! No matter what you've faced—the trials, tragedies, and traumas you've been through—like the butterfly, you can emerge free, beautiful, and integrated into the version of yourself that our Creator always intended.

Don't ignore your audacious dreams and aspirational goals. They are the clues to your heart's passions. Yes, we are living in uncertain, volatile times. But this is YOUR time, a time of opportunity and possibility. Each one of us is being called upon to bring our creativity, courage, caring, and confidence to fulfill our purpose.

For any woman reading these words who is waiting for permission, or a perfect scenario, or for more qualifications to be a leader, receive this truth: *You're already enough.*

You're already a leader if:

1. You feel called to lead
2. The work you're doing is tangibly impacting lives
3. You're a trailblazer: the only one in your lane doing what you do
4. You proactively take action that has a direct outcome for many

That's it! We are each created uniquely with distinct life experiences, passions, and talents that when allowed to fully blossom make us brilliant. And that brilliance gives us the power we need to create a meaningful impact, leave our imprint in life, establish a legacy, and make a difference.

Here are just a few types of leadership activities you may be engaging in right now that you may discredit that count as evidence of your leadership:

- Taking the initiative on a project
- Facilitating meetings
- Presenting your ideas to a group
- Rallying others around a common cause
- Taking the responsibility to lead a group of at least one person in an activity
- Partnering with others to accomplish a shared goal

Get the drift? Your leadership potential is there, but it is often buried in what seem to be mundane tasks. Your unique blend of skills, talents, knowledge, and strengths equip and qualify you to add value like no one else can.

There's no special formula, mold, or template that qualifies you to lead—no specific personality type, mix of strengths, enneagram number, marital status, socioeconomic status, age, or geography. You are simply called to lead or not.

Maybe your path to leadership has been unconventional, bumpy, challenging, sudden, or slow. Perhaps you lead in an arena where there is no one who looks like you, where you're the first. It doesn't matter. None of these things disqualify you.

You were born to make an impact in the world and to open the door to fresh, innovative, even disruptive possibilities. You are born to lead, sister!

To get a sense of your particular brand of leadership, hop over and take a quick assessment I created to help you begin to build your leadership brand: https://www.theunveiledway.com/what-is-your-leadership-brand.

Defining Influence

You can't lead without influence. John Maxwell famously said that "leadership IS influence." Influence is about impacting people's thoughts, actions, and decisions. When you're influential, you're shaping someone's life.

Perhaps you work in a corporation, a nonprofit, a government position, in academia, in the public sector, in ministry, or in your own business. Think of your work history and who you've influenced along the way. Because of your presence, mentoring, managing, encouraging, or expertise in your field, who has gained something tangible as a result?

It may surprise you to see that you've already been influential. With the rise of social media, the word "influencer" has come to mean someone with tens of thousands of followers or more, someone who commands attention in people's feeds, someone who can get lots of people to like and agree with what they are putting online. While that definition of influence may be true for social media, in real life, the magnitude of your influence is relative. Maybe you've influenced just one person in your work. That does not make you any less influential.

I want to underscore the importance of owning your lane, your arena, your niche. Your lane is probably not going to look like the next woman's lane. And that's how it should be.

Given the sphere of influence you command, how are you doing? Who cares about what you have to say? Who depends on your feedback? Whose career do you have the authority to shape? If you can come up with at least one person for any of those questions, then you have influence, my friend.

The way you define what leveling up your influence and impact looks like is personal. Your definition of influence can be any of the following:

- Getting greater recognition
- Owning your own business
- Seeing the many lives touched by your work
- Increasing your income
- Leading a certain number of people
- Getting a particular title
- Having a recognizable name or brand
- Achieving a certain status
- Being wealthy
- Being generous with your wealth
- Being seen as a subject matter expert (SME) or thought leader in your field
- Publishing a book

The list is endless.

Are You Ready to Rise?

You deserve to feel free and confident bringing your full self to work every single day. You need to know that who you are is enough and that you don't need to "add value" to feel worthy of your contributions.

You need to change the narrative, flip the script, turn the station, and tune in to the one that says, "Yes, I can!" You need to believe you deserve a life and career that nurtures, emboldens, energizes, and fulfills you, capitalizing on the very things that you love and are good at doing. Serving and leading the people God has put in your path to lead. Having the courage to follow the call.

What if you truly believed that you are the one you've been waiting for? That your time is now to do that scary thing that's been in your heart for years? That you're meant to step into your influence for such a time as this?

Sometimes we are the biggest barriers to our blessings. Our imposter syndrome, feelings of inadequacy, insecurity, fears—all of these impede our potential.

You, sister, are meant to rise. In your arena, in the way you are specially shaped to impact your sphere. Don't let that gap between where you are now and where you want to be in your career expand any further before you act.

The time is NOW!

Whether you're a high-achiever saddled with imposter syndrome, a senior executive grappling with your leadership brand, a decision-maker playing small for so long you no longer have confidence in your leadership potential, or a trail-blazer who's gotten comfortable playing second fiddle, it's time to step up and unveil your brilliance.

This book is organized into three "pegs" (like closet hooks) to help you hang and unveil your inner brilliance as a leader, influencer, and trailblazer and shine like the star you are.

Each chapter discusses a topic I've found foundational to address for women who desire to have impactful leadership in their arena. And I've weaved in image and style tips and stories so you can bring your cute game to the table too.

The first peg, "Know," helps you understand your purpose and unique design and emboldens you to cultivate your confidence authentically so you can stand on solid ground. A huge part of this stage is learning how to silence the imposter in your mind and discarding the self-limiting mindsets that have held you back in the past. The chapters in Know will give you clarity and self-awareness and help you understand the strengths and shortcomings you bring into your arena. There is a lot in this section that, if integrated, will help you grow tremendously. Take your time as you read as this section sets the foundation for the rest of the book.

The second peg, "Show," is all about stepping out of the shadows into the spotlight so we can all witness your magnificence. This section stretches you out of your comfort zones and defaults so you feel equipped and qualified to walk your secret sauce right down the runway, making your superpowers visible, vouched for, and valued.

In the final peg, "Glow," I encourage you to press pause so you can discern the best ways to thrive as a leader, leveraging all the brilliance you have to offer. This empowering section arms you with thoughts, takeaways, and tools to get the support and self-care you will need to endure in your journey as a woman of influence, whose *glow* will be sustained. This section ends as a rallying cry for you to PLAY BIG because it's YOUR time to shine. By this section, you will have everything you need to make your mark and shoot your shot—to Glow unapologetically!

Throughout this book, I share many stories about my life—my unveiling journey. My rocky start from a child into an awkwardly tall, self-conscious teen who wanted to be invisible. My struggle as a young woman crippled with performing, pleasing, perfecting, and playing small so she could be accepted. My reckoning as a woman navigating life and Corporate America who slowly began to unveil the star she always was. And my emergence as a more seasoned, mature woman, a leader who champions and empowers other leaders.

I share these anecdotes, so you know that I've also stumbled, fallen, gotten back up, and stumbled all over again to become the much more confident, self-assured woman I am today, one who understands the challenges so many women face all too well.

In these pages, you'll read stories of other women too. Women in the public eye and women who I've worked with whose stories will inspire and motivate you.

I wrote *Frumpy to Fabulous: Flaunting It* over a decade ago to help women show up as the best version of themselves, empowering them to Flaunt It, and arming them with the tools and techniques to do just that.[2]

My goals in this book are similar—to empower you to lead in your arena with authenticity and confidence in your brilliance.

My hope is that this book encourages, champions, educates, and motivates you, dear reader, to unveil your unique brand of brilliance so you can serve your sphere exceptionally.

If you're tired of the status quo, fed up with dimming your light to make others comfortable, frustrated with working below your pay grade, or at the end of your rope because you're ready to break free from the box that has contained your amazingness for so long, now is your time to let all that go.

Now is your time to step up, speak out, stand up, and show up for the world to see your brilliant magnificence in its full glory, red carpet style.

It's your time, girl! Soar to the heights you've dreamed of, blaze your singular trail, play bigger, serve your sphere with your superpowers, and make your mark.

Are you ready to shine like the brilliant star you are? Let's get going!

KNOW

"The most fundamental aggression to ourselves, the most fundamental harm we can do to ourselves, is to remain ignorant by not having the courage and the respect to look at ourselves honestly and gently."

~ Pema Chödrön

Chapter 1

From Frumpy to Fabulous:
Get Clarity for Your Calling

"We need to understand that there is no formula for how women should lead their lives. That is why we must respect the choices that each woman makes for herself and her family. Every woman deserves the chance to realize her God-given potential."

~ Hillary Clinton

IN MY WORK AS AN image consultant, I encountered many women who admitted they were on the frumpy spectrum. This is why they needed help! Many of these women wanted to look and feel better about themselves, but they just didn't know how or where to start.

One of my popular offerings was an image consultation session. I'd spend around five hours with a woman, helping her understand how to dress in ways that flattered her body in styles that aligned with her preferences. This was a very customized, personalized session that was all about what the woman wanted and desired image-wise.

I'd start the session by pouring over her images of celebrity and model photos that showed how she desired to look, then photos of how she currently dressed, and finally clothing she would never be caught wearing. I wanted to get a very clear sense of her personal style. I would ask questions to dig deeper about why she liked or disliked a particular look. Was it the silhouette, the colors, the pattern, the way the outfit was pulled together, or the fit? Based on her responses, I would get a sense of where she aspired to be style-wise and we'd agree on a path to get her there.

Going from frumpy to fabulous is a journey of exploration, reinvention, and gaining clarity about your image aspirations. If you feel like you're in frumpy land, consider the last time you felt fabulous. What was different and why do you think you changed?

For a woman to go from frumpy to (her) fabulous, she had to get truly clear on what she liked in the first place. Her tastes, preferences, and leanings mattered. As her image consultant, I had my own tastes and style. But I would make it clear in that first session that my tastes had nothing to do with my client's proclivities. The two hours or so we spent dissecting her style were ALL about her desires.

When women come to me in a career transition, getting clarity around their career goals is a logical place to start. Raise your hand if you've been in the same field for a few years and have stumbled from role to role with no clear strategy about how you're going to get from where you are to where you want to be.

Many women struggle with this issue. Our careers can take on a life of their own, and the next thing we know, a decade has passed and we wonder how on earth we got stuck in the role we have. Unfortunately, without clarity and a strategy, this is the result.

Clarity gives you the vision for the result you want, and strategy gives you the roadmap to get there.

One of the important points I made at the outset for *Frumpy to Fabulous: Flaunting It* was the importance of intention.[1] Without intention, all our thoughts and ideas are just that—stuff rolling around in our minds with no anchor. For women to achieve their image goals, dressing with intention mattered. My tagline, "Presence with a Purpose," underscored the intentionality necessary for our image to support our purpose.

We each have varied image goals—conveying a professional image at work, attracting a mate, securing a more visible role, looking more confident, projecting a sexy vibe, conveying authority, and so on. But once we are clear on our goals, we can get to work making it a reality.

As the Brilliance Unveiler, my work helping women get clarity for their calling is like the mission I had as an image consultant. It's about co-creating a vision for a woman's ideal role based on her strengths, values, and passions. Typically, where your strengths, passions, and values intersect is your sweet spot, the cue to your calling, or as I like to put it, the arena where your brilliance can shine. It's the space where you bring your best to your role, whether you're in a corporate environment; a nonprofit; your own business, endeavor, or movement; or a ministry setting.

Having the clarity to understand your brilliance is game-changing. When you operate from this space, you're unstoppable. Your brilliance is what I refer to as your "Woo." It's your "wow" factor, your secret sauce, your unique value proposition, your superpower, and your distinct excellence. When you're working from your brilliance, your contribution is powerful and unique, and you become known as a standout contributor. When you are working from your brilliance, you raise the bar for everyone around you. In your brilliance, you blaze trails, and your influence has a legacy-making impact. It's your Woo that you use to fulfill your calling.

I define "calling" as the thing that God uniquely wired and shaped us to be and to do in this world. It's leveraging our individual talents, strengths, and passions to serve the world. Calling is very close to purpose, and I use these words interchangeably.

Your calling often shows up as a desire to create, build, inspire, lead, mobilize, or make an impact. It is extremely specific to how you are shaped and designed, the experiences you've had, the skills you've acquired, and the types of things that light you up. Your calling is your God-ordained purpose. In his book *The Call*, author Os Guinness sums up calling like this, "There is no calling without a caller."[2] You are *called* to your calling, which is what makes it so powerful.

When you are walking in your calling, it will challenge you, inspire you, humble you, and ultimately free you. When you determine your God-given calling, your life starts to make more sense. Working in your calling, you feel satisfaction and contentment that is beyond understanding, and you are well on the path to leaving a transformational legacy.

You don't just want to have a career. You want to pursue a calling. In a career you are typically focused on yourself, but in your calling, you are in service to others. In your calling, you are operating from the highest, finest vision of yourself, and therefore you shine in it. It is that thing you must do, which is why it is a calling. It calls *you!*

I've seen women break into quiet tears when they consider the cost of not walking in their calling and purpose. Not just the cost to themselves but the even greater cost to the people they're meant to impact. This is deep, important stuff that we just can't dismiss as wishful thinking or fantasy.

Your calling is your why, the reason you exist, your purpose. When you gain clarity about your specific calling, everything changes. When you're clear about your calling and the way your strengths can be stewarded to fulfill that purpose, the power in your voice becomes undeniable. This is because you're standing on the foundation of your truth and what you're called to do. Your voice then resonates with the people, sphere, or audience you're meant to influence because you are speaking from your innate brilliance and your specific purpose.

If your calling is fuzzy, misdirected, or lacking focus, then you won't be able to have that bull's-eye vision about your impact. Clarity of calling is the foundation for your impact in the marketplace. And that's powerful!

Let's explore how to get clarity for your calling. I've developed what I refer to as the three "backbone" pieces for your calling wardrobe—pillars that are foundational to finding your calling. Just like your wardrobe must have backbone pieces to come together, so does your calling. Consider these backbone pieces the foundation from which your calling wardrobe is built upon.

Three Backbone Pieces of Calling: Passions, Strengths, & Values

Passions

When I became aware of image consulting as a field, it was like I had finally found *my* calling. I just knew I could ace this. Shoot, I had spent most of my life prepping for it. Learning to dress my six-foot frame was an art and a science, and I had cracked the code. I didn't just know how to dress my body; I knew how to help other people dress theirs. I had shopped for my family in the US, bringing suitcases of clothes back to the Caribbean, and understood how to flatter figure types different from mine and how to bring out the best in each person. It was so natural for me that I didn't think much of it. Until I learned I could make money from it.

This would be my dream job. I loved clothes, accessories, looking good, shopping, and empowering others, especially women, and I knew every fashion trick and tip from decades of reading beauty magazines. I had this! I jumped in headfirst, learning everything I could about becoming an image consultant. After tons of research and training to be an image consultant, my business Elan Image Management was born. To everyone's surprise but mine, I left my lucrative marketing research career to build a business in a little-known niche industry known as image consulting.

Elan Image Management was the culmination of everything I had endured in my life with my own self-image, self-advocacy, and the role fashion and beauty played in giving me confidence. I became enthusiastic about helping other women find their true beauty, working with their attributes. After all, I learned how to dress my gangly frame at a young age. I learned how to use makeup to bring out my best features. I had spent decades of my adult life pouring over fashion magazines, and I knew every trick in the book to camouflage, highlight, and accentuate. This career must have been made for me!

What gave me the gall, you may wonder, as an immigrant Black woman to think I could do this and be successful? Especially given that I had no cushion after buying my home a few years earlier, no support or mentor showing me the way, and few folks cheering me on from the sidelines. Folks around me were either shocked or silent. Whether it was because I had become used to charting my own course, advocating for myself, or was just darn full of myself, I pursued this dream like it was the calling on my life I believed it was. I was truly on my own, but for some reason that made me want to pursue my passion even more.

My brand, The Image Diva, slowly caught on. Even though the country was in the Great Recession, I had clients signing up for my services in droves. I was riding high, writing, speaking, conducting workshops, giving seminars, and doing TV interviews. I was pouring into my clients—women who, like me, had lost their shine, or never knew they had the power to look and feel great or command the attention of their choosing. I felt it was my life's work to empower and liberate women from the mindsets and lack of knowledge that kept them in an image rut.

It was exciting, validating, and empowering work. I had found my voice and my power, and it felt amazing! My clients saw me as their guide, their champion, and their empowerer. I believed in my message that our image conveys who we are and how others perceive us. My tagline, "Presence with a Purpose," supported the notion that we should dress with intention. That our image speaks for us before we say a word. And in an environment where women were starting to believe in their power but were still objectified, we could take control of our image and others' perceptions of us. I didn't just talk the talk, I walked it. I showed up to every event, seminar, speaking engagement, and TV interview as The Image Diva.

Those first few years were expansive and exhilarating. I worked individually with hundreds of women in just a few years and created a vast amount of content. In 2010, I took things up another notch by penning and self-publishing my book, *Frumpy to Fabulous: Flaunting It. Your Ultimate Guide to Effortless Style.*[3] Even though I did this all with my own might and self-reliance, the Lord chose to bless me anyway and the book quickly became an Amazon best-seller, topping the Fashion & Beauty and Self-Esteem charts for weeks. With sales worldwide, women knew my name all over the world. I seemed to have finally found the secret to success, certainly by the world's standards.

I share this story to demonstrate the momentum-inducing power of passion! Passion is the first backbone piece I use when helping women get clarity for their calling.

Your passions are part of the way God uniquely designed, shaped, and wired you. Your passions are those things that give you energy, light you up, or motivate you to keep going. Your passions are usually things you care deeply about. They are the things that make you get out of bed early in the morning on a cold, rainy day.

Passion lives in your heart. It's what you love, and it matters. Understanding your passion starts with giving yourself the grace and space to know who you are, what you want, and what ignites you.

Do you feel pumped up and motivated to get the ball rolling each day? Are you making the impact you want? Do you believe you're operating in the arena best suited to your skills and talents? If you answer no to these questions, it may be time to do a bit of exploration around your passions.

Doing the type of work that makes you feel excited is an integral aspect of operating in your brilliance. When you can draw from your passions, you feel energized. This energy gives you the bandwidth to do what it takes to be successful.

Debunk the myth that you can't enjoy your work *and* make good money doing so. You don't have to sacrifice fulfilling, satisfying work to command a strong salary. You can. But first, you have to understand what fulfills and stirs your heart.

Your passions give you the momentum you need when things get tough, as they surely will. Your passion fuels your energy and drives you to pursue your calling. Howard Thurman, civil rights activist, philosopher, and author put it this way, "Don't ask what the world needs. Ask what makes you come alive and do it. Because what the world needs is people who have come alive."

When you are fully engaged with your passion, you're not obsessing about what you can't do, what you don't have, or what you're afraid of because you are so excited about the possibility of what you can accomplish. Author Amy McLaren articulates how passion motivates us to abandon our fears: "We become so connected to what we love that we might momentarily leave behind things like fear, self-doubt, perfectionism, and all that other stuff that would normally get in our way."[4]

To get crystal clear clarity on your passion, please set aside time to respond to the questions below. Feel free to jot your answers down in a separate notebook, or right here in the spaces below.

Read through the list one time to get a gist of the questions, then go back to thoughtfully respond. Don't feel pressured to answer every question. Just get to a point where you have clarity on what you're passionate about.

1. In what ways do you enjoy helping others?

   _____

   _____

2. What makes you feel fully alive when you're doing it? What activities give you a feeling of being in the sweet spot of life?

   _____

   _____

3. What do you spend time reading, researching, or learning about the most? What makes you interested in these things?

   _____

   _____

4. What experiences have you had that left you passionately energized? What's common among these experiences?

   _____

   _____

5. If you had a year to live, what would be most important for you to do?

   _____

   _____

6. What are the issues, subjects, principles, or causes that you can talk about for hours and hours?

   _____

   _____

7. What activities are you self-motivated to do?

   _____

   _____

8. What have you done in your life that you'd love to do more of?

_____

_____

9. Do you have a dream of helping others in some way that would cause you deep regret if you never took the risk to go for it?

_____

_____

10. What accomplishments or legacy would have ultimate significance for you?

_____

_____

As you reflect on these questions, know that it is possible to *develop* a passion for something you enjoy doing. You don't have to wait to discover passion. You can dive right in and develop it or grow into it.

It's important to find ways to engage with your passions instead of simply acknowledging them. Often just being curious and following where your curiosity leads you is a great place to start. If your passion isn't immediately obvious to you, you can tap into the wisdom and observations or your inner circle. When and where have your people seen you shine?

Finding passion can be elusive, so you must be intentional about developing passion by dabbling or exploring different things so that passion can find you.

I love how McLaren frames the ripple effect of living in alignment with our passions: "When we lean in and say yes to our lives from a place of passion, we reinforce the very best of who we are. We amplify our strengths and gifts, and we become magnets of possibility. Life starts to flow more effortlessly, and even when there are challenges, we discover resources to handle them."[Ibid]

Passion is the foundation of fulfilling your calling and bringing the best of your brilliance to your purpose.

Strengths

Knowing the power in your strengths is foundational; this is why it's the second backbone piece. By leaning into your strengths, stepping into them, leveraging them, and understanding that those talents combine to create your superpowers, you'll gain clarity about your purpose and calling.

When many seasoned professional women get to a certain point in their careers, they forget the talents, skills, strengths, and capabilities that got them to their current level of success in the first place. Some women may have never even recognized their gifts and superpowers and how they could use them to make the desired impact in their arena. They go through their careers stumbling into new roles, shapeshifting themselves, and struggling all the while to claim their unique brilliance.

If you don't know the key to your brilliance, then you won't be able to value, leverage, or honor it. You won't be able to see yourself as special, unique, brilliant, gifted, talented, or accomplished unless you claim your strengths.

There are a few reasons women fail to recognize their strengths or to grasp the power in their unique abilities.

The first tricky thing about strengths is that they come so easily and effortlessly to you. Because of this, you may take your strengths for granted or fail to recognize them as strengths. You ignore, undervalue, or dismiss them as not a big deal. But in doing so, you end up devaluing your contributions, never capitalizing on the abilities that make you amazing.

Second, when you can't articulate your unique giftedness, you won't get the affirmation you want from your peers and bosses. When you fail to honor your gifts, those around you will have a tough time honoring them as well, which ends up making your strengths hidden and invisible.

Third, the perfectionists among us (we'll be tackling that topic later) may try to be great at things that are outside their natural, God-given strengths. Trying to cultivate attributes that are outside your "sweet spot" is an uphill battle that often leads to frustration, burnout, or bitterness. However, drawing from your strengths allows you to operate from a space where things flow naturally, and success is more effortless.

You can only live in your brilliance when you work from your strengths. Until you can clearly see your strengths by examining your career trajectory and highlighting the skills, talents, perspectives, and expertise you own, it will be difficult for you to have confidence in yourself as a leader and a trailblazer.

To start to examine your natural talents and strengths, it may be helpful to do a comprehensive inventory of your career to date. As you do this examination, it is helpful to answer a few salient questions. Depending on your level of self-awareness, you may struggle with some of the questions. That's OK! Just keep reflecting and pondering your life and career for insights into your innate strengths. You may also want to get the help of a trusted friend, family member, or coworker for their perspectives. Don't rush through your answers. You want to take your time here.

Again feel free to jot your thoughts down below.

1. What lights you up? What do you love learning about?

   _____

   _____

2. What is effortless for you? What seems to come naturally to you?

   _____

   _____

3. What activities make you feel like you're in "the zone" where ideas, inspiration, and creativity just flow?

   _____

   _____

4. What do you want to do more of? Less of? Why?

   _____

   _____

5. What skills, strengths, or gifts have those who know you well complimented you about or asked for your help with?

   _____

   _____

6. What special awards or recognition have you received in your professional career?

_____

_____

7. What kinds of roles or responsibilities do you enjoy and feel good at?

_____

_____

8. Which types of roles or activities do you know are *not* a good fit for you?

_____

_____

In his workbook, *Your Oxygen Mask on First*, author and coach Kevin Lawrence lays out a helpful worksheet for this examination, with a focus on successes.[5] He believes when we're in our sweet spot, we leave behind clues. To examine your patterns of success and understand your natural abilities, he recommends looking at your track record across your life by completing what he dubs your Historical Sweet Spots Grid. Get a blank paper and draw three columns labeled Achievement, Natural Ability, and Environment.

In the Achievement column, write your five top achievements in work and life to date. In the Natural Ability column, note for each achievement what natural ability made you succeed. Lastly, in the Environment column, pinpoint the environmental factors that helped you succeed. These factors can be things like work situations, whether you worked alone or with a team, if you had the freedom to be creative, etc.

After you've completed the grid, reflect on your responses. On another piece of paper, write in two columns what energizes you and what drains you. These responses indicate when you are operating in an area of strength versus weakness. When I completed this exercise, it was no surprise to discover that I love to create, collaborate, coach, and curate. It didn't hurt that I could come up with an alliteration to synthesize my sweet spots (see what I did there?).

These two exercises will help you identify your key strengths. In addition, a formal assessment I strongly believe in is Gallup's CliftonStrengths Assessment. If you do nothing else, take this assessment. It has been a game-changer for me and my clients. This is one of the most esteemed and extensively researched assessments used by many companies to help them form teams, set up individuals for success, and cultivate leaders.

I will address this topic of strengths in more detail in a later chapter. But for now, use the information you're gathering to get the clarity you need to identify your calling.

Values

The third backbone piece is your values. Your values define the way you live your life. They determine your priorities, your position on issues, and the basis of your principles.

Your values are deeply personal, often spiritual, and can be culturally focused or anchored in the norms of your family of origin. Your values determine what you are willing and not willing to sacrifice, and they drive your behavior in all facets of your life. They define what is most important to you and form the framework you use in decision-making. They are the driving force behind what you do and what you are passionate about.

Honoring your values helps you live a more fulfilling life by engendering healthy self-esteem, reflecting the highest principles of your mind, and mirroring your core spiritual beliefs. When you act in opposition to your core values, however, you often feel frustrated, depressed, dissatisfied, resentful, and out of alignment with yourself. In fact, it is impossible to be fulfilled and know true joy if you are not honoring your values. This is because they are your compass, your true north.

The importance of our values is so underrated. We all make important decisions using principles and criteria that matter to us, but often we do this unconsciously, unaware of the key tenets that guide us or how they shape our behavior.

Becoming aware of your values is an important aspect of determining your sweet spot because when you live and operate in alignment with your values, you're going to be positioned to thrive.

Elvis Presley (yes, that one) explains it this way, "Values are like fingerprints. Nobody's are the same, but you leave them all over everything you do." It's so true. But I would also add that they're like invisible fingerprints, which is why we're so prone to be blind to their role in our lives.

Knowing your values helps you understand what to say yes to and what to turn down because they are like guardrails, helping you navigate challenging decisions or circumstances. When you make decisions aware of how your values play into them, you're going to be at peace. You also won't feel guilty about your decision because you'll understand why you chose what you did.

As a leader, your values may include things like excellence, authenticity, achievement, making a difference, or innovation. These values represent what is most important to you and guide your actions. When realized, your values provide you with a sense of purpose and fulfillment. Your core values directly impact how you perceive and relate to your role and impact your ability to make sound, guilt-free decisions. As your North Star, your values guide, direct, and affirm your choices.

Observing the outpouring of condolences after the late Justice Ruth Bader Ginsburg passed in September 2020, it was obvious that this unstoppable woman lived a life true to her core values. In the obituaries, words like "advocate for equity," "feminist icon," "indomitable," "purposeful," and "trailblazer" came up repeatedly.

When Justice Ginsburg spoke of virtues like equality and equity, her words did not ring hollow. This is true for our values—they cannot ring hollow. Our values are the anchor and guide that keep us girded with our beliefs and principles. They set the tone of our life.

RBG's commitment to gender equality showed up in the legacy she left behind. She dismantled sexist legal structures by speaking truth to power. RBG understood that some principles transcend politics, that some values transcend party, and she fought for those principles and values. Her life demonstrates that living aligned with our values is a life lived on purpose, where legacy-making is created.

First, our values inspire us to hold a greater, grander vision of ourselves and our role in the world, often leading to game-changing priorities that have enduring impact. RBG's impact was clear after her passing. Reacting to the news of her death, celebrity Felicity Jones tweeted, "Ruth Bader Ginsburg gave us hope, a public figure who stood for integrity and justice—a responsibility she did not wear lightly. She will be missed not only as a beacon of light in these difficult times but for her razor-sharp wit and extraordinary humanity." Reese Witherspoon tweeted, "May your legacy be our motivation to be actively in pursuit of true justice for all."

Staying true to her values is what allowed Justice Bader Ginsburg to craft her legendary dissents shaping the future legal landscape, challenging the status quo, and fighting for what she believed in her heart to be right—an advocate for others. As Justice, she understood that enduring change happens one step at a time. The cases that she won have served for decades as the foundation for the legal analysis of sex-based discrimination and the continued fight for equality under the law. She paved the way for women and helped lay the groundwork for the legal recognition of other minority gender-based groups. "With an incomparable and indelible legacy, Ruth Bader Ginsburg will forever be known as a woman of brilliance, a Justice of courage, and a human of deep conviction," Meghan Markle wrote in remembrance of the icon.[6]

Second, our values anchor us in times of trial. They are the source of our indomitable spirit, our courage, our fortitude. Because we are living for ideals greater than our personal wants and desires, we can keep getting up and moving forward. As a young woman, Bader Ginsburg graduated at the top of her class from Columbia Law School, but she couldn't get hired because of her gender. She didn't let it deter her. She channeled her energy into education and became a law professor at Rutgers University while volunteering with the American Civil Liberties Union, taking on cases that challenged gender discrimination.

While she had her share of hardships and obstacles, she never lost sight of her purpose, her "why." This posture does not happen by chance. It is an intentional pursuit of excellence driven by one's values, which allows one to transcend the pain of suffering, hardship, or disappointment with equanimity.

Finally, our values weave through our life's pursuits, goals, and achievements, all of which determine our legacy. This is true of RBG. She was indomitable, persevering when men tried to hold her back. Her staunchly pro-women, pro-immigration, and pro-minority verdicts are legendary. She always strived to overturn civil-rights violations, no matter who they affected. In all her professional pursuits, she fought for people's rights, changing America for the better.

Former President Bill Clinton, who appointed the jurist to the Supreme Court in 1993, tweeted, "her life and landmark opinions moved us closer to a more perfect union." French President Emmanuel Macron tweeted, "Throughout her entire life, Ruth Bader Ginsburg fought for justice, gender equality, and the respect for fundamental rights. Her outstanding legacy shall be our inspiration for a long time to come."

Ruth Bader Ginsburg's life demonstrates that a life lived according to our values is one lived in integrity, authenticity, and courage. Her legacy showcases what happens when a purpose-driven individual fulfills her calling and leaves a larger-than-life, generational impact. Perhaps the quote from Ernest Hemmingway's *For Whom the Bell Tolls* sums up RBG's approach to life: "Today is only one day in all the days that will ever be. But what will happen in all the other days that will ever come can depend on what you do today."[7]

Great icons, including Nelson Mandela, Helen Keller, and Abraham Lincoln, left the world changed by the footprints they left for us to follow. Why? Because their lives were shaped by their values. Their convictions rang true as they sacrificed their comforts and often their privileges for much nobler, higher causes. Their legacies are rich and full and inspire us to be bigger and better than we would be if left to our own devices.

I recently read a story in my daily devotional that I hadn't heard before. Many years ago, Abel Mutai, a Kenyan runner competing in an international cross-country race, was just a few yards from victory. But somehow, confused by the course's signage, he thought he'd already crossed the finish line, so he stopped just short of finishing.

In second place was Spanish runner Iván Fernández Anaya, who saw Mutai's mistake. Instead of taking advantage of Mutai's error and claiming victory, Anaya stayed behind and, using gestures, guided Mutai forward to a gold-medal win.

When reporters asked Anaya why he purposefully lost the race, he insisted that Mutai deserved the win, not him. "I didn't deserve to win it. I did what I had to do. He was the rightful winner. He created a gap that I couldn't have closed if he hadn't made a mistake. As soon as I saw he was stopping, I knew I wasn't going to pass him."

Anaya chose integrity over victory.

In the devotional, the writer said, "If we abandon our integrity, short-term 'wins' actually yield defeat. But when fidelity and truthfulness shape us in God's power, we slowly become people of deep character who lead genuinely good lives."[8]

As a leadership coach, the Brilliance Unveiler, I hold women accountable to the professional goals they envision for themselves because I know these goals are their legacies in the making. The achievement of our grandest dreams and visions enables us to inspire the generations that follow. It is important to understand how these dreams are fulfilled by honoring our core values.

There are many tactics and tools you can use to unearth your values. I like to go with a reflective process, which encourages you to dig deep to discern what matters to you. To learn more and to use a process I've developed to call out your core values, download my free resource "Clarity for Your Calling Guide." You can find it at: https://www.theunveiledway.com/clarity-for-your-calling-subscribe.[9]

The Sweet Spot of Your Calling

Now that you have the three backbone pieces of your passions, strengths, and values in your calling wardrobe, what new awareness do you possess? How do these three come together for you?

The intersection of these three backbone pieces is very important. The area where your passions, strengths, and values coincide is a clue to your specific calling. Yes, my friend!

As you bring the pieces together, consider the following questions:

1. What do the people around me need?

   _____

   _____

2. What am I designed and experienced to do to help fill this need?

   _____

   _____

3. What can I do to make a difference and have an impact?

   _____

   _____

4. What's the cost of not doing what I am called to do?

   _____

   _____

5. What outcome would be the most tangible expression of my purpose?

   _____

   _____

6. What next steps can I take to cultivate my calling?

   _____

   _____

7. What clarity do I still need?

   _____

   _____

As I mentioned earlier, getting clarity for your calling gets you on the path where you can begin to map out your career vision strategically and intentionally. Knowing your arena and knowing what it looks like to operate in your strengths, helps you see your way forward so you don't end up stuck in a career path that is not designed for you.

A final point about calling. So often, your calling is way bigger than you. It may intimidate you or even seem impossible to achieve. That is a clue that you're on the right track! Ava DuVernay slam dunks it this way, "If your dream only includes you, then it's too small."

When you're committed to pursuing your calling, a whole new world of things you want to pursue opens up to you. Your calling may be just beyond your understanding, and it may require a serious stretch, but it is so compelling that you are driven outside your comfort zone to take the steps to fulfill it. Because you know in your heart you must.

If you're in the process of reevaluating your career or going through a career transition, this is the optimal time to gain greater clarity about your calling. It's that proverbial fork in the road where you can take the path that changes everything or continue down the path you've been on.

I want to encourage you to step onto that less-traveled path, that bolder, unknown, and scary one. The one that is rife with uncertainty and discomfort. Because maybe, on the other side of that path, is the satisfaction and fulfillment you've been waiting for your whole life.

Maybe corralling all your courage to fulfill your calling will help you blaze a new trail for others to follow. (I see you, trailblazer!)

What's amazing about being clear about your calling is that it has the power to free you from a career that has left you unfulfilled, wanting more, and wondering why you lost your zeal along the way.

Look, if you're reading this book, you're looking for something different. You know you're meant to do something that will create lasting, enduring change for the people you are called to serve. You've already taken a step onto another path. Keep going, trusting your instincts and paying attention to the signs and clues along the way. Don't dismiss the long-held desires of your heart. They're real and true.

I want to end this chapter with a beautiful, inspirational parable called "The Three Trees" by an unknown writer that I've paraphrased below.

There were three trees on a mountain who had big, bold, bodacious dreams about their calling. The first tree dreamed of being fashioned into the most beautiful chest filled with the finest treasures. The second tree wanted to be the strongest ship in the world, "traveling mighty waters and carrying powerful kings." The third tree, however, hoped it would never have to leave the mountaintop because it wanted to grow so tall that people would look up to the heavens and think of God.

After a few years, three woodcutters climbed to the mountain top. As the first woodcutter chopped the first tree, he remarked about its beauty, so the first tree thought its dream would come true. The second woodcutter remarked about the second tree's strength, so the second tree thought it would get its dream. The poor third tree kept hoping it would not be chopped down, but alas, the third woodcutter chopped it down, not noticing anything special about it.

The woodcutter brought the first tree to a carpenter's shop, but it was fashioned into a feedbox, coated with sawdust and filled with hay for hungry farm animals, not a beautiful chest. The second tree was taken to a shipyard but was hammered and sawed into a simple fishing boat, not a mighty ship. It was taken to a little lake, not the ocean as it hoped. The third tree was confused when the woodcutter cut her into strong beams and left her in a lumberyard.

Time passed, and the three trees nearly forgot their dreams.

But one night, a young woman placed her newborn baby in the feedbox that was the first tree. "This manger is beautiful," she said. And suddenly the first tree knew he was holding the greatest treasure in the world.

Another evening, a tired traveler and his friends packed themselves into the small old fishing boat that was the second tree. As it sailed across the lake, the traveler fell asleep. Soon a raging storm arose, scaring the little tree because she knew she was too small to survive such a storm. The sleeping man woke up and with his words, "Peace. Be still," the storm stopped as quickly as it had begun. Then, the second tree knew she was carrying the greatest king of all—the King of Heaven and Earth!

One Friday morning, the third tree was shocked when her beams were yanked from the forgotten woodpile. Fashioned into a cross, she was carried through an angry crowd. Soldiers nailed a man's hands and feet to her. But on Sunday morning, when the sun rose and the earth trembled with joy beneath her, the third tree knew that God's love had changed everything and every time people thought of the third tree, they *would* think of God.[10]

This story brings humble tears to my eyes every time I read it. Regardless of your faith, I hope it resonates for you too, dear reader.

All the trees had dreams. They had callings. But it looked like their callings would never come to fruition because things turned out so differently than they had imagined. Yet, at the right time, each tree achieved its vision—exceedingly, abundantly greater than it could have ever imagined. God was faithful to use their gifts and heart's desires to fulfill their vision for His glory.

So it is with us. God has gifted each of us so uniquely and distinctively. He has a purpose and a call for each of us. And if we are obedient to that call, we will do the good things God purposed for us long ago, and in so doing bring Him the glory!

With your calling, you can hope for a renewed desire and momentum to achieve those goals and dreams you may have put on the back burner. You can expect to feel excitement at discovering how God has uniquely shaped you and how you can use your gifts to impact the lives of others in meaningful ways.

Your brilliance is yours. When you shine, you do so as only you can. Believe that you can be in a career or a business that is satisfying, gratifying, and rewarding which positions you for the impact you're meant to make!

Chapter 2

Stand Tall:
Cultivate Your Confidence

"No one can make you feel inferior without your consent."

~ Eleanor Roosevelt

A
S AN ELEVEN-YEAR-OLD, I went through a growth spurt that left me a good head taller than all the children at my school. This didn't help my confidence at all. But mercifully, the kids at school were kind to me and didn't see my giraffe status as something to bully. That had to be God. But at five feet and eleven inches, I felt terribly awkward.

I was uncomfortable with the attention my height attracted, yet I couldn't hide it. My confidence was weak back then, so the only thing I knew to do to keep me out of the spotlight was to diminish my presence. I was shy and quiet and mostly kept my thoughts to myself. I blended in as much as my frame would allow. I never spoke up in class unless I had to. My M.O. back then was to do everything I could to deflect attention away from me.

In high school, I got braces to rein in my very prominent front teeth, so I stopped smiling too. About that time, zits were waging war on my cheeks, so not only did I feel freakishly tall but unattractive as well. I was easily the tallest girl in school, so I contorted myself to blend in, not stick out, and not command attention. It must have worked because, aside from my few friends, I was left alone.

During that time there was an art teacher who must have seen through my guise. She was a petite woman, and she was not even my teacher, but every time she passed me in the hallways, she'd look up to me and say, "Tall girls are the prettiest," with a big smile on her face. I never knew what to say to her, and I'm sure I just looked away in embarrassment, but her words settled somewhere in my heart and bore tiny seeds of worthiness.

My mother, bless her heart, was a skilled seamstress and would sew outfits for me for special occasions. In my opinion they were hit or miss (she'd disagree), particularly the time she made this bright orange, drop-waist dress with puffed sleeves for me to attend a birthday party.

That dress was everything I was trying to steer clear of—from the attention-getting hue to the silhouette that made me look like a long potato sack. I hated the dress but had no other option but to wear it to the party. I *had* to take matters into my own hands.

I started pouring over my Mother's *Glamour* magazines for hacks. I would save my allowance to buy clothes that I liked that flattered my lean, leggy frame. I was particularly fond of Kate Jackson's style in *Charlie's Angels*, who was also tall and thin, so I began looking for cool, baggy tops and pleated trousers to emulate her look. (Yeah, I know I'm dating myself with that reference!) I started frosting my hair and curling the edges up like Farrah Fawcett.

All these fixes helped me feel a bit more confident not just about my looks but also about myself. I remember attending my high school's May festival—the big event of the year—wearing a beige V-neck, baggy blouse with my khaki, pleated slacks and actually feeling something close to attractive.

Clothes became a refuge, a way to help shape others' perceptions of me. I liked the fact that I got to control the narrative. I could inform someone's impression of me by my fashion choices, and the power of that planted a seed that would start to blossom decades later.

When I turned seventeen, my shape had filled out in lovely feminine ways. The braces were gone, and I'd now fully mastered the art of makeup to accentuate my eyes. I lost the flip hairstyle and started rocking two long braids on the sides of my head, way ahead of the trend that is now rampant. I had grown into my stature and started feeling the power in my presence. Something amazing was happening—I was blossoming!

And other people started to notice too. One day I was shopping in Port-of-Spain (Trinidad's capital) wearing my favorite yellow, straight-legged slacks paired with a red, floral shirt my mother had made that I liked accentuated with a gold belt. A young girl no more than seven years old tugged on my hand. When I turned to look down at her, she smiled brightly up at me and said, "Miss, yuh nice."

I was taken aback. By that time, I'd gotten used to the stares that were now stares of awe and not shock at my height, but this little girl admiring me like that hit me differently. I'll never forget that moment. It's like that young lovely saw in me what I was starting to feel.

She had poured into me with those three simple words. I smiled back at her and moved on my way. I simply had no words. But what I wished my younger self was empowered to do then was tell that sweet girl that she too was nice! Really, really nice! That she was special just as she was. That she was beautiful with her pretty smile and barrette plaits.

A few years later, when I came to the United States to attend Rutgers University, I had a boyfriend and I had grown into my statuesque six-foot-one frame. I had curves in all the right places, and my height, which was not necessarily seen as an attractive attribute in Trinidad, suddenly caused heads to turn and strangers on campus to approach me asking, "Are you a model?" My surprised expression would invariably prompt the second question, "Do you play basketball?" I would shake my head no to both questions, but this happened so many times that I realized in this new country I was an "it" girl—tall, slim, pretty, and with an exotic accent to boot. I sure had come a long way!

I now had learned the skill of shaping my image to make people see me as attractive, confident, and cool. But my insides still had a lot of catching up to do. At my core, I was still an insecure, people-pleasing, young lady who was not confident about herself.

I used my appearance like a shield. It helped me feel in control. I told myself if I looked pulled together, attractive, and poised, then I would be accepted, liked, and respected. The times I didn't feel that way, my inner critic had a field day. I would feel myself shrinking, avoiding eye contact, and feeling incredibly insecure if I felt I missed the mark with my image. I thought I had control over how people perceived me. But the truth is I didn't at all.

Fashion was a refuge, a tool, a hack, but it could not fix what was broken inside of me. Confidence is an inner game, and until I acknowledged the unhealthy mindsets, poor self-image, and low feelings of self-worth, all the external stuff was just window-dressing. This I would understand later in life.

Image and Confidence

One of the fastest paths to boosting our confidence as women is feeling secure about how we look. This was my story as a young woman. My confidence was based on how attractive and appealing I thought I looked. It was based on external validation and others' perceptions of my image. But that is shaky ground to center one's confidence in.

In my image consulting work, many women came to me seeking help with their image because they wanted to feel more confident. It's like we all read the "Confidence Manual 101," where it said that in order to get confident, we must work on our appearance and image.

However, the truth is that our image is just a tiny part of the story. Yes, our appearance can help us feel more confident about ourselves. But if that is not paired with healthy, solid, self-esteem, appearance only goes so far.

There are so many stories of beautiful women in the public eye who struggle with poor confidence. Women like Jennifer Aniston, Lady Gaga, Jennifer Lopez, and others are gorgeous and seem to have it all—looks, talent, success, wealth— yet no matter how beautiful the world says they are, it doesn't matter if they don't feel beautiful on the inside too.

Image and appearance do matter, and they do help boost our confidence. My work with hundreds of women proves that. But one of the reasons I got into leadership coaching is because of my own journey of reckoning with my image and knowing that as a tall, pretty, and smart woman, deep down my worth was overly attached to my looks and others' perceptions of me. And when those looks "failed" me, my confidence took a nosedive. The instability and fickleness of letting my looks dictate my level of confidence was exhausting.

I had been doing inner work to strengthen my self-esteem since my twenties, but I needed to go deeper so I could get to the place where I felt confident in who I was, regardless of how I looked.

A Lack of Confidence Can Derail Your Career

How you step into your work and passions as a leader, or a woman aspiring to leadership, is predicated on your level of confidence. Your confidence quotient will inform how you lead because it shapes your interactions with others and influences how you perceive yourself as a leader.

A confident leader is not afraid of making tough decisions, going against popular opinion, or shaking things up. A leader lacking confidence, on the other hand, may come across as people-pleasing, risk-averse, or too easily swayed by the loudest voices in the room.

If you want to be a woman of influence, you've got to be confident. If you're insecure or lacking confidence, you won't be bold, you won't make those big moves, take those leaps or those risks required if you're serious about making an impact. You will hide in the background, not raise your hand, not speak up, and your impact will not be realized.

If you're going to make an impact or have influence, confidence is everything. But most of us have areas where we feel insecure, where we have a deficit, or where we fall short, and these can wreak havoc on our confidence if we don't address them.

One of my clients, Sherry, came to me severely lacking in confidence. She was an accomplished woman in her forties, newly divorced, with three young children under the age of fifteen. Even though she experienced success early on in her career as a vice president of marketing for a well-known nonprofit, she found it challenging to fit into her new role.

When she contacted me, she had already changed jobs twice in the past three years, one where she was fired, so her confidence had taken a beating. She found herself struggling to communicate and feeling like she had no authority or clout in her new position, one which she had accepted at a significantly lower salary than she'd earned three years ago in a position beneath her pay grade. And yet here she was still struggling, thinking that her previous success was not merited.

She came to me wanting to learn how to communicate better, but I knew her challenge ran much deeper than that. She was failing in her communications with her team and the owner of the firm she worked for now because she no longer believed in her capabilities. Her self-doubt and low self-esteem were very evident. She was intimidated in staff meetings and felt powerless and voiceless in her role.

Deep down Sherry knew she had the skills and capabilities. She was comfortable with her marketing expertise but not in speaking up for herself. Her most recent career experiences had triggered deep-rooted issues from her past which threatened not just to derail her success in her current role but in her life as well. She had lost her sense of authority and agency.

Sherry wanted to feel more comfortable being a leader and leveraging her ideas, creativity, and skills. She wanted to have more influence and maximize the impact she knew she was capable of. But first, we had to address the issues that forfeited her confidence and influence.

Low confidence is prevalent among women, especially in the workplace. So many top performers, leaders, and high achievers don't recognize their accomplishments, triumphs, and wins and struggle deep down with feeling confident.

But it's our confidence that sways people and commands their attention. It's our confidence that gets us a seat at the table. It's our confidence that garners us respect and popularity. Some researchers argue that confidence matters even more than competence!

Your confidence is nonnegotiable. To be impactful and make your unique mark, you must believe that you've got what it takes. You must know deep within that you're qualified, equipped, and competent to fulfill the greatest vision for your life.

In their book *The Confidence Code*, the authors write that when women aren't confident, we don't succeed: "We can't even envision the work we could be doing, or the levels we could reach or the satisfaction we could have. We can't even contribute fully to a system that is in great need of female leadership."[1]

The authors make the case that confidence is not just about feeling good about ourselves or thinking we're killing it. More importantly, confidence is the belief that we can create a successful outcome in any given situation, despite the obstacles in our way. It's our assurance and faith in ourselves to realize our goals which allows us to take the often bold steps required to achieve them.

A confident woman isn't sandbagged by crippling self-doubt, obsessed with overthinking. She isn't over preparing, or overly concerned about what others think of her. She's on purpose, on a mission to do her "Do" and doesn't waste time or energy agonizing over whether she'll fail because failure to her is just part of the ride!

For me, this summary in their book really captures the essence of confidence: "Confidence occurs when the insidious self-perception that you aren't able is trumped by the stark reality of your achievements." Right?

Your confidence is solidified by your actions because your actions demonstrate what you're capable of doing and accomplishing. Your confidence helps you get outside your comfort zone and do hard, risky things because you believe you can overcome, conquer, and deliver.

A Posture of Confidence

In a keynote talk I gave last year for a career symposium, I asked the women in attendance to indicate which one of ten success saboteurs limited their success. There were about one hundred women across a variety of industries in attendance, including recent graduates and seasoned professionals. The most common saboteur selected was lack of confidence, followed by imposter syndrome and perfectionism.

From my experience working with women, I knew a lack of confidence was a common career-limiting behavior, so I devoted an entire segment of my presentation to cultivating confidence. I believe cultivating our confidence is the foundational aspect of rising above and beyond in our workplace.

One of my main slides illustrated the differences between a confident woman versus one who isn't.

A confident woman:

- Speaks her truth
- Is not afraid to show vulnerability
- Is curious
- Takes responsibility for her actions
- Gives compliments
- Is a risk taker

Conversely, a woman lacking confidence exhibits these behaviors:

- Worries about what others think
- Is always guarded
- Acts like a knower
- Makes excuses
- Seeks validation
- Is a people-pleaser

Let's break down these behaviors in more detail.

Speaks Her Truth / Worries What Others Think

A confident woman stands up for her beliefs even in the face of criticism. She stands firm in her truth, grounded in her principles, values, and integrity. While she may receive pushback or vitriol, she does not back down. She stays the course.

When a woman lacks confidence, she focuses more on how she's perceived rather than what she truly believes. When you worry about what others think, you lose focus on the things that make you shine, and you try to shape your behavior to please others.

This behavior is known as people-pleasing, which I address in more detail later. There are, what I call, three gremlins many women must tackle in work and life in general—the gremlins of performing, pleasing, and perfecting. Letting these gremlins run the show leads to frustration, burnout, and resentment.

While perfectionism, performing, and people-pleasing are gremlins many of us deal with, we must focus instead on what we can bring to the table. We must play to our strengths so our brilliance can be unveiled.

Not Afraid to Show Vulnerability / Always Guarded

A post on Instagram by Brittney Cobb summarized the adverse effects of not sharing how we truly feel. "Not speaking up, refusing to say what you're feeling or thinking, shrinking your voice, pretending to be unaffected—reinforces fear. Fear of not getting the result you want, fear of damaging relationships, fear of what the response will be. But if you stay attached to the outcome, you will almost always be paralyzed by it… You will sacrifice your well-being for a false sense of safety. You'll stay stuck. As you learn to assert yourself, your confidence grows, your relationships become more authentic, your ability to tolerate uncertainty increases & the less shame you will feel."[2] #Truth

Brené Brown broke onto the scene over a decade ago, challenging us all to open up to vulnerability because, in doing so, we find freedom, belonging, and true connection. The very nature of vulnerability requires us to be fortified inside. To come from a space of strong self-worth, confidence, and truth.

On the other hand, being guarded means coming from a place where you are armored up, lacking transparency, and not being authentic about what you think, feel, or believe. You put on a facade of strength, tolerance, or even confidence, but that façade is not who you truly are.

When you're guarded, there is no room for authentic connection and your guarded default is typically a subconscious behavioral mechanism you develop in childhood to protect yourself from being hurt. This survival tactic has a noble purpose when we don't have the tools or resources to address things more holistically.

But if you keep being guarded throughout your life, your growth, potential, and satisfaction will be severely limited. And a guarded person can't be confident because they're never showing up in spaces authentically.

It's tough to admit when you've screwed up, when you've failed, or when you've made a mistake. These are all extremely vulnerable actions. But a confident woman understands the mettle required in vulnerability and can draw from her storehouse of courage to admit her missteps, speak truth to power, and more.

A guarded woman lacking confidence tends to be defined by her *A*s, as I like to refer to them: her awards, accolades, achievements, accomplishments, and acknowledgments. Yes, those *A*s are impressive. You accept them, you take them in, but you don't let that define who you are, and you don't let them drive you to succeed. Your drive must come from a deeper place than just those *A*s.

Much of what I'm talking about is a mind versus a heart posture. Mind posture says, "*I think my worth is in my A*s." That's not a good place to be because guess what? You won't always get the *A*s. And when you don't get an *A*, you crumble and fall apart. So you have to have your worth in something deeper.

And that's where your heart posture is. For me, my heart posture is my faith. I'm a Christian. I believe that God defines who I am as a beloved daughter, designed and meant to do good things He has prepared in advance for me. Knowing this gives me an inner confidence that belies my struggles or challenges. For you, your heart posture might be something else. Whatever it is, it must be something that you can firmly ground and grow roots in, not something random, fleeting, or unsustainable like an achievement, award, or validation.

Is Curious / Acts like a Knower

Having a posture of curiosity is being open, expansive, inclusive, and comfortable in uncertainty. But many people resist curiosity because, to thrive, curiosity means getting comfortable with uncertainty, vulnerability, and not knowing. The latter are tough spaces for a woman lacking confidence to hang out.

As a coach in training, I was taught to form my questions with a curiosity mindset versus an information-gathering one. With a curiosity mindset, I could observe my client in fascination and view our coaching conversation as a path where insights, learnings, and discovery could thrive.

However, with an information-gathering style of questioning, I take on a role as the expert, as the knower, as the one directing the conversation and coming up with recommendations. This is a controlling tactic and one that does not project confidence as much as one-upmanship.

Imagine sitting at Starbucks and chatting with a friend about a challenge you're going through. Your friend leans in as you're talking, engrossed in what you're saying. Instead of giving you advice or trying to make you feel better with off-the-cuff comments, they say things like, "I hear you," "How does that make you feel?" "Tell me more about that part?" and "How can I support you?"

You feel seen and heard which makes you want to share even more with your friend. You feel she gets you, that she understands, and this draws you closer to her in friendship.

Imagine that same scenario, but instead of your friend being curious about your story, they assail you with questions like, "What do you mean?" "Why did you do that?" "How is that going to solve your issues?" and "You should do XYZ." How do you feel in this scenario? Do you feel heard or like you were just in an inquisition?

While curiosity strengthens relational bonds, being the knower builds walls that repel intimacy. With curiosity, there is exploration that uncovers and exposes, digs deeper, considers, and reflects.

If you want to cultivate confidence, you must learn to stop asking questions as the expert knower. Instead, ask questions simply out of curiosity. This puts you in a mindset of not being attached to a response so you can maintain a curious stance throughout a conversation.

Asking "What if...?" and "How might you...?" questions generate more creative ways of tackling issues. As a coach, when a client makes a statement that I know has the potential to unveil layers of "stuff" beneath it, I ask a question like, "Say more about that," or make a direct observation such as, "I'm wondering whether..." or "What's the real issue at play here?" or "What do you make of this situation?" These open-ended questions elicit deeper levels of exploration which lead to fresh insights and perspectives.

In her book *Lead Like a Woman*, author Deborah Smith Pegues shares this response from award-winning filmmaker Ava DuVernay on how her confidence is grounded in not being the knower and instead inviting curiosity: "My confidence comes from knowing that I don't know everything... I walk in with no problem saying, 'I don't know the answer to that. Let's find out together,' or, 'What do you think about that?' 'Hmmm, I'm not sure about that; let me think about it some more.' None of those things is diminishing. They actually give you power. No one knows everything."[3] I agree.

Takes Responsibility for Her Actions / Makes Excuses

It takes a lot of gumption to fess up when things go south. But it is an act of integrity to do so. And while others may be disappointed by your misstep, they will respect you for speaking up and owning your part in it.

Passing the blame to others, sidestepping your responsibility in a debacle, or making excuses does not make a leader.

Leaders often have to take the fall for their team even when they are not directly responsible for the failure. Leadership demands courage, authenticity, compassion, and resilience. If you're passing the buck to make yourself look good, your perceived win will be short-lived. And worse, those who know the truth of the situation will lose respect for you.

When you take responsibility for your actions, the good and the bad ones, you project inner confidence that emanates outward. When you make excuses, or always deflect blame, over time this tendency raises questions about your integrity. And in my opinion, if you are perceived as lacking integrity, you will never project confidence.

Gives Compliments / Seeks Validation

How can we be generous with our praise, telling someone how great they are and celebrating what they have accomplished as opposed to always fishing for compliments ourselves? It starts with intentionality. Being generous with praise stems from the confidence that you're brilliant in your lane and you're not in competition with anyone else. It means having an abundance versus a scarcity mindset. When we can be generous with our praise and affirmations, it speaks to our strong sense of self. It speaks to our leadership posture.

Someone smart produced the expression, "Comparison is the thief of joy." Stop comparing yourself to the next person. Let go of the comparison trap and focus on your capabilities, strengths, and skills. We are all designed to do different things. We are created to have a different influence. Comparing yourself to other women does not validate you because it stems from a scarcity worldview and is a losing game.

In her latest book *Atlas of the Heart*, Brené Brown devotes a whole chapter to the emotions associated with comparison—emotions like envy, resentment, and jealousy. She writes, "Comparison says, 'Be like everyone else, but better.'"[4] She talks about how, at its worst, comparison is competitive by nature, wanting to win and be the best. But this type of thinking often leads to fear, anger, shame, or sadness.

When a woman lacks confidence, she's always seeking approval and validation from others. I love what Brittney Cobb has to say about this: "Leaving yourself to gain approval or acceptance from others won't benefit you in the long run. But it will reinforce the lack of safety & abandonment you fear. Constantly seeking external validation (approval from others) puts you in the position to be controlled, taken advantage of & manipulated by other people. It puts others at the forefront of your unspoken needs & leaves you resentful, angry & feeling alone... Internal validation (approval of self) will keep you grounded & can be sustained over time."[5]

Constantly needing validation, praise, or approval is a sign of insecurity. Don't be that woman.

Risk-Taker / People-Pleaser

Risk-taking matters, because to move into the area of brilliance that you are meant to be in, you're going to have to take risks. You'll need to risk failure and getting it wrong. You'll need to risk not being perfect and messing things up. But that risk-taking is what gets you to the next level in your rise. It's what gets you to the next trajectory, the next upward arena in view. When others see you taking risks, your confidence quotient increases in their eyes. And you will feel more emboldened yourself.

When a woman lacks confidence, she will work even harder to prove she belongs and deserves a seat at the table. She will put in more time, do the grunt work, and become a doormat because inside she is telling herself that the more she does, the more she will be recognized for the value she brings. She will become the expert in every task required in her role to avoid negative feedback or criticism—in effect taking on people-pleasing behavior.

The problem is that although mastering all the minute details of her job may allow her to keep her current job, it's not the aspiring strategy toward the true career she envisions for herself down the road. Leaders don't get bogged down in the minutiae; they lead!

If you find yourself overworking, placating, or micro-doing, check yourself. Are you becoming indispensable to the role you currently have instead of positioning yourself for the one you want to have in the future?

When a woman is confident, and not overcompensating, she can focus on doing her job well enough while simultaneously spending time building important relationships and elevating her visibility, keeping her eye on the next role she aspires to. She can master her job while recognizing and valuing her contributions.

Opting to people-please is opting to play it safe and play small. You cannot keep abandoning yourself to placate others and expect to walk in alignment with your purpose. It just doesn't work that way. Always toeing the line may make you more likable in the short run, but in the long run, you will not be perceived as having the courage, confidence, or command to lead.

Walking Tall

By now it may be fairly obvious that confidence ultimately stems from our feelings of worth and value. It's a self-esteem issue. When we feel unworthy or have low self-esteem, issues like imposter syndrome, insecurity, inadequacy, perfectionism, people-pleasing, or being performative arise. Until we address those issues, we'll struggle with our confidence.

The gender biases we encounter at work don't help us either. McKinsey and Company's "Women in the Workplace 2021" report highlights that even though there have been significant gains made since 2016, women continue to have a worse day-to-day experience at work than men and "are more likely than men to have (our) competence questioned and (our) authority undermined."[6]

A Women's Leadership study by KPMG uncovered the following alarming statistics:

- 73% of women don't pursue job opportunities beyond their level of experience
- 65% won't ask for a promotion
- 61% don't ask for a raise they feel they deserve
- 56% fail to ask for a new role or position[7]

Because of these challenges and because we have so many things working against us, it's even more imperative that women display confidence if they're desiring to lead and make an impact. A woman's confidence is not just for her. It's for all those she leads. Her example of confidence inspires and motivates those around her.

If you struggle with confidence, as most of us do at some point, adopt one or more of the strategies below to convey greater self-assurance and command in your sphere of influence.

1. Play to Your Strengths

You will see this thread of playing to your strengths throughout this book because I believe so strongly in the power of claiming and leveraging where we are gifted. I devoted a chapter to strengths later because they are foundational for growing confidence.

Playing to your strengths matters, but you can't play to what you don't believe. You must claim your TAGS—your talents, abilities, gifts, and strengths. Your TAGS are like your name tag. Claim them!

It's time for women to claim their strengths and not hide from them or hide them. Why do so many of us believe we're arrogant if we own our exceptionality? Where do we get this message that we are not all great and valuable? That only a certain few of us can be this way?

Unfortunately, many of us have been conditioned to believe it's arrogant to acknowledge our giftedness. What would it look like if more of us celebrated and embraced that we're amazing in our brilliance? What if we dared entertain the thought that we can each be uniquely amazing and that such a thought doesn't have to be reserved for a precious few?

I agree with author and entrepreneur Reshma Saujani who wrote that "we need to stop trying to wrestle for power, respect, and opportunities from others and instead bravely make them for ourselves."[8]

When you know you bring value, it gives you leverage. Most of us have areas where we feel insecure, but our confidence comes from being our own best champions, believing in our worth and value, and knowing what we bring to our role.

God has gifted each of us in unique and wonderful ways and has crafted us with particular abilities, talents, and gifts—our TAGS. When we develop our God-given strengths and use them to serve other people, we can accomplish unbelievable things.

Plus, when our work aligns with our strengths and talents, we receive more meaning, purpose, and fulfillment from it. But when we try to operate outside our talents, or if we use our abilities in ways God didn't intend, we're headed for a life filled with anxiety, frustration, and failure.

In *The Gifts of Imperfection*, Brené Brown articulates this point so well: "Self-doubt undermines the process of finding our gifts and sharing them with the world. Moreover, if developing and sharing our gifts is how we honor God, self-doubt is letting our fear undermine our faith."[9]

Permit yourself to value and honor the TAGS you bring and how they add value to your role and strengthen your impact.

2. Be Mindful of Your Mindset

Confidence is mostly an inner game, which is why managing your thoughts matters.

Carol Dweck's groundbreaking book on mindset demonstrates that people with a growth mindset see intelligence and competence as strengths that can be built over time. They believe that the path to mastery is based on continuous growth and learning. When they fail, rather than withdrawing or becoming discouraged, they double down on the task at hand.

In contrast, those with a fixed mindset are focused on performing well and being smart. They see intelligence and skill as black and white. Either you're good at science or not. A great speaker or not. When they're faced with a setback, their confidence tumbles and they will go to great lengths to avoid that failure again.[10]

Adopting a growth mindset positions you to be open and willing to learn and grow. It makes you less afraid to fail. But a fixed mindset keeps you stuck, timid, and insecure.

You will cultivate greater confidence when you stay in a learning posture that allows for mistakes and uncertainty versus a performative posture focused on perfecting, pleasing, and performing. The latter is about grinding and hustling. The former is about extending grace and generosity toward oneself and others.

We've all been through a lot with COVID-19—we've all been challenged. In times of crisis, our inner self is unveiled. Are you resilient and hopeful or are you feeling hopeless and unsettled? When life is throwing lemons at you, are you making lemonade or are you stomping on the lemons thinking that will make it all go away? How can you replace negative, defeatist thinking with positivity and hope? What does a possibility mindset usher in for you this year? Are you paying attention to what God is trying to do in your life? Do you even see it? Do you believe it? What's holding you back?

3. Take Up Space

Taking up space has to do with making your presence felt and known. I am over six feet tall. But I used to want to curl up in a ball and be invisible. I had to learn to own my height and stand in its full strength and power.

What I didn't know growing up was that my stature afforded me a privilege I didn't yet understand—my height is a natural confidence gainer! People automatically assume I have more gravitas when they meet me because I take up a lot of vertical space.

But making my presence known also has to do with the confidence I feel inside when I own my height and "take up space" with it. I shared a story in my last book about practicing the Mountain Pose in yoga and learning how to *feel* the power of standing tall and strong like a mountain. Standing solidly like a mountain is SO powerful and exudes the type of confidence you just can't fake. The type of confidence that makes people look at you with respect, admiration, or awe because they feel and see your confidence.

But you don't have to be super tall or large to leverage this strategy. It doesn't matter what size you are, walking tall is all about your energy and how you channel it. And it's about how you feel about yourself coming through your physical presence. Your posture and poise also play a role here. Walk tall no matter what your height or size.

If you're small or short physically, another strategy I've used with clients is to have them imagine themselves in a larger frame, particularly in interactions where they may feel intimidated by someone larger or with more clout. Just visually picturing yourself in that meeting with Mr. Larger Than Life in a bigger, more powerful, or more confident frame than your natural one can make an enormous difference in how you come across in reality. It's all about your self-perception, after all.

Moreover, when you bring your A-game to work, amplify your voice, use your authority, and speak truth to power, you're making your presence known and experienced. And THAT takes up space, my dear, and projects the best type of confidence!

This is exactly what former tennis ace and United States Tennis Association President Katrina Adams acknowledges. She navigates many spaces where she has to showcase her authority and states, "Commanding the room is not an entitlement; it's the product of being prepared. I bring my knowledge of a subject, as well as my creativity. God has made this particular place for me, and it's up to me to rise to the occasion by demonstrating my talent and worth, knowing that I often represent more than just myself."[11]

Taking up space is such an effective strategy that we'll address it in a later chapter on leadership presence. In the meantime, consider what it would look like if you walked taller?

4. Practice Power Posing

Power posing is adopting the stances associated with confidence, power, and achievement—your chest lifted, head held high, arms either up or propped on the hips like Wonder Woman.

Social psychologist Amy Cuddy's research found that sitting and standing in confident postures changes your physiology and helps you feel more confident. She discovered that others will perceive you as confident too because in these poses you are taking up more physical space and spreading out your body in powerful stances. In these stances, the stress hormone (cortisol) decreases and our dominance hormone (testosterone) increases. These hormonal changes increase our energy and our sense of well-being, making us feel and look more confident.[12]

In the Victory Pose power pose, your hands are raised up and apart over your head, resembling a giant "V," with your head held high and proud. The gift of power posing is that it can immediately boost your confidence, even when you don't feel it.

I've started seminars having attendees power pose for a couple of minutes. Not only does it ignite and get them engaged right away, it also helps me feel more confident and in charge when taking the mic.

Trust me, this works! Try to engage in power posing for at least two minutes a day.

5. Communicate with Clarity

An effective and articulate communicator naturally projects confidence. When a person fumbles their words, doesn't land their points, or talks in circles, it leaves others confused, bewildered, and frustrated, which doesn't build confidence for anyone.

There is nothing more frustrating than communicating with someone who is unable to articulate what they need from you. The people you lead, work, and interact with must know what is expected of them. The easiest way to do this is to let them know. Be direct, communicate your expectations, and be clear about what "done" looks like.

Managing your team's expectations helps promote a culture of empowerment where people are clear about their roles, what's expected of them, and understand what success looks like. Empowered people have more confidence, feel more comfortable taking risks, and produce more because their performance comes from a place of agency and ability rather than stress and competitiveness.

Your communication skills also need to work for you in less-than-ideal situations. Your ability to succinctly communicate with clarity and confidence, as well as your ability to be an active listener will serve you well, even when you are engaged in tough conversations.

If you struggle with communicating, take stock of what is going on within you. Do you feel in over your head? Are you lacking internal confidence in your abilities? Are you unprepared for your conversations or presentations? Are you anxious? Or is it something else?

Once you understand the root cause, you're better able to address it. You may need professional help from a coach or therapist to help you work on your self-esteem or perceived lack of competency. You can enroll in a public speaking course to gain communication skills. Or maybe you just need to give yourself the margin to better prepare for work activities that require your communications to be on point.

6. Set Clear Boundaries

A confident woman is not afraid of making tough decisions or speaking her truth. She's not afraid of going against popular opinion or self-advocating. She is clear about what she will and will not tolerate. She's got solid boundaries.

Your boundaries are where you draw the line regarding behaviors you will tolerate and those you won't. They are your nonnegotiables, your hard nos. Your boundaries communicate to your coworkers, clients, and bosses what you will and won't accept, and what the consequences are for disrespecting those lines.

An absence of clear boundaries breeds insecurity, because when our boundary lines are fuzzy and others step all over them, we get upset and resentful, which then leads to a lack of confidence in how we are perceived or how we handled a particular situation. When we have clear, defined, respectable boundaries, people take us seriously. And we can get on with our lives and our work without worrying about others crossing those lines.

Healthy boundaries and confidence go hand in hand because you can only assert your boundaries when you're confident in who you are. In her best-selling book *Set Boundaries, Find Peace*, author Nedra Glover Tawwab writes that boundary setting has two components: verbally communicating your needs, then actively upholding the boundary you communicated. Communicating requires you to make assertive, clear statements about what is acceptable to you. Taking action means letting the violator know they crossed your boundary and backing that up with some type of consequence for dishonoring your boundary.[13]

From this lens it's easy to see why setting and maintaining boundaries is a confidence-building activity. If you often find yourself feeling resentful, overwhelmed, burnt out, or avoiding certain people or activities, consider whether these feelings are showing up because you have not set or maintained healthy boundaries.

7. Act As If (You're Confident)

"Acting as If" is a simple technique I use when coaching. It encourages clients to think, act, and feel as if they have a desired state, such as confidence. When using this technique, I'm inviting my client to speak from a future state and embody the behaviors, attitudes, and actions that are true in that state.

For example, if a woman is desiring to project more confidence, I would invite her to imagine herself acting confidently. I would have her imagine herself as that confident leader in her day-to-day activities, speaking, acting, and dressing the part of the confident leader she envisions herself to be. This combo of visualization and "Acting as If" helps her create a vision of her ideal future and allows her to live that image out in her life today as if it were true.

Internally, what is happening inside our brain when engaging in this work is a change to the neural pathways. By repeatedly focusing, imagining, and "trying on" new behaviors aligned with our goals, we create new neural pathways that, over time, become stronger than the old ones that kept us stuck or insecure.

But "Acting as If" needs a true perspective shift to move from just play-acting to real transformation. This technique isn't as effective if you don't *believe* in your vision of yourself and if you don't *think you can* do what it takes.

"Acting as If" is most effective when paired with visualization and affirmation. With affirmation, you can visualize your goal as already complete and use affirming statements to reinforce your new beliefs. Confident affirmations can include statements such as, "I am capable, competent, and confident in my role," or, "I believe I can X and I will," or one of my personal scripture favorites, "I can do all things through Christ who strengthens me" (Philippians 4:13).

Once the visualization and affirmations are clear and intentional, reflecting on questions like the ones below can help you solidify your new, confident persona as you practice "Acting as If" you're already confident:

- How would I react to people and situations if I am confident?
- How would I approach my work?
- What would my behaviors and mannerisms look like?
- How would other people respond to the confident version of me?

I used the "Acting as If" strategy over a decade ago when I was terrified to give my first presentation as an image consultant. I knew in my heart that I had to be willing to get out there and speak in front of groups if I wanted to be successful at increasing brand awareness and potentially snag new clients. But in my corporate career as a market researcher, I had managed to fly below the radar and not present as often as my peers. Now here I was, about to give a presentation in front of a group of thirty professionals, and it was all up to me to sink or swim.

I made sure I dressed the part of a successful entrepreneur, and on the entire drive to the event, I affirmed that I was competent, capable, confident, and knowledgeable about the subject. Moreover, days before the presentation I visualized myself giving a successful talk.

When game time rolled around, I got in front of the group and, to my surprise, I morphed into a woman I had never experienced myself being before. This woman was confident and competent, yes, but more than that, she was fun and passionate and charming. She was having a blast and even made jokes! Acting as if I was confident had transformed me from a terrified, insecure speaker to an engaging, bold, and successful one.

Confidence, Confidence, Confidence

Some people are naturally confident, but most of us struggle to feel confident in one or more areas of our lives. But be encouraged—confidence is a muscle you can strengthen with practice and repetition using many of the ideas I shared above.

Here are a few more confidence-building behaviors that speak for themselves:

1. Smile
2. Take in positive feedback
3. Celebrate your wins
4. Make eye contact
5. Exercise
6. Do something challenging
7. Own your brilliance
8. Dress intentionally
9. Be authentically you and believe that's enough

Your confidence can be your superpower. Build it up so that it's greater than anyone else's doubts in you or your abilities.

Believe you can be successful, competent, and accomplished. Stop apologizing, equivocating, and hesitating and act with assurance. Who you are and what you do is more than enough.

And yes, be confident enough to walk tall in your competencies, skills, and expertise so folks recognize your awesomeness for what it is. Banish the lie that it's arrogant or obnoxious to put your confidence on full display, because honestly, most women default to the opposite end of the spectrum and wonder why they're not more successful.

Look at all the successful, high-ranking men around. You think they got to that level by playing down their brilliance? Girl, just the opposite! Men do well at tooting their horn. It's time we do the same and not feel guilty about it. Game on!

Chapter 3

Fashion Fades, Style is Eternal:
Serve with Your Superpowers

"When I dare to be powerful—to use my strength in the service of my vision, then it becomes less and less important whether I am afraid."

~ Audre Lorde

FASHION TRENDS COME and go, but our sense of style is ours and ours alone. In my past work, I used the famous quote attributed to Coco Chanel, "Fashion Fades but Style is Eternal," to underscore to women the importance of their style as a peg in their "Presence with a Purpose." Our style has as much to do with who we are as how we want to look. When a woman has a solid, distinctive style, she is presenting herself to the world standing firmly in who she is as a woman, what she stands for, and what you can expect when interacting with her.

Style icons like Princess Diana, Audrey Hepburn, Sarah Jessica Parker, Michelle Obama, Gwen Stefani, and Rihanna (to name a few) capture our attention and awe with their stunning, exquisite representations of their image through their fashion choices. Their distinctive looks were so powerful that they often gave birth to new fashion trends. They used fashion to shape our perceptions of who they are as women, but it was their sense of style that we all tried to emulate.

If you've been on this Earth for a few decades, you'll know that fashion trends come, go, and come back again. As Solomon says in the book of Ecclesiastes, "There is nothing new under the sun," and this is certainly true for fashion.

Many factors influence our style and often fashion trends are the least of them. Our lifestyle, ethnicity, culture, experiences, personality, preferences, and tastes are just a few of the things that inform how we express ourselves via our clothing choices. A woman with a keen sense of style knows who she is, embraces her body, and dresses in ways that are true for her. Her clothing becomes another way to express herself and her individuality.

A woman who lets fashion trends dictate her wardrobe choices may look cute in the moment, but she won't be memorable. What makes a woman memorable is her art of dressing according to *her* style regardless of what trend is in or out of favor. Audrey Hepburn's love of a simple, neutral color pallet paired with clean strong lines distinguished her style. Her style gave emergence to The Little Black Dress (LBD), still a fashion staple decades after she blazed the red carpets.

My former image consultant self would advise that if you didn't have an LBD in your closet for the impromptu cocktail affair or upscale dinner date, your wardrobe was woefully inadequate as it would be missing a key backbone piece. This is testimony to the enduring aspect of style—it stands the test of time. True style is ageless and timeless.

You are unique and valuable, sister. We need your style, your gifts, your talents, your brilliance. Your impact matters. But it can only take root once you own and embrace the ways you're exceptionally wired to make your impact. To step into your influence, make your mark, and leave your imprint, you need to value and celebrate your strengths.

Just as style is to fashion, so are your strengths to your career. Your career may change, evolve, or level up, but your strengths are your strengths. Once you identify and keep cultivating them, they will serve you throughout your life and career.

The power we hold when we can name, claim, and aim our strengths strategically in our career cannot be understated. In a previous chapter, we talked about how many women fail to recognize their strengths, so they disregard them.

Here's the key takeaway I want you to glean: Your strengths are the key to your superpowers and the pathway to operating in your brilliance as a leader.

When I first started branding my coaching business, The Unveiled Way, the tagline that came readily to me was, "Let Your Light Shine." I've always been about women showcasing their brilliance. In letting our light shine, we give other women permission to do the same. Imagine if we all showed up in our spaces as stars shining brightly, magnificently, in our unique brilliance. Just imagine how powerful, revolutionary, and spectacular that would be.

Wouldn't you want to be one of those amazing stars? You are the one with the authority to claim your gifts. No one can do it for you.

We walked through how to identify your strengths earlier, so in this chapter, let's cover why understanding your strengths is so important and how you can begin to not only name your top strengths but claim and aim them as well.

First, let's start with a parable, "The Parable of the Talents," which illustrates the importance of stewarding our talents and why doing so is not just good for our career but is part of our ultimate purpose as women gifted with special skills and talents.

Your Talents, Your Stewardship

The "Parable of the Talents" is the story about a wealthy master who goes on a trip and entrusts his three servants with his wealth, giving each one talents "according to their ability." The first gets five talents, the second gets two, and the third gets one. The master is gone a long time, and when he returns, he calls each servant to account for the talents entrusted to them. The first two servants doubled their talents by investing them in fruitful enterprises, pleasing their master who praises them each with the words, "Well done, good and faithful servant."

However, the third servant, fearful and overly vigilant, had buried his one talent. The master was furious with him, taking away the talent and giving it to the first servant who had originally been given the most talents. The third servant is further punished and thrown out of his master's presence and into "that place there will be weeping and gnashing of teeth." *Yikes!*

This story confounded me for the longest time because I thought the punishment of the third servant seemed unusually harsh. Wasn't it prudent to play it safe and not risk losing the one talent? The cool thing about parables, though, is that there are usually multiple layers of meaning. For instance, the "talents" in the parable can mean money, property, our unique talents, and gifts, or even a Christian's calling to spread the gospel.

But let's explore the parable through the lens of our unique talents and gifts and why engaging and optimizing those talents helps us and others thrive.

We are given talents according to our abilities.

When you think of how you are wired and what things you are especially good at, take comfort in knowing that you have exactly what you need to fulfill your purpose. In the parable, each servant was given a share of talent based on their ability. Similarly, God blesses you with strengths, interests, and passions that make you exceptional at what you do, if you are working, leading, or serving in the areas of your unique gifting. This could be in your career, business, nonprofit, ministry, or personal life. You *do* have the right talents in the right quantities to fulfill God's purpose in you.

When you operate from your strengths, you can be more efficient, effective, successful, and satisfied. This is biblical but also practical. The decades of research behind Gallup's CliftonStrengths Assessment demonstrate that playing to our strengths and managing our areas of weakness is the pathway to success.

We have a responsibility to steward our talents well.

One of the strongest takeaways from the "Parable of the Talents" is the importance of stewardship. We aren't created to have all these gifts and talents only to have them sit and collect cobwebs inside us. There is a purpose for our existence, even if we don't understand the full weight of it just yet. At a minimum, our gifts should be used to add to the good in the lives of others. As the parable demonstrates, the master is pleased when the talents were multiplied to bless his estate.

So what does stewardship mean? In 1 Peter 4:10 it says, "Each of you should use whatever gift you have received to serve others, as faithful stewards of God's grace in its various forms." Stewardship means doing your best to maximize the opportunities your talents provide, and in so doing create value for others. Do you have a talent for singing? Make music. Do you have a gift for bringing things to life with paint? Then create art. Do you have a talent for crunching numbers? Get trained in accounting so you can help others balance their books or file their taxes. Do you have a way with words? Find subjects you're passionate about and speak or write so you can give others a new perspective or share wisdom in your unique way.

The exact talent doesn't matter, but how you maximize it to bless others does! Notice the use of the word "maximize." That is intentional. It implies a multiplying factor that points back to the parable. The servants who pleased their master multiplied their talents by a factor of two. We are called to multiply our talent as well. This is good stewardship.

There are consequences to hiding or misusing our talents.

In the parable, the one-talent servant who hid his talent is severely punished. The lesson is that hiding, abusing, or misusing our talents has consequences, sometimes dire ones. I think of Molly Bloom, the subject of the 2017 movie *Molly's Game*. Molly was a young championship skier on a path to becoming a qualified Olympian until an injury left her unable to compete. Intelligent, savvy, and a "go-getter," she, unfortunately, chose to let her disappointment redirect her talents into forming an illegal celebrity poker ring, which almost got her convicted with a heavy prison sentence. She got off with fines and community service. However, her integrity, name, and personal life suffered from her actions. She had misused her talents, her unique brand of giftedness, and paid steep consequences.[1]

Some of us hide our talents for a myriad of reasons—fear of failure, fear of success, low self-esteem, perfectionism. While the consequences may not seem dire on the surface, the spark that leads to our ingenuity, greatness, or exceptionality dies inside us when we don't embrace our gifts.

Scripture says, "In the same way, let your light shine before others, that they may see your good deeds and glorify your Father in heaven" (Math 5:16).[2] We don't exist here on Earth to fulfill our desires. I believe we are each created as God's masterpiece, formed with a purpose, with gifts meant to serve others and display God's glory.

When we bring our talents to the fore, we allow ourselves and others to benefit. A singer who doesn't sing for an audience, an artist who does not show his creations to others, a chef who only cooks her amazing concoctions for herself—each one is hiding or burying their gift. This is so obvious in creative pursuits, but it is true in every other domain as well. Our gifts are meant to be shared, not hoarded. The more we are generous with sharing, the more we bless and are blessed in return. This is the principle of reciprocity and generosity working hand in hand.

Playing small, dimming our lights, and not thriving in our talents is not God's grand design for us. He expects us to build upon our innate gifts so that we can make the most of what we've been given. This is how we demonstrate our faithfulness to Him. Just like the master was pleased with the two servants who multiplied their given talents, so is God pleased when we faithfully steward our talents and push back against playing small.

Don't compare your talent with others' talents.

A surefire way to stop the blossoming of our talents is to compare how well we're doing with others who have similar talents. Your gift is yours to express in the unique way only you can, based on your experiences, interests, and knowledge. Just like no two artists paint the same way or no two singers sound alike, in all areas of our gifting we are to bring our special flavor to the mix. Comparing yourself to another person is a trap. For many women, I believe one of the biggest barriers to discovering their purpose is their fascination with another person fulfilling theirs.

Was the master less pleased with the servant who doubled his two talents to four compared to the one who increased his to ten? You need to do you and not be worried about what the next woman with your talent does with hers.

Perhaps it's helpful to remember that your talent is not just about you—it's a way you bless others as well. Knowing this should take the competitive pressure off and motivate you to stay in your lane and excel in your amazing way.

Take time to reflect on your talents and strengths and the ways you can engage them to maximize their power, knowing that when you give your gifts room to blossom, you start creating fields of flowers that everyone can enjoy!

In their decades of research building the CliftonStrengths community, Gallup found that the chances of another person having the same top five talents in the same order as yours is one in thirty-three million. Let the magnitude of that sink in.

Playing to Your Strengths

I want to underscore again what we are defining as a talent or strength. Your strengths are areas of aptitude, giftedness, talent, or skill that come naturally to you. It's those things that others often compliment you on. It's the abilities that come so easily to you, that when you're in the zone, it doesn't even feel like you're working. It's that gift you take for granted because it comes so effortlessly that you don't even think about it as your strength. In addition, your strengths are the things you love doing so much that you would even do them for free.

In their CliftonStrengths work, Gallup defines talent as "a natural way of thinking, feeling, and behaving that can be productively applied." They define a strength as the "consistent, near-perfect performance on an activity" to such a degree that one's performance in that activity is considered world-class. Gallup's work is founded on the principle that when knowledge, skills, and practice are applied to a *talent* it is refined and becomes a *strength*.

The term "signature strengths" was coined by Gallup as a groundbreaking outcome of their CliftonStrengths Assessment. Each of the thirty-four areas of talent Gallup measures has the potential to become a strength if they rank in the top ten or fifteen dominant talents in your assessment results.

In Gallup's lexicon, my dominant talents include abilities such as "Intellection," "Ideation," and "Connectedness." Because I have engaged these talents for most of my adult life, they have become solid strengths that show up in a myriad of ways in my life. One of those is writing, which has always been a passion of mine.

In high school I took pride in writing papers for history class, knowing that I had a gift for stringing my thoughts together, making my points land hard, and producing robust conclusions. I didn't know it at the time, but I was using a combination of my "Connectedness," and "Intellection" talents to grow in my writing ability. Later in my career, I always found ways to make writing a key part of my role.

As a market researcher, I wrote proposals, questionnaires, reports, and presentations, highlighting my talent and love of writing. Later as an image consultant, I found ways to write via my blog and monthly newsletters. The icing on the cake was authoring my first book *Frumpy to Fabulous: Flaunting It,*[3] which became an Amazon bestseller!

You too can find ways to align your talents with your calling. For example, you may have a hospitality talent. Taking this talent and applying it to a ministry or nonprofit venture allows you to use your unique expression of hospitality to bless others. This is what Ritz Carlton founder Horst Schulze did to build a global hotel chain renowned for its excellence in customer service and a model of exceptionality in the industry. He did this by becoming excellent in his hospitality gifting. By maximizing his talents, he not only thrived but became immensely successful, blessing his employees and guests in the process.

I created the acronym ZEAL to give you a few clues for knowing when you are operating in a strength:

- **Zone.** When you're in the zone, you catch on to an activity quickly. Being in the zone is the feeling that you were born to do the activity. It is effortless and comes easily to you. In this endeavor, you're a natural and in the zone when you're doing it. Conversely, slow learning is an indicator of a nonexistent strength.
- **Excellence.** When you are leveraging your strength in an activity, you are excellent at it. Think about how Michael Jordan dunks a basketball or how Serena Williams serves killer aces in tennis. They are masters. This excellence is not a one-time thing but a feat they can accomplish repeatedly.

- **Amusement/Enjoyment.** When you are strong in an area, you typically enjoy doing it too. These are the activities we get jazzed about. This describes me when I'm writing. I can work on a piece of writing for hours and lose track of time. If it doesn't feel good when you're doing an activity, you are not engaging a strength.
- **Longing.** You have a deep longing to do the activity—this is the pull or attraction to one activity over another. I so love the satisfaction I get when I write that scheduling time to write is a priority because it brings me pleasure and satisfaction.

You can experience ZEAL for any strength. If you discover ZEAL in an activity, I recommend you examine how you can use this to your advantage in your career. Knowing your strengths also provides insight on how best to interact with your colleagues so you shine in your role.

Think of your signature strengths as a platform from which you can maximize, rise, and thrive. Gaining clarity about your strengths gives you the foundation for designing a strategic career plan. But more importantly, knowing your strengths gives you the confidence to define your career on your terms.

In *Frumpy to Fabulous, Flaunting It*, I describe seven core styles that help women identify their signature styles. Each of those styles, from Traditionalist to Diva, are templates that women can use to build their unique signature style. I emphasize the importance of going beyond what a woman might think is her signature but is really just her default, or "should," style—the style she adopts to conform to societal, cultural, or business norms. So many women I worked with struggled with this.

Just like I'm outlining here the importance of understanding your signature strengths, uncovering your signature style is the key to dressing with confidence. Your signature style is distinct, unique, and personal. You know you've found your signature when you feel and know it at a gut level. When you're rocking your unique style, you'll walk, talk, and act differently, you'll feel amazing, and you'll get compliments—all because you are drawing from what is true for you. We get similar outcomes when we're operating from our signature strengths.

Many women are so used to having their potential downplayed, their voices silenced, or their viewpoints shoved to the side they end up in roles where they bear the brunt of the grunt work without the visibility or recognition they deserve for the things they can bring to the table. In effect, they become indispensable for work that undervalues their potential. It is also likely that they are not engaging their strengths.

To flip the script, women must take control and be intentional about building a personal brand that showcases the brilliance they wish to be known for. Building your brand starts with knowing your strengths, engaging them in your work, and ensuring that you get the credit for what you contribute.

When you are clear about leveraging the strengths that bring your brilliance to the fore, a few more things fall into place:

1. You know which roles to say yes to and which ones to turn down.
2. You know which project to volunteer for.
3. You have a better sense of what new skills to acquire, or what additional qualifications you can work toward.
4. You know who to enlist as mentors and champions.

The clarity and confidence you gain in this process are transformative. When you can identify, embrace, engage, and maximize your signature strengths, and fold these into your brand identity, my friend, you will be well on your way to becoming a career trailblazer.

Seeing Your Talents for the Strengths They Are

The Johari window is a technique that helps people better understand their relationship with themselves and others. It is used in both a self-help context and in a group or corporate setting to improve individual and team performance. I believe it can be a powerful way to explore and highlight your awareness of your strengths and how they are perceived by others.

The Johari window shows the overlap between things we know about ourselves and the things others know about us. There are four panes in the window: Arena, Blind Spot, Façade, and Unknown, each one based on the knowledge known to you and those who know you.

Using this framework as a way to examine your awareness of your strengths is an eye-opening endeavor. Examining your top strengths (if you've completed the CliftonStrengths Assessment or the exercises I outlined earlier), you can easily fill in many of the quadrants.

For example, the Arena is the quadrant, or windowpane of strengths that are known both to you and the people who know you. What talent or strength do you often display that is easily known to others? Using the CliftonStrengths lingo, talents like "Learner" (fascinated with learning new things), "Positivity" (a glass half-full perspective), or "Responsibility" (takes ownership) are typically obvious to others since they are traits that can clearly show up our behavior and attitudes. The Arena pane is the quickest one to populate because you are already self-aware of these strengths and know that others are too.

The Blind Spot pane is trickier because, as the name implies, in this quadrant are the strengths, abilities, and talents that others can see and even admire in us but that we remain unaware of. Most people are particularly good at pointing out their own weaknesses, but they can be blind to their strengths. The things that are effortless to us never seem like the things we need to acknowledge. But nothing is further from the truth!

For example, one of my top five strengths is "Maximizer." Before I did the CliftonStrengths Assessment, I was blind to this talent. I knew I cared about doing things well, that I preferred to spend my time and energy on the things I did well, rather than trying to overcome the areas I fall short, and that I had a natural gift for discovering people's unique and distinct gifts and superpowers. But I did not acknowledge this as a strength.

Understanding the nature of this talent and knowing this was a top talent opened a whole new realm of revelation for me. I could look back on my life and see how this strength played a role in all areas of my life. My "Maximizer" strength served me well. The people around me, especially those who collaborated with me, my clients and colleagues, would have observed this strength in me too. And while the word "Maximizer" would not have been the label they used, words like excellent, high-quality, and motivational have been associated with me for a long time.

Working with clients on their strengths, I've observed how often they are both blind and often dismissive of their most powerful talents. When you look at your top strengths, which ones do you observe with confusion or cynicism? Which ones seem like much ado about nothing to you? This will give you a clue as to the strengths you need to learn more about, embrace, and leverage in your career or business.

The third pane, Façade, is populated with the strengths known to you but hidden from others. Why would you choose to hide a strength and not make it known, you may wonder? One scenario could be that you want to catch people off guard with an area of talent. Another reason could be that you are not proud of the strength.

Let's take a strength like "Empathy," one of the thirty-four CliftonStrengths themes. In some environments, empathy can be seen as a weakness. Even though research has shown that having empathy is one of the most coveted leadership traits—so much so that there are courses on cultivating empathy—a person may decide to hide their empathy because of cultural norms or family dynamics. People with "Empathy" in their top strengths can be seen as too soft, "bleeding hearts," and too sensitive. While these labels themselves are unkind and insensitive, a person with empathy can choose to put up a facade of thick skin to avoid being seen in a negative light.

With workplace norms changing and research showing the benefits of having empathy, the stereotypes of the trait are going away. But even more to the point, if there is any strength or trait that is innate to you that you feel the need to hide, I invite you to consider the cost of not putting your fully integrated self out front and center. The encouragement here is for you to express your full authentic self. Only in authenticity can you make true connections. When we hide parts of ourselves, especially in an area of talent, the cost of dissatisfaction, disconnection, and self-loathing is too high.

The fourth pane in the window is Unknown. This includes information, skills, and behaviors that are unknown about you to yourself and to others. This includes undiscovered talents or areas of giftedness that have never had the opportunity to see the light of day. Looking at your top strengths, are there any that completely catch you off guard? Are there strengths that emerge that you do not recognize in yourself and that no one has commented on? The chance of this occurring in your top strengths is pretty unlikely.

Fill this quadrant Unknown with an opportunity or a latent talent or potential in your career. You may have certain capabilities within you which you may not have explored due to a lack of suitable opportunity, confidence, or training. One of my clients has "WOO" (winning others over) in her top CliftonStrengths. As an engineer working in a lab, her WOO talents did not have a place to emerge or shine. Learning about WOO allowed her to see areas in her personal and social life where the talent showed up, but she did not realize it as a talent. And in her career, her WOO wasn't evident either.

But armed with this new knowledge, we talked about ways she could capitalize and leverage WOO in her new role. She could be the point person for visiting new sites across the country where the technology she was the expert in needed maintenance. With her WOO, she could quickly get support and agreement from these new teams because her gift enables her to win others over—to WOO them.

Uncovering the behaviors and traits that are hidden from you so you can acknowledge or address them is an important aspect of self-awareness, growth, and personal/professional development. It is also one of the advantages of doing strengths work as you come to appreciate the talents and aptitudes that are innate to you that you may take for granted. Strength awareness helps you not only understand but acknowledge your talents so you can start mobilizing them in all areas of your life.

Naming, Claiming, Aiming Your Strengths

Have you ever felt tired of being overlooked, undervalued, and underestimated in your career? Many women feel this way in their jobs. We work hard all the time, grinding and pushing forward but not getting the valuation we feel we deserve. However, the secret to career success, I believe, is all about playing to our strengths.

Gallup uses the Name, Claim, and Aim framework for leveraging the best of our strengths in our work:

Naming your strengths is all about identifying the talent themes innate to you that can be transformed into a strength.

Claiming focuses on embracing and living out your strengths so they become part of the way you operate in your role.

Aiming is about mobilizing your strengths and strategically leveraging them in your position so you are known for the skills that you love and do well.

One of my client's top strengths is "Developer" (seeing and developing the potential in other people) and "Empathy" (being able to put yourself in someone else's shoes).

Guess what her life calling is? She's an addiction counselor, and it's perfect for her strengths. She's also a foster mom. All our aptitudes and skillsets not only work in our work life but they also work in our home life as well because this is how we are naturally wired.

Conversely, we all have shortcomings. However, it would be a futile effort to convert those shortcomings into strengths. A smarter and more effective strategy is to manage your weaknesses by collaborating with someone who is gifted in that area or by amplifying the strengths you do have that can achieve a similar result.

The lowest talent theme for me is WOO. Winning others over is my thirty-fourth talent, which means I am not great at influencing people that way. If I use my energy and resources to try to be a person that has WOO, it's a losing battle. I just don't have the talent. If I needed WOO, the smart strategy would be to either partner or collaborate with somebody who has WOO as a top strength or decide to work around that shortcoming.

Even though I'm not good at winning people over, I am good at creating strong bonds and forming authentic, genuine connections with my "Connectedness" and "Relator" talents, (my #6 and #7). This is why coaching is one of my areas of brilliance—it's all about one-on-one connection, and I'm down for that!

In an interview on Craig Groeschel's *Leadership* podcast, author and activist Christine Caine articulated this so well when Groeschel asked her if she thought it was best to delegate or develop a weakness. Caine said that it would be insecure for a leader to think they had to be better than everyone with everything in their organization. "It's a relief!" she said. "I can work on the things I'm good at, and I can allow people to flourish in their own strengths and never see that as a threat to me."[4]

Caine founded The A21 Campaign in 2008, a nonprofit, non-governmental organization that combats human trafficking. Caine's strategy to staff up the areas where she and her husband Nick fall short in their organization with area experts allows her to surround herself with a cadre of employees who are excelling in their sweet spots. This arrangement makes for an exceptional organization that delivers on its promises in excellence, servicing so many victims and their families.

You can only be in your brilliance when you know what your strengths are and when you play to them by applying those strengths to the very fabric of your work. Drawing from your signature strengths allows you to operate in a space where success is effortless. Your work becomes more satisfying and more meaningful because you're doing the thing you were shaped and designed to do. That's the beauty of our strengths.

When you can engage, maximize, and mobilize your strengths in your career, you are primed and positioned for the success you deserve. Moreover, knowing your strengths gives you the confidence to define your career trajectory on your terms.

In my strengths journey, claiming my top talent of "Strategic" has been transformative. It's what makes me an agile decision-maker and helps me to play out scenario's steps ahead of the average person. Understanding this as my top strength reminds me I have to be mindful of getting too ahead of those around me otherwise what I am saying will appear confusing. My understanding of how this strength shows up in me helps me to be a better communicator of my ideas! I champion strengths because I have seen them play out in my life and in the lives of countless clients who can finally grasp their secret sauce and direct their careers in the area of their specific brilliance.

You can operate in your sphere of brilliance by clearly identifying what makes you YOU—understanding what gifts and abilities you bring to your role or platform and honoring and leveraging these talents to perform at your highest and best.

Your people need you to show up in your brilliance. Your exceptionality and distinctiveness are needed! It's time to recognize more clearly what you have to offer. This is why I am so passionate about strengths work. Strengths help us understand how we do what we do so well and effortlessly. And instead of taking your gifts for granted, claiming your strengths allows you to finally appreciate and value them as everyone else does.

Your Intuition: A Hidden Superpower

According to the *Oxford Dictionary*, intuition is the ability to understand something immediately, without the need for conscious reasoning. It's the thing you know or consider likely from instinctive feeling rather than conscious reasoning.

As women, our intuition, gut instincts, discernment, or "knowing" has been strong within us since we were kids, but many of us learned to deny it. We learn to trust others' reactions before our intuition, to question what we sense or *know* because we think, *"Who am I to be right?"*

For many of you, your gut instincts are strong, yet you have learned from past experiences to turn down its volume until you no longer hear it. Sometimes you learned to silence the voice inside you because you are afraid of what you'd understand—what would be unveiled.

Ladies, hear me loud and clear when I say this: YOUR INTUITION IS A SUPERPOWER!

When we make decisions based on our instincts or intuition, others may dismiss us as irrational. But recent neuroscience research has found that these instincts may be more rational than thought.

According to an article in *Psychology Today*, there is something called physical intelligence (or PQ) which is awareness of and attentiveness to our physical presence. But PQ is also about paying attention to what our body is telling us.

The article underscores that considering all our intelligence, our IQ, EQ, and PQ, allows us to listen to our heads, hearts, and bodies. We make better decisions: "When we're listening to all available channels through which we process information, including our guts, we can tap into information that may otherwise remain obscured. In some cases, listening to our gut may also help us realize something more quickly."[5]

In the past couple of years, I have learned to tune into my intuition, and I've strengthened that muscle. It is liberating and powerful to leverage this gift in my life.

Building your muscle of intuition and learning to value it over what your logic says is right is challenging but so important. I call it learning to defer to your heart versus your head.

One of my clients is good at reading people. I encouraged her to trust her gut instincts and not let her very smart brain "logic" her out of what she knew to be true about a person, *especially* when it didn't make sense. She was learning to exercise her intuition muscle and the stronger it got, the more powerfully it showed up. This ability my client has, to pick up on the feelings, moods, and spirit of other people, is referred to as "empathic accuracy."

I encourage you, especially if you're naturally high in empathy, to get familiar with your intuition, to trust and follow it. To all you extremely smart, strategic-thinking women: know that your intuition is WAY smarter than your logic. Our logic often gets tainted by fear, "what would other people think" questioning, or second-guessing. Intuition, on the other hand, is pure and unfettered by those limitations.

It's important to pay attention to your environment when trying to strengthen your intuition. The more data you have about your environment, the more your intuitive side has to play with and the more it will powerfully inform your actions.

Reflect on the times in the past when you knew something strongly, when you felt deep down it was true, but you didn't listen to it. How did that work out for you? I'll bet that you discovered that your gut instincts were right all along! If you have this gift, I'm sure this has happened many times.

Flip the script and begin to value your intuition like you value your other gifts. Your intuition gives you knowledge and discernment that is beyond your understanding. I believe it is a gift from the Holy Spirit. And I believe, as women, we are blessed by this gift more than men are because the Lord knew we would need a back door to figure stuff out! But that knowledge can only be accessed if we value it, trust it, and use it.

Take time to pay attention to how your intuition comes to you. One of my friends shared how she can't fully explain her intuition like this: "Sometimes I just get these nuggets, and my boss would ask me to write it down or to send him a link. But I couldn't do that because it just comes to me. It's not coming from me; I am the vessel." I TOTALLY get that because it's often how I experience intuition too.

My intuition comes as a deep knowing in my heart and gut that lands a specific way in my body. Now when I have that prompt, I don't second guess or try to figure it out. I just take the action or heed the warning my intuition is making me aware of. And when I do, it can feel almost supernatural because my intuition always makes sense *after* the fact.

Sometimes your intuition can be more subtle and the only way to describe it is a deep "knowing." When something is in alignment with your instincts, it may feel in harmony with you—nourishing, peaceful or enriching. Conversely, when something feels "off," it may feel uncomfortable, jarring even, or like a flattening in your spirit.

Your instincts will often defy logic. Sometimes your gut instincts may make you doubt yourself or think that you're crazy. But this is just your logic trying to protect you from what it cannot comprehend. Your logic is bound by limitations, but your instincts aren't. Your instincts are untethered to everything but the belief that anything is possible.

As Nelson Mandela famously said, "It's only impossible until it's done." Your doubts may seem more real than your instincts, but this is exactly why you must have faith and press into them even more.

Your *knowing* tells you whether something is just not right and what to avoid or turn away from. In your work, your intuition tells you who you can trust, who you can collaborate or do business with, and which people are genuinely for you.

Intuition can also show up as visions. For women with visionary abilities, it's important to pay attention to your dreams and to observe symbolic images that repeatedly emerge. According to an article by Doctor Lissa Rankin, "When the cognitive mind is busy, it can override the intuitive right brain and the subconscious mind, the wellspring of intuition. But when you're sleeping, your cognitive mind rests and opens space for the subconscious mind to signal you in dreams."[6]

One of my clients kept seeing ducks in her dreams, hundreds of ducks. This symbolism spoke to a message from God about His provision for her. Another time she observed a hawk circling her property, which she interpreted as an expansion of her vision about her purpose in life. Because she understood her gifts, she knew to pay attention to these animal symbols.

I have another client who has visions into the future for herself and others. What she communicates to those she has visions about never seems to make sense in the moment. Yet years later her vision materializes. She now knows to trust her visions and understands she's often way ahead of herself and other folks. When she has these hunches about the future, she journals about them and then checks in later to see if she was right. And she almost always is. With patience and humility, she can take the steps in her own life to see these big, bold visions come to fruition years later.

Trusting your intuition may be difficult at first if you're not used to exercising this muscle or turning up its volume. Because it may have been invalidated in the past, you need to learn how to validate it for yourself. Be patient and give your intuition time to grow and flourish in you.

Dr. Rankin also shares that being in the creative space in our minds emboldens our instincts. Activities like painting, scrapbooking, drawing, pottery making, or free-flow journaling quiets the cognitive mind and allows our intuition to become more audible inside us.

She also suggests that we tune into our feelings regularly, stating "The mind thinks, always chattering away, arguing with itself like a crazy person. Intuition, on the other hand, feels. If you're not sure whether you're listening to your fearful mind or your trustworthy intuition, see if you can differentiate whether you're thinking or feeling."[Ibid]

You are equipped with an intuition that is potent, trustworthy, and aligned with your truth. But it's your choice to value and leverage it as the superpower it is. When you do, you will experience the ease, flow, attunement, peace, and confidence that comes when you act in alignment with your inner knowing.

Own Your Brilliance

One day as I was coming out of the grocery, I saw a huge sign on a truck that said in big bold letters on the back "DESTINED FOR GREATNESS." It stopped me in my tracks. *Is this a message for me from God?*

I believe it was, but guess what? I haven't told anyone that story before because it seemed so presumptuous and arrogant to even think that. It can be so easy for us as women to talk ourselves out of owning our value and greatness.

Let this quote from Kathy Caprino's book, *The Most Powerful You*, ignite that fire in your belly to embrace your exceptionality and distinctiveness and share it with the world. Kathy writes:

> "Know that you are amazing (every individual on the planet is), and the world needs your talents desperately. Can you trust and accept the fact that you are special and unique and that it's time to recognize more clearly just what you have to offer others and the world?
>
> It's not arrogant or selfish to recognize and appreciate that you have greatness inside of you. Just the opposite. When you leverage your wonderful talents and abilities in service of others, you're finally making the difference you're meant to and you're helping others in the process. You've stopped wasting time and are now standing firmly in the truth of why you came here to this planet at this time to make a positive difference and make your mark and leave the world a better place. And you will also be more able to help future generations and other women in the world rise and grow as you rise. And that is a life-changing experience in and of itself.

The success and fulfillment you long for will come to you only when you can recognize greatness in yourself and begin to share it more powerfully.

Remember, in the end, it's up to each of us to identify clearly and powerfully what we have to offer in the world, and make use of it, in service of others. No one is going to do that for you. But when you finally decide and commit to honoring and leveraging your talents, and when you believe that it's possible for you to create a professional life you'll love and be proud of, and take brave actions (different from anything you've done in the past) to move closer to that vision, then your future will inevitably improve, and you will finally see new ways and opportunities that will allow your talents and gifts to burst forth."[7]

That deserves an "Amen!"

When you leverage all your amazing TAGS (talents, abilities, gifts, and strengths) in service of others, you're finally making the impact you're meant to make and helping others in the process.

It's up to you to identify and showcase what you have to offer—your unique value proposition. No one else can do that for you. Only when you decide to honor and share your talents with others will you be able to make your mark, leave your imprint, and have a ripple effect on generations of people.

Commit today to allow your star to rise and use your spectacular gifts to let your light shine in service to your sphere. You're magnificent in your uniqueness. Start owning your brilliance!

To recap, here are the key points about strengths:

- The path to professional success centers on building a foundation that capitalizes on your signature strengths. These strengths allow you to bring the best of your brilliance to work.
- Most people don't recognize their strengths for what they are because they come so easily to them. You can only be in your brilliance when you work from your strengths.
- Drawing from your signature strengths allows you to operate in a space where success is more effortless. Your strengths allow you to engage, maximize, and mobilize your gifts.
- Knowing your strengths gives you the confidence to define your career trajectory on your terms.

The Disney movie *Encanto* has a wonderful storyline that relates to the subject of this chapter. (Warning: spoiler alert!) The movie is essentially the story of Mirabel coming to terms with her worth as a young woman. She is the only member of her charmed, magical family, the Madrigals, who does not have a special gift or superpower, and this makes her struggle with feeling worthy and accepted.

When she goes on a hunt to understand why their magical house "Casita" is falling apart and why her family's individual powers are weakening, she discovers a truth that changes not just her life but that of her entire family: the true miracle is the family itself, not their gifts.

Near the end of the movie, when the family matriarch, their Abuela, finally reckons with her failings, she says to young Mirabel, "The miracle is not some magic that you've got. The miracle is you. Not some gift, just you." And this is exactly the message Mirabel needs to reclaim her identity as a beloved daughter and finally embrace herself and connect wholeheartedly to her gifted family. She sees that she doesn't need a special superpower to feel worthy; she just needs to be her amazing, naturally smart, curious, caring, quirky self.

In short, *Encanto* is a story of Mirabel trying to find her own magic and realizing it resides in who she is. And it is the story of a magical family realizing that the true source of their magic lies within them.[8]

Hear this, reader: Your gifts and strengths are amazing! But they are just tools you use to display your brilliance to the world, to make your impact. You, just as you are, are always enough. Your shine is not about your gifts, but about the essence of who you are.

Chapter 4

Beauty from the Inside Out:
Confront Your Imposter

"I am so beautiful, sometimes people weep when they see me. And it has nothing to do with what I look like really; it is just that I gave myself the power to say that I am beautiful, and if I could do that, maybe there is hope for them too. And the great divide between the beautiful and the ugly will cease to be. Because we are all what we choose."

~ Margaret Cho

AT TWENTY-FIVE YEARS old, I was given a once-in-a-lifetime full scholarship to attend Cambridge University. This was an opportunity to cross continents and study with some of the brightest minds in the world. Even though it was overwhelming and intimidating at first, I knew this to be the gift it was—more freedom and independence than I'd ever known. I would get to experience what it was like to be myself unfettered, carve an authentic identity, and foster friendships among the most diverse community I would ever encounter. I was so ready for this, despite my fears.

But the fears were almost crippling. During the first few months of my program, I was practically immobilized by imposter syndrome. I didn't *really* fit in with this cadre of students. Sure, I graduated magna cum laude from Rutgers

University—a performance which was certainly responsible for the scholarship grant in the first place.

But I was so sure this opportunity was some fluke, an error on the part of admissions, that I would sit in my econometrics class glazed over because the gremlins in my head were screaming. They yelled things like, *"You're not that smart, you're just book smart." "These guys have what it takes, but you don't." "Who do you think you are, thinking you can graduate from such a prestigious university?" "They made a mistake. They meant to select some other Jobity."* These thoughts and others were my unwanted companions as I sat in my classes, sure that I would fail and wondering how I would face the embarrassment that would heap on me back home.

My feelings of inadequacy started when I attended an orientation for all the master's students who were a part of the economics department—about one hundred students from around the world. They were all SO smart, "academic smart." We mingled together outside the Marshall Library of Economics. I was feeling fairly confident as I perused the room. I looked good (as usual), and I looked forward to exchanging polite banter with my peers.

One guy, a tall redhead, awkwardly came up to me in an overzealous sort of way and held out his hand in introduction. After the usual name and country exchange, he immediately cut to the chase and asked me whether I believed in Marxist economic theory or Keynesian. I stood there stunned, looking at him blankly. I'm thinking, *No!! I just got here man, are you kidding me? No one had EVER asked me a question like this before. I truly have no idea how to begin to answer this. Oh no! Try to look smart, Natalie. At least pretend you're thinking of a valid answer. Don't blow your cover so soon. Think fast. Think!*

I feigned an expression that, I hoped, suggested thoughtfulness as I tried to drum up a response. When none came, I looked around the room trying to find something, anything, to distract him so I could artfully change the subject.

He was not fooled. Mr. Redhead took my inability to articulate an intelligent response to his question as proof that I was not worthy of further inquiry and unceremoniously moved on to his next victim. I felt exposed and foolish. The perfectionist and people-pleaser in me immediately started berating myself for not paying more attention in classes. *What's wrong with me? Why hadn't I remembered this stuff?*

This was Cambridge University after all, and as I would come to discover, the rules of the game were going to be different. I could not count on my excellent memorization ability or superb multiple-choice test-taking skills to ace these courses. I would have to dig a whole lot deeper. But before I came to this humble awareness, I would resort to my old gremlin buddies: debilitating overwhelm and fear.

After that fateful orientation, when I realized the exceptionality of geniuses around me, I resigned myself to failure. In that period of my life, there was no middle ground—it was either success or failure, and my default was the latter. I sat in econometrics class every week for a good three months before I dared even open the textbook. I was convinced I would not be able to grasp any of it. I was convinced that I did not belong there. My imposter, my inner saboteur, was "running roughshod" in my mind. But I did not know about such things back then.

As an image consultant, I encountered so many women who were stuck in an image rut because their self-perception was distorted by a faulty mindset, poor self-image, or deep-seated insecurities. This became so pronounced the more women I worked with that I had to devote part of my consultations to helping them shift their mindset and self-image so that their new fashion choices would be sustainable. If we didn't tackle what I called their "image saboteurs," no enduring progress could be made.

It was the reason why, in *Frumpy to Fabulous: Flaunting It*, I devoted an entire chapter to these challenges.[1] They showed up in a variety of ways, but the common root was that the saboteur kept the woman stuck in her style rut. Often, the saboteur also limited the changes she could make. The only way to transform her look was to combat the saboteur and help tap into her beauty and sense of self from the inside out.

When I was interviewed about my book, I was always asked which chapter was my favorite. Hands down, the chapter "Beauty from the Inside Out" was my answer because I knew many other style, fashion, and image books did not talk about the inner work we all needed to do to be able to "Flaunt It." And to me, this inner mindset work was a foundational aspect of helping a woman go from frumpy to fabulous.

In the book, I defined image saboteurs as long-held beliefs or ways of thinking that result in barriers or challenges to one's self-image. The way to get rid of them is to acknowledge their power, confront the lie masquerading as truth, and shift the focus to healthier perspectives.

Combatting a woman's image saboteurs was life changing. I witnessed testimony after testimony of women freed from the bondage of their twisted thinking, then making dramatic changes to their style and image presentation that helped them achieve not just their image goals but their life goals as well.

A few of the common image saboteurs I encountered, and my suggestions for helping my clients combat them and shift to a healthier mindset, included the following:

- **I don't like the way I look.**
  - This thinking stems from a distorted and inaccurate perception of beauty based on what the media and pop culture says is beautiful. Women need to refuse to allow themselves to be judged by the rigid, monolithic standard of beauty that pervades our culture and stand strong in their unique expressions of beauty.

- **I need to lose weight.**
  - I don't know any woman who hasn't uttered these words at one point in her life. Our obsession with our weight is tied to what the fashion gurus and celebrities tout in our faces. But the truth is that the average size for US women is a healthy size 12, not a size 2. Nothing is wrong with being a size 2 if that's healthy for you, but most women just aren't built like that. If we are always striving to get to our "ideal" weight, we'll never enjoy being who we are right now. Yes, eat healthily and be fit, but know that body acceptance starts within.

- **My mother always said…**
  - There are many variations to this refrain. But typically a woman can be stuck because of something her mother or loved one said to her as a girl that she dragged with her into adulthood. The power of those formative voices is strong, ladies, but we can't let them hold us back. If you find yourself saying, "I can't wear skirts," for example, ask yourself, why not? If you don't have a valid comeback, chances are you're dealing with a saboteur. And you just gotta kick that gremlin to the curb.

- **I don't feel comfortable standing out.**
  - Ah, this saboteur is so tricky because it can seem so legitimate, right? Women can fool themselves into thinking they like being invisible because it's what feels comfortable. I worked with so many beautiful women who were afraid to shine. There are many roots to this saboteur, but the common truth is that women feel they need to choose between looking natural and authentic and polished and stylish. These don't need to be either/or propositions. Like I wrote in *Frumpy to Fabulous*, having flair doesn't mean you're a diva and dressing less than your best doesn't mean you're being authentic. Invisibility in any form should never be an option. If you're choosing to blend in, it's usually because you're dealing with self-esteem issues or imposter syndrome. We'll get into THAT phenomenon in

a bit, but for now, let your light shine through in the way you present yourself, whether that looks like stopping folks dead in their tracks with your fabulousness or by being quietly understated but still standing solid in your beauty.

- **I am too busy.**
  - If there's ever an excuse that can get old, this one is it! It's so easy to tell ourselves that it's our busyness that makes us neglect paying attention to our looks. But is that really true or is it your default cop-out? Being too busy should never be an excuse for looking frumpy. The truth is we prioritize the things we value. Maybe you're in a season where the way you look is not just that important to you. Own that then. When you're ready to make your image a priority, I know you'll find the time to do so.

- **I'm afraid of unwanted attention.**
  - This saboteur is painful to hear because it typically means that a woman has suffered hurt, trauma, or abuse in her life tied to her image. Sadly, many women have. The #MeToo movement founded by Tarana Burke has made women more empowered to reclaim their authority over their bodies, lives, and heartbreaking backstories. Praise the Lord for that! Prayerfully, with the new inner freedom many women experience in sharing their stories, women can feel freer to fearlessly channel their femininity and sexuality, without worrying that they'll be preyed on because of it. We can hope for this.

- **Who cares how I look?**
  - Uhh, we care, because how you look gives us cues about who you are and what you're about. I always started my "Dressing for Success" presentations with a slide that showed the data from decades-old research that proved that we're judged in the first sixty seconds of interaction predominantly based on how we look. If you want others to perceive you as a smart, successful leader with a purpose, guess what? How you show up matters. And not just at work either. And the other truth? Deep down you DO care about how you look. No woman chooses to show up frumpy because that's her goal. If you're struggling in this area, get help. There are image consultants, stylists, and wardrobe gurus out there whose mission is to help you elevate your image and display the best version of you possible. Don't stay stuck.

The Power of Our Mindset

The stories we tell ourselves and the narratives we choose to believe can keep us stuck not just with our image but with our career. I bullet-pointed the image saboteurs in the last section so you could track the things you may have said to yourself (or still do) regarding your image. Project some of these same excuses and more into your career sphere and you will open a Pandora's box of mindset struggles that can sabotage your desired impact and influence and keep you trapped in a role that no longer serves you.

It may be easy to dismiss the image saboteurs mentioned above as trivial because you may trick yourself into thinking they don't impact your bottom line—your money, your success, your impact. However, struggles in one area of our lives don't just camp out there, they spread into our whole life and undermine the very things that matter to us. Unless, of course, we cut them down at the root and address the issue.

Carol Dweck's book *Mindset,* which I referenced in chapter two, outlines research proving that children and adults who believe they're capable of change and improvement—those who adopt a growth versus a fixed mindset—are more likely to excel than those who believe their potential has a limit and who focus on what they're not good at. In the book, she demonstrates via countless examples how success in our lives can be dramatically impacted by how we perceive our talents and abilities.[2]

Fixed mindset people are those who believe their abilities are fixed—they are who they are and they accept that as an unchangeable fact. These folks are far less likely to flourish in their endeavors than their growth mindset peers.

People with a growth mindset believe their abilities can be developed and refined and that there's a margin to grow and evolve with education, training, practice, and dedication. They don't place limits on their potential and are likely to excel and be among the best in all sectors of life.

The table on the next page highlights the key differences between these two mindsets.

Glancing between these two ways of thinking, the powerful impact our mindset has on how we view the world and our response to challenges becomes obvious.

If you find yourself tracking more with the attitudes in the fixed mindset column, you'll need to work hard to open up your mind to new possibilities, perspectives, and postures of being. This chapter will give you plenty of tools, examples, and insight to do so. I also strongly recommend you check out Dweck's book to convince you even further that now is the time to address your mindset challenges.

Fixed Mindset	Growth Mindset
Avoids challenges	Embraces challenges
Believes intelligence is set in stone	Believes intelligence can be developed
Gives up easily	Persists when faced with setbacks
Sees effort as pointless	Sees effort as a path to excellence
Feels threatened by others' success	Inspired and motivated by others' success
Focused on proving themselves over and over	Not focused on how others see them
Concerned about making mistakes and failing	See mistakes and failure as part of the journey
Believes success comes immediately or not at all	Understands success comes with focused effort
Allows failure to define them	Allows failure to refine them
Focused on outcomes and not the learning experience along the way	Focused on learning and growing more than the outcomes
Ignores constructive criticism	Learns from constructive criticism
Plateaus early and never achieves their true potential	Reaches higher levels of achievement
Ashamed of perceived imperfections/weaknesses	Sees perceived imperfections/weaknesses as part of being human

On the other hand, if you're more growth mindset oriented, bravo! However, this doesn't mean you won't struggle with fear or limiting beliefs. It simply means you're naturally more open to changing them.

Our mindsets and the narratives we tell ourselves and believe to be true profoundly influence our success and our confidence, especially in our careers. An unhealthy mindset is a prime breeding ground for conditions like imposter syndrome and similar behaviors that sabotage and derail our ambitions and ability to thrive. Just as my image consulting clients had to take charge of their image saboteurs before they could harness the power of their fabulousness, so too in their professional arena, women have to reclaim the truth of who they are, own their brilliance, and operate in their confidence and authority if they are to have their desired impact.

You can keep making excuses about why you cannot move up fast enough through the ranks or get your business off the ground, or you can use the ideas, tools, and tips I share in this chapter and beyond to start changing your mindset around your value and self-worth so they no longer hinder you.

So let's address this imposter now so that you can get busy banishing the imposter and getting to the business of unveiling your amazing brilliance unfettered. Then, and only then, you can shine fully and exceptionally serve your sphere.

That Sneaky Imposter

Most ambitious, purpose-driven women want their contributions to matter. They want their impact to make a tangible difference in others' lives. They want to be respected for their expertise and talents. They want their strengths to be engaged and leveraged to the fullest, so they are fully utilized in their role. But sometimes their imposter gets in the way.

According to an article published in *NBC News*, the term imposter syndrome was first used in 1978 by psychologists looking for a better explanation about why high-achieving women often attributed their success to luck rather than their accomplishment.[3] Essentially, imposter syndrome describes the psychological discomfort women feel with acknowledging their role in their success. Imposter syndrome manifests itself in different ways professionally, but most women cite feeling like a fraud or an imposter who doesn't deserve their accomplishments, coupled with the anxiety of being discovered as a fake by their employers and colleagues.

To manage the voice in our heads that tell us we're not enough, we try to do more, to hustle for our worth by pleasing, performing, and perfecting—that three-headed monster that keeps us grinding to prove we're enough—except somehow it always makes us fall short. The gremlin always makes us hustle even more until we burn out or quit.

As I shared at the beginning of this chapter, imposter syndrome showed up in my life as crippling self-doubt and performance anxiety, despite evidence showing my accomplishments and successes. In college, even though I was acing most of my courses, every time I took an exam, I thought I'd failed. My friends and family thought I was being dramatic, but in truth I doubted myself every single time. Then I'd get the A or B+ and brush it off as a close call, only to repeat the same reaction with the next exam.

In my early career as a market researcher, I was plagued with fears that I'd be fired because of poor performance. Then I'd get my yearly review and be floored by the glowing accolades in direct opposition to my fears. Over time and with considerable personal development work, I got better at accepting my successes and believing that I was capable of excellence.

Valerie Young wrote an entire book on imposter syndrome. She shares that people struggling with imposter syndrome "have seriously misguided notions about what it takes to be competent." Even though someone may look successful and be perceived as smart and accomplished, if they struggle with imposter syndrome, they're going to believe that they're "merely passing for competent," or worse, dread the moment when they'll be revealed as "an incompetent sham."

Young goes on to explain that "despite often overwhelming evidence of their abilities impostors dismiss them as merely a matter of luck, timing, outside help, charm—even computer error. Because people who have the impostor syndrome feel that they've somehow managed to slip through the system undetected, in their mind, it's just a matter of time before they're found out."[4]

I can relate. For months I thought my acceptance into Cambridge University on a full scholarship must have been some type of technological glitch. Even though my last name is not a common one, I thought for sure they must have meant to accept another Jobity. There was just no way I could be that smart! It's rough admitting this now, but that's truly what I thought.

After my encounter with Mr. Redhead during the orientation mixer for students in the economics-related programs, I resigned myself to failing my program. For months I didn't even make the effort to study because I was so convinced I wasn't smart enough to comprehend these new subjects. And I would surely have failed if it were not for the support and encouragement of two African male friends who helped me believe in my competency. But that story is for another book.

What causes imposter syndrome to rear its ugly head? Some experts say the pressure of rising to new challenges can often make people question their experience, credibility, and skillset, paving the way to impostor syndrome. New successes or opportunities like a new job, a promotion, or other career milestones are triggers.

Social worker Cara Maksimow explains it this way, "The person who achieved this level of success begins to have negative thoughts that the success was not earned. These negative thoughts, which are often referred to as 'cognitive distortions,' are based on fear and anxiety and not based on objective facts."[5]

Sharon's Story

This was the case with my client Sharon. Sharon was a successful twenty-year veteran who worked for a global company and had recently been promoted to a leadership position when we first started working together. She came to me struggling with her confidence, unable to articulate her strengths, and feeling insecure about how she communicated in meetings. She felt ill-equipped and unqualified for her new leadership role, which was made more unbearable because she was paired up with a confident, highly communicative peer, Brian, who she felt outshone her at every opportunity. Sharon was desperate for a lifeline, wanting to be able to succeed but having little faith that she had what it took.

Sharon was struggling with imposter syndrome big time. If she did not rein it in, it would most certainly have derailed her success. One of the areas we agreed to focus on in the beginning was working on helping her name, claim, and aim her strengths so her confidence could grow. Her top CliftonStrengths was "Relator." Since she was an introvert, she struggled to understand and own this as her superpower. As we dug deeper into her past career and life experiences, she slowly started to believe this was a strength and began to engage it more in her interactions, especially with Brian.

As her confidence grew, she saw Brian's shortfalls and could see how her contributions had value. "He is really good at summarizing points and coming across as if he has it all together, but he's weak in implementation," she observed during one of our sessions. "I am the one who gets stuff done, who mobilizes resources. He's just great at talking a good game."

A few months in, Sharon's self-perception became more accurate and she became more engaged and driven, energized now about her strengths. We then started tackling her imposter, who we named Sally so we could confront the imposter head-on. Sally was the negative voice in Sharon's head, the doubter, the underminer. Sally said things like, "Who do you think you are?" and "You're in way over your head." Sally was empowered when Sharon was facing a new challenge or when she suffered a setback, which would make Sally's voice louder and more frequent.

In our coaching sessions, Sharon came to understand the nature of this voice and its triggers. As an immigrant of color from an African country where women are groomed to take a backseat to their male peers and where their career aspirations can be highly scrutinized, it made sense why Sharon struggled so much in her new, more visible role that she shared with a man.

According to writer Sheryl Nance-Nash, fear, doubt, and insecurity—the hallmarks of imposter syndrome—impact women of color even more than their white counterparts. This is because of the psychological impact of systemic racism which creates a mindset that we are not good enough. Nance-Nash cites a quote from psychotherapist and executive coach Brian Daniel Norton to explain, "When you experience systemic oppression or are directly or indirectly told your whole life that you are less-than or undeserving of success and you begin to achieve things in a way that goes against a long-standing narrative in the mind, imposter syndrome will occur."[6]

Moreover, the fact that women of color are not adequately represented in corporate environments makes the ones that are in those environments feel that much more pressure to perform and excel because they are carrying the burden of perceptions about their whole race on their backs. "The lack of role models for marginalized communities has a major impact on making people feel like they do—or don't—belong in these corporate environments," writes Nance-Nash.

Sharon was living this experience as a Black woman in a senior leadership role. But the more she claimed her strengths, celebrated every small win, stretched herself, and challenged her old ways of thinking, her imposter Sally shrunk, and a new narrative began to take root. A narrative that said things like, "I deserve to be here," "I've got this," "I can communicate authentically and powerfully once I am armed with knowledge," and similar empowering, positive thoughts.

Before long, these thoughts became so pervasive that we named the new voice in her head Samantha to acknowledge that a new neural pathway had formed in her brain. This was huge! In less than six months, Sharon had not only grown in confidence and authority, but she started to see her influence elevate.

Amazingly, eight months into her new role, Sharon got wind that she was going to be promoted again, this time in a role where she would not have to compete for visibility. Now that she was more comfortable and confident in her position, the thought of a promotion did not scare her. In fact, she was thrilled. This new position was perfectly aligned with her strengths, expertise, and passions. She could now believe that she earned and deserved this role because she now saw herself and her competencies more objectively.

But her story gets even better. In a highly visible meeting with all of the company's C-suite executives, it was announced that Sharon was not going to be promoted to a senior director position but to a vice president role, making her one of the handful of female vice presidents in the company!

After Sharon had been in her new vice president role for a few months, she was tasked with chairing and leading dozens of meetings across the country with the company's key business units. Her role involved using her "Relator" strengths to be perceived as a trusted partner among key company stakeholders. Using this strength, paired with her "Strategic" and "Individualization" strengths, she customized each of those meetings to the culture and nuances specific to each team.

Leading those meetings leveled her up even more. While Sally still makes an appearance here and there, Samantha is the voice that is mostly in the background now. Sharon confronted her imposter, and her imposter had to shrink way back so she could become the leader she was designed to be.

Facing Your Imposter Head On

While imposter syndrome is an equal opportunity disorder, impacting 70 percent of the US population, it does appear to impact women more than men. Also, certain characteristics, like being the firstborn, can make imposter syndrome more likely to emerge. As was the case in my upbringing as the eldest, I was expected to be the model child, and when I made mistakes, I was criticized harshly for them. The guilt and shame of not being perfect made me view myself as bad, unworthy of approval or accolades. This was a prime breeding ground for imposter syndrome behavior to develop within me.

Imposter syndrome held me back for so many years. My career as a market researcher plateaued until I gained the confidence and freedom to believe I deserved every success—shoot, that I had earned every success! Until I shook off that imposter on my back that said I was not good enough, I couldn't shine. I could not reach or even dream of higher aspirations. I would never have had the guts to finally abandon my market research career and pursue my dream of entrepreneurship as an image consultant if I had let imposter syndrome keep me playing small. And hear this ladies; I was not only afraid of failing in my career, I was also afraid of succeeding. If I succeeded, the light would shine more brightly on me, making me feel even more pressure to perform perfectly.

If what you've read so far sounds like you, know that you don't have to continue to make imposter syndrome define you or your career goals. Let my testimony inspire and encourage you—you can get past it, learn to manage it, and catch yourself before you spiral out of control. But it will take some work.

Dr. Lisa Orbé-Austin and Dr. Richard Orbé-Austin, executive coaches and psychologists, wrote a book that tackles imposter syndrome in detail.[7] In a presentation that Dr. Lisa Orbé-Austin gave to the Institute of Coaching on imposter syndrome, she acknowledged that imposter syndrome worsens when we become more visible or have greater stakes in our professional game and that part of minimizing the potency of the imposter is to internalize our successes, rather than attributing them to luck, overwork, or a mistake. She cited a 2020 KPMG study showing that 75 percent of executive women suffer from imposter syndrome in their careers.[8]

That's a lot of us, ladies! That's why I'm spending so much time on this topic. Orbé-Austin cites four hallmarks of this type of thinking:

1. A lot of diligence and hard work ethic which can border on overwork
2. A feeling of intellectual inauthenticity so that you downplay your accomplishments
3. Having high emotional intelligence (or EQ) and not trusting it, viewing it instead as deceptive
4. A need to seek out mentorship for external validation

Orbé-Austin says that women who struggle with imposter syndrome achieve and accomplish a lot, but they struggle with the fear of being a fraud, and this fear can become debilitating. These women tend to work harder and spend more time on tasks, especially when they've received any type of negative feedback. And for women of color, Orbé-Austin confirms that we have a double dose of imposter syndrome because of the added cultural, professional, or organizational messages that reinforce that we don't belong. These external messages make us feel that much more like frauds.[Ibid]

In the professional arena, specific triggers for women of color include:

- Discrimination
- Microaggressions
- Isolation
- Lack of mentors
- Inequitable treatment
- Gaslighting

As a Black woman who understands these issues personally, when I work with women of color who struggle with imposter syndrome, as many of us do, I know it's important for me to hold a sacred space that helps them feel visible, valued, and vouched for. Having a coach of color can facilitate greater and faster transformation because of their shared lived experiences in this context.

A piece in *Business Insider*, has a checklist of warning signs to tell if you're being hijacked by imposter syndrome. Key ones include:

- You're unable to internalize your achievements and you downplay your accomplishments
- You fear being "found out" or being exposed as inexperienced or untalented
- You avoid feedback
- You're reluctant to ask for help
- You turn down new opportunities
- You second-guess your decisions
- You're overworked to the point of burnout because you need to prove you're "enough"
- You fail to start or finish projects
- You set incredibly challenging goals and feel disappointed when you fall short[9]

I believe it's important to take away the stigma, misperceptions, and lack of knowledge around imposter syndrome so we can address it. Make no mistake—the doubt, insecurity, and stress from imposter syndrome can thwart our career trajectories because they prevent us from seeking out leadership positions that have more visibility and influence.

To give you a kick start, here are a few solutions that worked for me and others. Harnessing the power of these strategies can help you claim your power back and take control of your career success.

1. **Replace perfectionism with power.** The saying goes, "Perfection is the enemy of done." It is also the enemy of good enough. When you recognize that there is no perfection on this side of eternity and embrace the truth that you are everything you're meant to be right here, right now, you can flip a finger at perfectionism-driven imposter syndrome. So you made a snafu in your presentation? It's not the end of the world. It only means you're human. So you didn't know the answer to the question posed by your boss? No one expects you to have all the answers, and you should not expect it of yourself either.

    You're not an imposter, my friend; you're just a woman with a purpose on her way to making her mark who makes a mistake here and there. Instead of striving to be perfect, strive to be authentic. The greatest leaders are authentic and humble. There is power and freedom in this! Own when you mess up and keep it moving.

2. **Identify and curate a "Strengths and Successes" inventory.** It should be obvious by now that I am a strong proponent of the CliftonStrengths Assessment. I believe it is an excellent tool to give you an objective perspective in the areas where you shine. But don't just take the assessment—take a deep dive into understanding each of your signature strengths and how you express them in your role. Then incorporate this new understanding into your work life so you refine and fine-tune how you express those strengths in all your activities. Take an objective look at everything you've achieved. Reflect on your grit, dedication, commitment, and resilience. Recall all the hard work you've put in to get to this echelon of your career. Embrace the fact that you got yourself here—your accomplishments are proof of that.

   This was a strategy I used with my client Melinda. In one of our sessions, I asked her to objectively recount the "facts," not her feelings, about her experiences. She listed off a myriad roles and accomplishments which, to anyone listening, proved she had all it took to be on a leadership team. Hearing herself talk about her achievements this way was the beginning of her mind breaking down the lies fueling her low self-esteem. After a few weeks, she felt more assured because her inventory of past successes showed she was NOT a fraud. Instead, her inventory demonstrated that she was exceptionally capable to perform in this capacity.

   With an objective inventory of your strengths and accomplishments throughout your career, you are better able to tackle your negative self-talk when imposter syndrome shows up. Seeing all your strengths, accomplishments, and wins professionally makes it harder to justify that it's all just luck. Refer to your "Strengths and Successes" inventory whenever you find yourself doubting your abilities and questioning your potential.

3. **Identify allies, mentors, and advocates in the workplace who believe in you and are supportive of you professionally.** Talk to them about your fears and solicit feedback from them about their experiences with doubt and insecurities. Even if your mentors don't have full-blown imposter syndrome, every successful woman has experienced doubt and low self-confidence. They will relate and help you see that they're not that different from you, which helps normalize your experiences. Imposter syndrome gains power when you believe it is personal to you. Talking about, acknowledging it, and listening to constructive feedback from other successful women will empower you to fight against it.

4. **Savor your successes and celebrate your wins.** All too often, ambitious women blow past their wins and milestone accomplishments without a thought and move onto the next challenge. Stop the madness! You must take time to savor your successes. Nailed that presentation? Celebrate it! Snagged that high-profile client? Celebrate it! Got the promotion you have been vying for months? Celebrate! When you celebrate and acknowledge your successes, you can leverage the confidence and fulfillment you feel to encourage even greater confidence and assurance in your abilities. Imposter syndrome has to back down in the face of the confidence, pride, and gratification that comes when you do well.

   One thing that works well for me is to keep a record of my wins in a gratitude journal. I document things that went well in my day every evening. This practice helps me reinforce that I'm thriving. So the simple activity of writing down your wins diverts your focus from your negative thoughts and toward the brilliance you bring to the table. Doing this helps you savor the wins that much more.

5. **Stop comparing yourself to others.** There is another saying, "Comparison kills." If you think this sounds extreme, it is not. Comparison is the thief of joy, creativity, ingenuity, peace, love, and contentment. If that's not a metaphorical death, I don't know what is. When you compare yourself with another person, you will always come up short (in your mind) and fuel that imposter syndrome energy. You are unique and amazing when you stay in your lane and focus on the traits and skills that you bring to the arena. Consciously fight the tendency to compare and measure yourself against others. Trust me, comparison is a waste of your valuable time and energy.

   Instead of using other professionals as a benchmark for your success, which only leaves you feeling inadequate, try to press deeper into what skills, talents, and expertise you can build on to make you even more effective in your role. Ask yourself what additional learning or experience will get you closer to achieving your ultimate vision for your professional impact. This practice will ground you and help you boost your feelings of confidence and control.

   You can also try using a reframe to shift your perspective. Using reframe is not about seeing the world through rose-tinted glasses; it's about thinking differently about a situation so that you feel more empowered and competent. A question to ask yourself when you're feeling inadequate is, "How can I view this situation from a more empowered mindset so that I feel more capable and in control of the situation?"

6. **Remember that you're not alone.** When you find yourself beating yourself up for your perceived inadequacy, remind yourself that some of the world's brightest and most successful people have experienced failure and career crumbling blunders, yet they got back up and stepped back into the game because they knew they had something valuable to offer. So do you.

   Oprah made, produced, and acted in movies that massively flopped, like *Beloved*. Martha Stewart went to jail, for heaven's sake, yet still managed to resurrect her career as a lifestyle guru. Maya Angelou experienced a myriad of failures as a teenager and young adult and only started writing books in her forties. She never gave up, despite her many blunders. Did she experience insecurity? Heck yes! Just read her memoirs.

   When you think of Oprah, Martha, and Maya, do you think of them as screw-ups? No, of course not. Treat yourself with the same level of grace and generosity, recognizing that so many women relate to you when you feel defeated in your career. But the only difference between a successful woman and an unsuccessful woman is how she responds to failures, real or perceived. In those moments when you're feeling low, remind yourself that making mistakes or failing doesn't make you an imposter—it makes you human like everyone else, even your most esteemed idols.

   In a recent *Time Magazine* feature, Michelle Obama interviewed record-breaking poet laureate Amanda Gorman. Gorman shared her struggles with imposter syndrome saying, "No matter how many speaking engagements I do, big audiences always trigger a little bit of impostor syndrome in me."[10]

   If you can relate, know you're in good company. Imposter syndrome tends to show up in places where we would like to play big, like in our careers, businesses, platforms, or ministries. While imposter syndrome is real, you can refuse to let it dull your ability to shine by taking control of the negative self-talk. Take a page out of Michelle Obama's and Amanda Gorman's playbook and shine even when imposter syndrome tries to tell you otherwise.

7. **Act as If.** This strategy should ring a bell too. Acting as If not only helps build confidence, but it also works really well on our imposters too. When I worked as an image consultant, I encouraged my clients to show up

every day as if they were dressed to meet their most important client or attend an important meeting. Our image not only communicates how we feel but it can also help mold others' perceptions of who we want to be. The way you dress, your poise, the way you speak, your non-verbal cues all communicate volumes about who you are as a professional. So why not leverage your image for maximum impact? Coupled with your inner game of "Acting as If," your image can help you dispel all your negative self-talk, so you believe you deserve a seat at ANY professional table.

8. **Observe your negative thoughts.** In her webinar presentation to the Institute of Coaching, Lisa Orbé-Austin talked about silencing your imposter by addressing your automatic negative thoughts, or ANTs. Examples of ANTs include labeling (such as telling yourself, "I'm stupid"), mind reading (thinking you can interpret what people think about you), fortune-telling (predicting negative outcomes), catastrophizing (expecting the worst-case scenario), comparison (see above), all or nothing thinking (if I don't get at least a B+, it means I've failed), overgeneralization, and discounting positives (I never do anything right).

   The tactic to correct this type of thinking is to observe the thoughts and recognize the imposter voice in your mind. Then do the following:

   1. Remind yourself that you are not your thoughts.
   2. Tell yourself you are just the observer of your thoughts.
   3. Know that having such thoughts does not make them true.

It's also helpful to think of the different perspectives in your situation that can challenge your ANTs.[11]

This strategy is probably best executed with professional support as it's so difficult to be objective in one's own situation, especially when the imposter is at large.

While there is no perfect hack to rid yourself indefinitely of imposter syndrome, practicing the strategies above will help you manage your bouts with the anxiety, self-doubt, lack of confidence, and insecurity that imposter syndrome fosters.

I believe you deserve to thrive doing work that plays to your strengths, energizes you, and allows you to bring your brilliance to the table every day while positively impacting those you lead, mentor, guide, or influence. Let's all work hard to kick that imposter to the curb so we can play big like we're called to!

The Quest for Perfection

In Valerie Young's book on imposter syndrome and its impact on women, she breaks down five different archetypes the imposter can take. One of these archetypes is the Perfectionist. She writes that because the perfectionist's focus is so singular, "when (they) fail to measure up to these unrealistically high standards, it only confirms (their) feelings of impostorism."[12]

We're talking about women who are highly gifted and competent, yet their unrealistic expectations for their performance derail their success over time. This perfectionistic behavior often involves thoughts such as, "I must perform at 100 percent all the time," or, as one of my clients put it, "I expect to be perfect in my work because any less than that is not good enough."

Young notes that perfectionists sometimes hold others to their extraordinarily unrealistic exacting standards. When perfectionists lead others, they tend to become that insufferable boss who is hypercritical, never satisfied, and has issues delegating because they think they're the only one who can get it "right."

According to Young, "Quality-wise, Perfectionists always go for the gold, the A+, the top spot. Anything less and you subject yourself to harsh inner criticism, often experiencing deep shame at your perceived "failure." Precisely because there is such shame in failing, you may avoid altogether attempting anything new or difficult."[Ibid]

This describes me many decades ago. I was a striver. In college I only cared about getting the As—anything less did seem like a failure to me. This all-or-nothing approach (one of the ANTs listed above) was so punitive, but I didn't see things any other way. I had gotten into the habit of equating my performance with my level of self-worth.

If you're a high achiever, perhaps you can relate. You get caught up in performing, pleasing, and perfecting, hustling for your worth in your achievements. You can't help but review that proposal for the tenth time to ensure you catch every grammatical error. Or you tweak your PowerPoint presentation to death, making sure all the fonts are the same type and size, that the colors blend well, and that all your bullets are the perfect length. No one will likely notice or care that you are spending time on these details, but you care. You care so much that if you try to stop yourself from obsessing over your deliverable, it's really hard. You get that knot in your stomach, you feel vulnerable, you feel unsettled, so you MUST review your deck or document one more time.

Young acknowledges that "perfectionism is a hard habit to break because it's self-reinforcing."[Ibid] Because the truth is, perfectionists do amazing work, they over-prepare, they deliver top-notch presentations, they are the top performers in their organizations, and typically function at the high level they think they must attain in their heads. And this performance, in turn, reinforces their drive to keep up the pace. Because their perfectionism pushes them to strive and achieve, they are often successful—on the outside.

"But it's a huge setup," Young writes, "because when you expect yourself and your work to always be perfect, it's a matter not of if you will be disappointed but when."[Ibid] The downside of perfectionism is that it's exhausting. The cycle never ends; because once perfectionists achieve a goal, they just raise the bar higher. The result is they never feel the satisfaction from their many successes because, in their minds, it's never enough.

Additionally, because perfectionism is unattainable, it becomes addictive. Perfectionists tell themselves the false narrative that if they are perfect, then they will finally feel worthy and approved. But that relief never comes because no one can live up to the standard of perfectionism, least of all themselves. So they constantly wash and repeat the cycle of trying to be perfect by performing and pleasing to gain approval to avoid the shame and judgment they feel inside.

This is the scenario my client Kelly struggled with. An overachiever by any standard, Kelly came to me recognizing that perfectionism was a problem for her, but she was so attached to this way of being that she didn't know how to change. Her career goal was to master everything confidently in her role. She was highly punitive and beat herself up for the slightest missteps, things no one else on her team would even notice. Kelly took her perceived "failures" to heart and would get caught up in self-condemnation, overthinking how to make things right.

Kelly acknowledged that even if her colleagues' positive impressions of her performance remained unaffected, it bugged her that *she* knew she didn't complete something perfectly. Because it meant she did not perform at the 100-percent level she expected of herself but at the 98-percent level. That 2-percent shortfall would diminish her achievement or win to such an extent that she didn't experience it as a win at all but as an underperformance. She would stew over small missteps and take a long time to move on from them.

Kelly was new in her role as a program manager, a role that required her to learn new scientific jargon and principles that were completely foreign to her. And yet, in just a few months, she was already killing it. I would joke with her that her brain was like a computer because she was able to absorb and retain a high quantity of data and categorize and store information that she could readily access in seconds.

Despite her superpowers, Kelly got incredibly nervous when she gave presentations and wasn't sure how her delivery would be perceived. She would agonize over what she believed to be stupid things she may have said as she gained knowledge in her role or if she didn't know the answer to a question posed to her. The typical learning curve that everyone goes through in a new role meant nothing to her—she expected to know everything immediately.

Kelly's competency was so remarkable that she got high praises from her colleagues and boss, who frequently remarked on her exceptional performance. They had never worked with a program manager with skills and abilities like hers.

Yet Kelly would share these truths with me with a type of begrudging acceptance. "Yeah, I guess this is a pretty good review, but there's still so much I don't know..." Until she felt she achieved her unrealistically high bar of success, the accolades didn't sink in.

Kelly loved her work and knew she was in the absolute right lane for her talents and abilities, but she wasn't fully satisfied because her struggles with perfectionism made her the victim of paralyzing procrastination, burnout, frequent headaches, anxiety, and constant negative self-monitoring. She also struggled when things "didn't make sense." When she had to operate in any type of gray area, she would have difficulty getting over the hump and going with the flow.

I tell clients like Kelly that striving for excellence is a worthy goal, but perfectionism is something altogether different. Perfectionism, at its core, is all about earning approval.

In *Dare to Lead*, Brené Brown explains, "Perfectionism is other-focused: *What will people think?* Perfectionism is a hustle." She further breaks down that perfectionism "fuels the thought that, '*If I look perfect and do everything perfectly, I can avoid or minimize the painful feelings of blame, judgment, and shame.*'"[13] In Kelly's case, her thinking was, "*If I can't master my role, it must be because I'm just not smart enough*," which then triggered feelings of anxiety, low self-worth, and insecurity.

Stopping the Madness

What then is the hack for perfectionists? Change can be hard because there is a tradeoff. Often the habits that hold us back as leaders are the same ones we've used to get us to our current level of success. We've become so familiar with engaging in the behavior we want to change that stepping out of that behavior causes discomfort and anxiety, which then prevents us from implementing the healthier behavior. This is because the short-term gain we get from engaging in the behavior keeps us tethered to it.

One of the principles Michael Bungay Stanier discusses at the beginning of his book *The Advice Trap* is a concept he calls Present You gains versus Future You costs. He explains, "Hard change involves saying no to some of what's worked for Present You. Saying no now enables you to say yes to the promise of future rewards. You're playing a longer-term, harder, bigger game, with a constant temptation to opt out for a short-term win."[14]

Even when we know a behavior like perfectionism is destructive eventually, we do get a short-term win from it. Perfectionists get to feel superior, better than those around them, and in the short term, feel perfect. This feels good—albeit only temporarily, which is why it's hard to stop. This immediate, small win, even though it's not really what the perfectionist wants, is what Bungay Stanier calls "a short-term boost for Present You." The cost? The bigger win for Future You.

For a perfectionist, that Future You can look like finally being able to manage your work-life balance as a leader because you're not sweating the small stuff. It can mean being able to truly delegate so you can focus less on doing and more on leading your team. For a woman like Kelly, using this technique can look like her envisioning an end to all the grinding and hustling and gaining the freedom to relax and enjoy her work. This Future You is free and liberated and has the margin to be a more effective and impactful leader. These are substantial benefits. But they're not immediate, and herein lies the challenge of changing.

The unfortunate reality is that Present You gains short-term benefits from not changing at the expense of a free and liberated Future You who is no longer striving for perfection. When you're set free from perfectionism, Future You can live from a more present, authentic, humble, and empathic place—all fundamental traits of great leaders.

Is this you, sister? This used to be me! I know you desperately want to change, but you feel stuck.

Coming to a new awareness of what I truly wanted out of life and who I wanted to be helped me evolve and grow out of most of my perfectionistic tendencies. What I'm saying to you, leader, is that there is hope. You can change too! You don't have to feel stuck in the perfectionism grind.

The first step is becoming clear about what you want and who you want to be as a leader. Envision yourself a year or two from now. How do you see yourself leading? What does a typical day look like? What do you spend your time doing? How do you want others to interact with you? What are your top leadership traits?

How do you relate to your work? What brings you joy? What do you sound like? What is your worth rooted in? How do you define success?

I coached Kelly around these questions, and it helped her to let go of some of the small stuff she was prone to sweat. It also helped her to move more quickly through tasks that didn't need her absolute best. Instead of procrastinating because everything she delivered had to be perfect, she could move forward, albeit reluctantly, to the next milestone.

Kelly's vision for herself in the future was limited to her current role. She really couldn't see herself doing anything better. She was clear she did not want to lead people; her anxiety around not being able to read her coworkers and peers' minds was tough enough! For her, a fulfilling career three years out meant doing the same type of work she currently did, but perhaps on a higher level. For Kelly, her leadership vision would be as an individual contributor.

You're not going to be motivated to change if you don't have a vision of what Future You looks like. So hear me now: this vision needs to be big, bright, and bold—in full technicolor in your mind.

Then when you feel yourself wanting to lean into perfectionism, take a moment. Ask yourself, *"Is trying to execute this task perfectly going to give Future Me what I want? Or is it going to just be the same ole, short-term win?"* Wrestling with this question honestly in the moment should help you to pivot and decide to score points for Future You. Every time you choose Future You over Present You, you allow yourself to change, mature, and evolve into the amazing leader and woman you already are.

Your perfectionism may have been ingrained into you from an early age. And it certainly helped you achieve success. But as you move up your career ladder, you'll find, as Kelly did, that the cost of not changing gets higher. The stress of keeping up a perfectionistic way of being amps up and spills over into your physical, mental, and emotional health.

Here are a few simple things you can do to change your behavior and the thinking that drives it:

1. **Accept that failure is part of the human experience.** Yes, success feels great, I know. But real success only comes when we are truly willing to accept that failure is an option, and that we will survive it. If we are to take the risks required of anyone wanting to make an impact, we must be open to failure. We must be open to the fact that everything is not under our control. Like everyone else, sometimes you will fail and that's OK. You can lean into failing forward and trust that you can and will recover.

2. **Accept that not everything you do deserves to get an A+.** Learn how to prioritize your efforts and energy so that you dedicate the best of your skills to the things that truly matter. For the rest of your endeavors, particularly those mundane tasks on your To-Do lists, your best effort will certainly be good enough.

3. **Learn to delegate.** Chances are that if you're a perfectionist, delegating does not come easily for you because it means relinquishing control of the outcome. Commit to delegating more, asking for, and receiving help. Try to see delegation as a way to empower others, to help them stretch and grow as you do. When you micromanage and try to control everything, you deny those around you the ability to serve and support you and may even enable them to rely on you. So, rather than enable, empower. The upshot is you'll get to use your skills the way they're intended and not get bogged down in tasks that are beneath your paygrade.

4. **Check your self-esteem.** All perfectionists depend on external validation to feel good about their performance, even ones like Kelly who are more self-punitive. Seeking external affirmation is a risky business because it depends on the fickle fancies of folks who often come and go with the tide. The only constant is our unwavering and unfailingly loving God and the "self" that we have allowed to either foster or flounder. Seeking self-approval begins and ends within. There is no shortcut, no fast track, no other way.

5. **Spend time loving on yourself.** Loving yourself will truly bolster your inner confidence. What do you say to yourself in your downtime? Are you building and lifting yourself up or tearing yourself down? Do you know that it doesn't matter who thinks you're awesome if you don't think you're awesome?

6. **Focus on progress, not perfection.** High achievers are often perfection seekers. But the truth is that none of us is perfect. Aiming for perfection is a losing game. Instead, aim for growth and learning. And learning some more. As a wise friend recently said to me, there is only winning or learning. Losing only happens when we don't learn from our mistakes. Believe that you don't always have to be the knower, you can be a learner.

7. **Recognize that you are so much greater.** You're greater than the "A" grade, the perfect five satisfaction rating, the exemplary performance. These are just metrics. But you are divinely YOU in all your expressions. The bible says you are God's masterpiece, created anew in Jesus Christ. Be not just satisfied but awed with that. You are enough, just as you are.

8. **Get out of your comfort zone.** Try taking small risks to see how you can perform different tasks and settings. Volunteer for stretch assignments that will take you a bit out of your comfort zone. You're not a superwoman but you are a woman with superb powers! When you find yourself struggling, consider the cost of holding onto your old, tired ways of behavior. What are you missing out on if you continue this way?

9. **Focus on excellence.** Excellence has nothing to do with perfection. The difference between perfection and excellence is that one is an unrealistic outcome, and the other is a way of being. In excellence, there is the healthy striving to put forth one's best effort. In perfectionism, it's all about doing things perfectly, and perfect doesn't exist. After all, who decides what's perfect? Perfection is a zero-sum game—it's all or nothing. Excellence is a posture, not a target. Excellence makes room for effort and the satisfaction that comes with that, regardless of the outcome.

10. **Loosen up!** Manage your expectations of what's required of you. An important part of Kelly's progress was understanding how her expectations of competency and performance for herself and others were much higher than was expected. Her mediocre was another person's adequate or good. This was a tough shift for her and one she continues to grow into. Once Kelly could relax her standards and leave wiggle room for a margin of error, she could extend grace to herself and others. Life is a marathon, not a sprint. Get those endurance muscles in gear and enjoy the long journey. And discover yourself along the way.

Recognizing the Gremlin

It should come as no surprise that perfectionists also tend to suffer from imposter syndrome. Successful, purpose-driven professionals with high aspirations can find themselves crippled with insecurity, doubting themselves even as they achieve milestone after milestone. In their distorted, "all or nothing" thinking, they have to be perfect or else they've failed.

If you find yourself struggling with fear, insecurity, or doubt—key signals that you may be a victim of imposter syndrome—check yourself by the following behaviors.

Playing small by not voicing your ideas or opinions.

- Remember that your silence sometimes speaks more loudly than your words. If you're being silent, make sure it's intentional and not because it's your default.

Waiting for permission or an invitation to take charge or lead.

- A woman becomes a leader by showing initiative, advocating for herself, or aligning herself with those who are her champions. These are active things, not passive. Remember others won't see your shine if you don't display it.

Doing work that will never make you stand out.

- Doing work that downplays your potential is the fastest path to getting into a rut. You can only be in your brilliance when you do work that plays to your strengths.

Allowing others to define your reputation.

- One of the secrets of brand building is taking control of your brand narrative. We'll get into more detail on that in a later chapter. For now, ask yourself what do you truly want to be known for.

Downplaying your accomplishments.

- I believe humility is a hallmark of leadership. However, ask yourself whether you're being humble or just being insecure.

When in doubt, keep in mind the posture of an impactful leader. An impactful leader:

- Walks her talk
- Perseveres and keeps her eyes focused on her vision even when she is challenged
- Gets it done, even if it means rolling up her sleeves at times
- Picks herself back up and keeps it moving after failure

- Sees the big picture and strives to impact real change
- Leverages her platform to amplify marginalized voices

Imposter syndrome is one of the biggest roadblocks I see women come up against when they're on the verge of showcasing their full brilliance. Whether it is because they're making a new career move, gaining more visibility in their role, embarking on a new venture, launching a website, nailing a large client, or on the brink of fulfilling a lifelong dream, the insecurities, inadequacies, and doubt that signal imposter syndrome can hijack their success.

So when the imposter starts getting loud in your head, saying that you're stupid or not good enough, respond with, "What the heck do you know?" And anchor yourself in the truth of who you are, your gifts and talents, and all the myriad of ways you have already made an impact.

SHOW

"Let's pursue a walk with God so close that the spotlights of this world—be they for us or against us—are eclipsed by His enormous shadow cast on our path."

~ Beth Moore

Chapter 5

Flaunt It:
Elevate Your Voice & Visibility

"More visibility is more power, but more vulnerability."

~ Ezra Furman

$\mathcal{M}$ANY YEARS AGO, before I'd left my marketing research career to become an image consultant, I went to see the Baltimore Symphony Orchestra in concert with my cousin and a couple of his friends. After the concert, we were all mingling in the lobby talking about the experience. As we were talking, a little old lady came up to me smiling widely. She was very short and had a full head of gray hair—she must have been in her seventies, but she was made up with her red lipstick. Looking up at me she said, "You are magnificent." I must have looked confused because I was sure I did not hear her correctly, so she said it again, this time so loudly that those around me heard her too, "YOU ARE MAGNIFICENT! THE WORLD NEEDS TO SEE YOU."

I was embarrassed and perplexed. Was she mad? What the heck did she mean? I still remember the look on her face. She was still smiling but now looking at me incredulously because it was clear that I didn't know what she was talking about. Smiling politely back and blushing I said, "Thank you very much," turning to look at my friends in disbelief. "Can you believe what she said?" I whispered to my cousin. But he shook his head at me saying, "Natalie, isn't that just what I've been trying to tell you the other day? You don't understand how amazing you are!"

He was right. I didn't understand what he'd been trying to tell me around that time, and I didn't have a clue what this nice lady meant. I remember doing a visual check-in with myself. I was wearing white fitted shirt and slacks. I wore my hair curly back then, and sure I thought I looked cute. But magnificent? That's a whole other level I couldn't comprehend.

I was so focused on how I looked on the outside that I didn't understand the power and light in my inner brilliance—that it was more radiant and magnificent than anything I had going for me on the outside!

Over the years I would turn her words around in my head and attempt to discern her intent. What I believe now is that she saw something in me, a glimmer of my light perhaps. She could probably sense I was an insecure woman. But she would have also observed my statuesque frame, and unlike many of the people I had known in my life, she took it upon herself to not just marvel at me from afar but to speak life into me. This was such a gift. I could not appreciate it at the time, but I do now.

Flaunting It is about living in the fullness of your brilliance—all of it—the physical, mental, behavioral, emotional, and spiritual aspects of who you are and how you express yourself and show up in the world.

Dictionary.com defines the word, "flaunt" as "displaying (something) ostentatiously, especially in order to provoke envy or admiration or to show defiance." Synonyms include, "parade," "exhibit," and "show-off." The opposite of flaunting is hiding.

When I wrote *Frumpy to Fabulous: Flaunting It*, I chose that title intentionally. I wanted women to feel confident about their expression of their particular beauty and fabulousness.[1] In order for women to "Flaunt It," I believed they had to have the confidence, knowledge, empowerment, and awareness of who they are and how they look.

I used the word in a tongue-in-cheek type of way, not so that women would be showy and obnoxious about their visual expression, but so they would dare to get out of their comfort zones and show the world who they truly are, in all their visual fabulousness.

But when I talk about "Flaunting It" in this book, I want you to understand the spirit of that word and how it speaks to your significance, your achievements, your impact, and your legacy.

This chapter is all about how to display your brilliance so that those who need to know are aware of your contributions. Yes, you kinda have to "Flaunt It" in your career to get to your desired destination.

Albert Einstein famously said, "Be a voice, not an echo." Those words are an invitation for you to stand in your power, use your voice, and be the change you want to see. It's a call to leverage the best of your TAGS to the benefit of your sphere. It's a clarion cry to speak your truth which may mean amplifying your accomplishments and advocating for yourself to get up the next rung or to win that cherished client or contract. It's about permitting yourself to be exceptional and extraordinary in your sweet spot and being so confident and comfortable in that space that no one can miss your shine!

Why Shine?

For a large portion of my life, I knew that I was playing small, but I didn't know how to thrive any other way. For the longest time I was scared to shine because, as a child who had felt invisible, diminished, and inherently flawed, I could not fathom the idea that I had magnificence and power.

The agency to voice my opinions and utter my point of view was not a part of my reality growing up, not merely because my own voice was silenced but because I didn't see it modeled in the women around me. While I had some glimpses of confident, self-assured, and emboldened women in the media—on TV and in magazines like *Essence* and *Cosmopolitan* which I devoured every month—they were as foreign in my everyday existence as seeing a snowflake on Trinidad soil. Mostly I saw women who asserted their authority by being controlling or obsequiously deferential, which I knew even at a young age was not really authority at all.

I *just* wanted to fit in. The fear of rejection became one of my core limiting beliefs. It hijacked my voice, making me hide my brilliance, withhold my point of view, and modify my behavior to make those around me comfortable. I suppressed my true needs and feigned self-sufficiency. I dimmed my magnificence so that I would not risk being abandoned. But that type of M.O. never works, does it? Instead, I settled into a state of mediocrity that only shifted when I dared to embrace the truth of who I truly was.

Life would not let me play *that* small. In fact, life catapulted me forward and upward despite my fears. I truly had only two choices: to let my spirit die inside or to go through the painful journey of being born again. The price of rebirth felt incredibly high. But I can say unequivocally that the reward for enduring and persevering was great. After being forced to reincarnate a few times in my life, I stand rooted and secure in the knowledge that I am enough, I am worthy, and that I am meant to shine. As a Christian, I am a daughter of a King, beloved, blameless, and a unique masterpiece. My Creator designed each star uniquely and names and calls them specifically (Ps 147:4). No one else can shine like I am meant to shine.

No one can shine like you are singularly meant to shine.

I encounter far too many women who are living with their lights dimmed like I used to. How can we soar like eagles to the heights God uniquely designed for us if we are imprisoned in any way, muted, or silenced, and trying to complete someone else's journey? We marvel at the beauty, grace, and exquisite delicacy of a butterfly. But trapped in its cocoon, how can it let us marvel at its magnificence? What is a flower without its bloom? Is it not a travesty of creation? If all the flowers around us refused to bloom, would we not wonder about the point? It is the same with each of us. We must be allowed to bloom, to soar, to flutter our wings, to sing our song, or else surely a piece of our soul perishes inside.

If there is one message I hope I convey to you through this book, it is that innately you are magnificent! Let yourself shine like the brilliant star you are, friend! We need to see your reflection of the glory of God, who shows glimmers of His glory through each one of us.

For so many years I let other people's opinions and judgments define me. As so much was leveled against me at a young age, I never developed the confidence and feelings of worth and self-esteem that most kids grow into. Instead of shaping my guidelines according to my true heart and spirit, I had set my guidelines according to yardsticks and self-protecting narratives of other broken human beings. I would learn in time that no one could write my story; no one could be the author of this narrative but God and me.

When I truly belong to and accept myself, I don't crave others' acceptance or cringe at their rejection. When my self-esteem is solid, I am whole, good, and worthy, regardless of others' perceptions, positive or negative. After decades of trying to fit in, to be cool, and be accepted, I can say that most often, I belong to myself. It is truly liberating! More and more, I care less and less what folks think.

To get to this level of self-assurance, I have had to keep building my foundation on what is lasting, eternal, and true. My identity needed to be rooted in my inheritance as a beloved child of God and my inherent worthiness as a human being with strengths and flaws. When I have honestly been able to stand secure in these truths, I *am* fully myself and able to shine.

I try to make it my business to speak life into other women, particularly younger women who cross my path. As scriptures say, life and death are truly in the power of the tongue—I saw this played out in my life and the lives of many women around me. Sometimes I feel silly with my affirmations. Sometimes women respond to me like I responded so many years ago to that woman at the

Baltimore Symphony Orchestra event. The women I affirm often act like I can't possibly be for real. But I know that if all I do is plant a little seed of worthiness, that would be enough. Then the next time someone affirms her, the seed will be nourished a bit more until, in time, she fully blooms and celebrates her awesomeness.

As Brené Brown says, we are hard-wired for connection. I'd like to believe that an integral part of that connection is being validated, encouraged, and empowered by those around us. I believe healthy connection with other humans is as vital as proper diet and nutrition. We need each other to grow into the best version of ourselves. We need each other to be inspired and elevated to greater heights. We need each other for belonging, to be heard, and to speak into the deep desires of our hearts.

Accepting invisibility and voicelessness requires a high price. I meet and encounter voiceless, disempowered women in my life far too often. How I wish I could take them all in my arms and reassure them that they are, indeed, enough, that their voice needs to be heard, their light is meant to shine. Not owning our voice and using our personal power is a trap that keeps us playing small, cowering, and deferring to others. This not only hurts us but those around us as well, who we're meant to bless with our light.

As Marianne Williamson's famous quote says, "We were born to make manifest the glory of God that is within us. It's not just in some of us; it's in everyone. And as we let our own light shine, we unconsciously give other people permission to do the same. As we are liberated from our own fear, our presence automatically liberates others."

When I wrote *Frumpy to Fabulous: Flaunting It*, I had come full circle—from a voice suppressed to one that rang loud, free, and true. I never imagined as a young girl that I would find the courage to let the world see me in full bloom. I couldn't have known the brilliance that lay dormant inside of me until I was brave and secure enough in myself to let it shine forth.

Magnify Your Voice

In her book *Ready to Rise*, author Jo Saxton explores the power of women owning their voice, using her experiences as a singer and the story of Deborah in the bible to highlight how we can leverage our voices for impact. Saxton says, "When we use our voices, our influence, when we show up in our lives and callings, others are strengthened, invited, and empowered to do the same."[2]

Saxton shows her readers how Deborah played big and used her voice because she was "secure enough to voice and articulate the broad scope of her leadership and influence in her society... There are times when the hardest voice to elevate is your own—especially if you are a woman, particularly if you're a woman on the margins. It's not always culturally acceptable to tell people the full extent of who you are."[Ibid] Those words resonated with me.

As an immigrant Black woman living in the United States, the things God put in my heart to do sometimes seemed like too much. I had so many "who does she think she is?" type of dreams and goals. It was (and sometimes still is) difficult to amplify my voice when culturally, as a Trinidadian, I was trained to defer to those senior and with more status than me, to stay in my lane, to not stand out and be different.

In the culture and times when I grew up, following the norm and the well-trodden path *was* the path. "Be a doctor, lawyer, or accountant," my father told me. "But don't you even think of doing psychology. I'm not going to support that. What can you even do with a degree like that?" So I humbly obliged and got my degree in accounting and economics, my heart knowing full well that even with my 3.8 GPA, I was not designed to be an accountant.

"There are times when using your voice means articulating who you are—the skills you bring and the impact you make." This line from Saxton's book is exactly what this chapter is about—getting comfortable with self-promotion. This is something many women naturally shy away from because they are afraid of how others will perceive their self-advocacy. "Don't get too big for your britches" or "a nail that sticks up gets hammered down" are messages many of us have received. These messages keep us tethered to a shrunken version of ourselves.

But when we try not to rock the boat—when we accommodate, people-please, and play small—we box ourselves into roles that are mismatched to our qualifications because, heaven forbid, we vie for the role or position we *truly* want. What would people think? Saxton shares that there have been times when it was easier to minimize her skills and dismiss her achievements for the sake of not inviting criticism or rejection. She learned that "apologizing for my voice has come at a cost" and that when "I minimize my credentials, I negotiate in accordance with my *perception* of someone's acceptance, not in recognition of my personal worth and value and contributions." Let that sink in, ladies.

Who are you becoming when you're not owning your capabilities, gifts, and expertise? What are you really saying when you mute, minimize, or downplay yourself? That you're not worthy, valuable, or important to be known in the full richness of your being?

Your voice is powerful! When you speak your truth, share your opinions, express your viewpoints, communicate your ideas, and are vulnerable with your feelings and thoughts, you are permitting yourself to take up space. You are allowing yourself to be seen, experienced, and known. And when you do that, you empower other people who share those thoughts, views, and opinions to feel heard and seen too. They know they are not alone in their experience because you've opened up your heart and mind through your voice. And they, too, start owning their magnificence, leveraging the gift of their voice in their sphere.

The poem "breathe" by Becky Hemsley speaks to how, as women, we've often been taught to deny or minimize ourselves to be who others think we should be. No wonder so many of us struggle with amplifying our voices and advocating for ourselves and others.

breathe

"she sat at the back and they said she was shy she led from the front and they hated her pride

they asked her advice and then questioned her guidance they branded her loud then were shocked by her silence

when she shared no ambition they said it was sad so she told them her dreams and they said she was mad

they told her they'd listen then covered their ears and gave her a hug whilst they laughed at her fears

and she listened to all of it thinking she should be the girl they told her to be best as she could

but one day she asked what was best for herself instead of trying to please everyone else

so she walked to the forest and stood with the trees she heard the wind whisper and dance with the leaves

and she spoke to the willow, the elm and the pine and she told them what she'd been told time after time

she told them she never felt nearly enough she was either too little or far, far too much

too loud or too quiet too fierce or too weak too wise or too foolish too bold or too meek *then she found a small clearing surrounded by firs and she stopped and she heard what the trees said to her*

and she sat there for hours not wanting to leave for the forest said nothing… it just let her breathe"[3]

Your voice is a vessel to reveal and communicate your brilliance so you can bless the world with it, just as you are. When you use your voice this way, you're saying, "This is who I am, this is what I can accomplish, and this is my vision for getting there." You're projecting confidence, worthiness, credibility, and authority. And we need to see you. Let your brilliance shine brightly and use your voice and vision to illuminate the path forward for those who need your guiding light.

Stacey Abrams is one of my heroines. When I think of the resilience, fortitude, and gumption of many successful women, she unquestionably comes to mind. After narrowly losing Georgia's gubernatorial race in 2018 (by less than 1.4 percentage points) because of voter restrictions in her state, Stacey immediately dusted herself off and got back to the work of fighting to give every Georgian access to the right to vote.

Because of her grassroots work, passion, and gravitas, she has been credited for President Biden's win in Georgia, marking the first time the state voted Democratic in a presidential election since 1992. And just a couple of months later, two Democratic representatives won their local elections, flipping control of the chamber.

According to Brooke Baldwin, Abrams has always used her voice to advocate for others, even when her authority was newly won. She notes that Abrams "did not hesitate to lift while she climbed." In her interview with Baldwin, Abrams shared that she gave away a quarter of the funds she raised while registering voters in Georgia to women-run groups doing similar work. Baldwin writes, "Abrams told me she wanted to make sure she didn't 'hoard' her access and power because then, she said, 'you become just as problematic as those who were against you.'"[4]

In November 2022, Abrams is running for Governor of Georgia again, not shrinking back from putting herself out there again with the world watching her. It's never been about herself, always what's been best for the people in her community and the country. She uses her platform, authority, and voice to advocate for those whose only political power is the vote in their hand.

On her current website, Abrams sums up her "why" in this statement: "I've never stopped fighting for Georgia. I've never lost faith that—together—we can build a brighter future for all of us. You should not lose that faith, either. Together, we can keep more money in families' pockets, help our communities prosper, and give our children the greatest opportunities to thrive. I'm running for governor because opportunity and success in Georgia shouldn't be determined by your zip code, background, or access to power. We are one Georgia."

If Abrams prevails, she will become the first Black governor in Georgia and the first Black woman elected governor in US history. If anyone can do it, she can.

Toot, Toot!

In her timely book *Woman of Influence*, author Jo Miller shares this nugget: "Your work does not speak for itself. You do."[5] I couldn't have articulated it better. When you keep your head down, you silence your voice and diminish your influence.

So many women have this mistaken perception that if they work long and hard enough as the consummate team player, they will get the recognition they deserve. While this is true for a fortunate few, most of us don't get this type of championing unless we lobby for it ourselves. And for women of color like myself, this is more often the reality than not.

This bears repeating: Working hard does not mean you will get the recognition you deserve. It usually means you'll get more unglamorous work dumped on you. Miller goes on to say that your contribution needs to be visible for recognition to occur. But it's only visible, ladies, if you intentionally make it so.

I agree with Deborah Smith Pegues who puts it this way, "In any arena where you want to succeed, you must be visible. Being visible means speaking up at meetings and owning your wins. Being invisible means avoiding conflict, minimizing accomplishments, and failing to speak up when you need to."[6] She cites an article based on Harvard Business Review research conducted to ring this point home. The article uses the term, "intentional invisibility" to describe how women often choose to stay in the shadows to avoid potential backlash.

According to the report, "Women employed this 'intentional invisibility' when they avoided conflict with colleagues, softened their assertiveness with niceness, and 'got stuff done' by quietly moving things forward without drawing attention to themselves. The consequence of this approach was that they often ended up feeling well-liked but underappreciated."[7]

To avoid being seen negatively by their colleagues, women often soften their personalities, downplay their assertiveness, and take on more passive professional postures so they can blend in. Even though women in the study recognized that invisibility could hurt their chances of being promoted, they hunkered down, avoiding the spotlight because they were concerned about the negative backlash they would face if they touted their achievements.

This is what is known as the double bind: women will be penalized if they're too soft and accommodating and penalized if they're too assertive and outspoken. Women who fear this backlash are less inclined to be vocal in claiming credit for their contributions.

Before you resign to staying quiet, consider whether this is truly a reality in your workplace culture or more about you. Sometimes the reason we are under-represented in leadership spaces is due to our own fears and insecurities.

To people-please, too many women bury their brilliance, creating missed opportunities for their companies and themselves. There's nothing obnoxious about owning what you do well. Once you know what your unique gifts and strengths are, get comfortable exposing and leveraging them in service to your organization. Your colleagues, peers, and bosses will never be able to leverage you and your skills if they don't know what they are.

Men have no issues amplifying their accomplishments—in fact, for them it is the name of the game! Women need to take a page out of their playbooks and learn to make their talents known to those who have the influence to advance them.

Consider the experiences you said no to because you were afraid. Or the innovative ideas you never shared because you felt they would be rejected. Or the opportunities to fast-track your career that you dismissed because you didn't think you were good enough.

If your imposter is not the reason you're hiding, it could be your mindset about self-promotion. We've all had the experience of being near a braggart, an over-the-top boaster who made it all about them and whose mission was hogging the spotlight. These people so grate against us that we swear we will never be like them. But in many cases we go to the opposite extreme of not saying enough about our contributions!

As I have been saying in this chapter, making your achievements visible, valued, and valuable is a vital career advancement strategy.

In my professional career, I have been guilty of not wanting to self-promote because I felt my peers and others would perceive it as boasting. Learn from me, ladies. Self-promotion, when done well, is not only a right but a responsibility if you truly believe you have something of value to offer your sphere.

Effectively Self-Promote

Effective self-promotion, far from being shameful, is a fundamental aspect of ensuring you get up the next rung of the career ladder. In their book *How Women*

Rise, leadership experts Sally Helgesen and Marshall Goldsmith write, "If you want to reach your highest potential, making your achievements visible, especially to those at senior levels, is as important as the actual tasks spelled out in your job description."[8]

One of my clients, Ellen, who is on the brink of breakthrough success in her role, recognized this reality the hard way when she realized her boss was not her advocate. She assumed her boss would tout her achievements because that's the way Ellen treats her team. For Ellen, self-promotion was very uncomfortable and felt inauthentic, but with our coaching sessions she started to view it in a new, positive light.

If we don't self-promote, there's more at stake too. Helgesen and Goldsmith make the point that staying out of the spotlight and muting your voice not only keeps you stuck in a role beneath your potential, but it can also diminish the satisfaction you feel in an otherwise fulfilling role. To elaborate on this point, they write, "If the praise you hope for is not forthcoming, you might feel unappreciated and under-acknowledged. You may start to resent not only the higher-ups who seem unaware of all the hard work you do but also colleagues who are skilled at getting noticed. You may then decide they're just showboats and congratulate yourself on being less self-centered, taking comfort in your own wonderfulness even as you stay in the shadows."

When you understand what you're good at and why you're good at it, you can promote and leverage this understanding in your position. Your bosses will not know how to leverage your skill set if they have no clue about the signature strengths you bring.

Hiding in the name of modesty doesn't serve anyone. Consider the flip side of not making your strengths, accomplishments, and wins known. If you have not shared your contributions, you can miss out on opportunities that are tailor-made for you. But it's not just you who will lose. Your organization and those it serves will miss out on the opportunity to benefit from your gifts as well.

Amplifying your accomplishments and qualifications does not make you self-absorbed or self-serving. Instead, this awareness communicates that you're great at self-promotion and ready to rise.

Your invisibility should not be an option. We're going to see you anyway, so why not let us see you shining brightly in your full magnificence?

In our coaching sessions, Ellen was able to shift her negative perception about self-promotion (which is not the same as boasting!) and identified a few powerful ways it could help her succeed in her new, much more visible role.

Here are some of Ellen's key takeaways.

Effective self-promotion:

- Inspires confidence about your capabilities in others.
- Allows people to learn about you from your perspective. Don't wait for your annual review to start tooting your horn. Schedule monthly or quarterly check-ins with your boss and others where you can assess your progress and get valuable feedback.
- Gives your colleagues and bosses insight into your strengths.
- Helps you take advantage of opportunities to share your expertise in visible ways.
- Allows you to be intentional and strategic about the traits and successes you want to bring to the fore.
- Increases your visibility in the ways you want to be known for.

Consider the reasons why getting ahead matters to you. Is your drive to reach the highest levels of your organization? Is it to serve your clients, leveraging your exceptional skill sets? Perhaps you believe that having a woman at the helm of your company would best serve your clients, and why should that woman not be you?

Whatever your reasons, if advancing in your career matters to you, you must get more comfortable selling yourself—not in a snake-oil salesperson type of way but in an authentic, confident, humble way. Self-promotion gets a bad rap among women, but it doesn't have to come from a prideful or inauthentic place. It can be anchored in humility and in service to your bigger vision. This context allowed Ellen not to feel "icky" in her quest to tout her accomplishments.

There's nothing obnoxious about being clear and direct about what you do well. When you stay mute and invisible, you silence your voice and sink your influence. And if you're reading this book, that's not the result you're aiming for.

When viewed through the lens of letting your light shine so others can see your brilliance, self-promotion is not just smart, it's essential. It's about allowing your impact to be felt and your influence to carry more weight.

Like I shared with Ellen, self-promotion does not have to be a zero-sum game—it can and should be a both/and deal where you highlight and showcase the accomplishments of others on your team AND you give yourself the same courtesy by shedding light on your own contributions.

Improving your visibility is an intentional and strategic task. When your skills are valued, when you have access to stretch assignments, and when you are known and liked by influential senior leaders, you are on track to more visibility in your position.

To give you a jump-start in self-promotion, here are a few strategies that will help you play large and boost your visibility and impact.

1. **Seek projects or engagements that shine the light on your skills and expertise.** Create career-defining moments by excelling in projects and assignments that showcase your strengths and point to your future career aspirations. Amplify the accomplishments that align with your greatest professional aspirations.

2. **Don't get saddled with "non-promotable" busywork.** Many women wear their ability to multitask like badges of honor. But being known as a producer does not get you the attention and respect you seek as a leader. Being good at something doesn't mean that it is good for you to do. Often these non-glamorous tasks and low-visible projects distract and interrupt us from achieving the initiatives that truly matter in our role.

    In an article for *Chief*, Dr. Laurie Weingart writes, "By default, (organizations) turn to women when (they) need non-promotable tasks done." Weingart continues that, sadly, "Women are often more likely to volunteer and say 'yes' to doing them when asked. It's a self-perpetuating cycle, and then we say 'yes' because of the fear of violating the expectation." What many women don't realize, however, is that these non-promotable tasks they do "helps their organizations but does nothing to advance their careers."

    Weingart notes that these non-promotable tasks are typically shorter-term, less visible assignments that need to be executed quickly. Often, they're behind the scenes and not directly tied to the organization's bottom line. For these reasons, getting bogged down by these tasks does nothing to advance your career and get you the visibility you deserve.[9]

    The hack to releasing ourselves from this cycle is committing to only engage in high-value assignments that impact the company's key initiatives or bottom line. We also need to be crystal clear about our yes so that it comes from a place of empowerment and not fear. Heed Jo Miller's warning and "don't become indispensable for work that downplays your potential."[10]

3. **Go outside your comfort zone and seek assignments that help you learn, grow, or stretch.** It's easy to stay in the familiar, in what's safe, what's comfortable. But that's not where growth happens. According to Jo Miller, "If you're not pushing the limits of your comfort zone—by raising your

hand for an assignment that's a stretch or a challenging new role—you're not exploiting the full capacity of your leadership potential." The truth is, if you want to grow and stretch as a leader, you've gotta take risks and you've gotta be brave! Sorry, ladies, but playing it safe does not get you the visibility you want. Miller asserts, "The ideal stretch should challenge you without defeating you, and it should draw you out of your comfort zone yet fall short of pushing you too far too soon."[Ibid]

4. **Communicate with proof.** When you're having a conversation where you're advocating for a raise or promotion, do your homework and come prepared. Understand and articulate clearly and specifically what you want and be clear about your boundaries going forward. Know the salary you have in mind and build a strong case with hard data to back it up. If you have documentation about how your contributions have advanced the company and its initiatives, don't be shy about bringing that information into your conversation.

   In the past, I've entered salary negotiations using these tactics. I did my research on competitive rates for similar roles in my region, given my education, years of experience, responsibilities, and achievements. I outlined all the projects I spearheaded, new business I won, ways I made a difference to my team, etc. and brought all these metrics and data into the meetings. I would speak confidently about the vision I had for myself in my new role and how my advancement and associated salary increase were not only wise and prudent for me and my career goals but for the company overall. It always worked.

5. **When considering new opportunities, ask yourself a few strategic questions:**

   a. Does this opportunity reinforce my leadership brand?
   b. Does it allow me to deliver valuable outcomes?
   c. Does it move me forward in my chosen career trajectory?
   d. Does it help me develop new skills that support where I am headed?
   e. Is this the right time for me to take on this initiative?
   f. Does this assignment align with my work-life balance goals?
   g. Does it make my value visible to leadership?
   h. Does it expand my network?
   i. Does it connect me to potential sponsors?

Reflecting on these questions will clarify the projects you want to say yes to and those you must decline because they don't move you forward in alignment with your vision.

6. **Part of self-promotion is learning how to amplify your accomplishments so that your delivery is positively received.** Again, being strategic will serve you well. A few pointers:

   a. Focus on the achievements that align with your career aspirations. In other words, don't try to talk about everything but the kitchen sink. That method dilutes your contribution.

   b. Find and use the channels of communication that resonate with you. For example, speaking, writing, presenting, podcasting, whitepapers, webinars, etc. Maximize the way you promote the things that you've done well by repurposing them. I do this all the time. I turn my blog posts into short-form LinkedIn posts or use them in my newsletter updates. You don't have to reinvent the wheel each time. Maximize, leverage, repurpose.

   c. Feature the recommendations, endorsements, and positive feedback you've received from sponsors, mentors, and colleagues who believe in your brilliance. I have many of my clients create what I call a "Success File"—an inventory of all their achievements, awards, and accolades (their As!) from emails, LinkedIn endorsements, personal notes, etc. This repository of wins is helpful when they need to provide positive proof of their successes. And it also comes in handy when they need to boost their confidence when the imposter in their head gets loud and tells them they're undeserving. In these moments, they pull out their Success File and remember why they're a superstar.

7. **Think big picture.** Start by articulating a vision of where you'd like your job to take you so you can give your managers and others context for what you desire down the road. In her book *The Most Powerful You*, author and executive coach Kathy Caprino shares this advice, "Explain how your vision at work ties into your personal mission… it's also important to step back and look at how this promotion—with its expanded role and contribution—will be fueled by your passion, purpose, and commitment to the organization's success. Talk about how this role aligns with what you care about most, and how it will help you achieve not only the top business

goals but your personal goals as well, for making a positive difference and leading in the way you dream of."[11]

There are even more ways to elevate your visibility. I curated a list of twenty tactics you can use as inspiration. You can download that list at www.theunveiledway.com/20-ways-to-elevate-your-visibility. Use the tactics that feel authentic to you. Try some of the ones that will stretch you too. The main point is to use your voice, authority, and influence for yourself.

And here's the thing. If you're a woman who has visibility, who's been able to command considerable influence in her organization, you have the power and authority to amplify the voices of the women around you. The more we make ourselves and our contributions visible, the more we can lift each other up! As a woman of influence, you can choose to lead by example and inspire the women in your sphere to let their unique light shine.

You have everything in you to be an impactful leader. Amp up your visibility with these strategies and notice how your peers and colleagues start treating you like the magnificent, super talented, game-changer you already are!

Elevating Your Visibility Requires Courage

I had an experience with visibility earlier this year that left me feeling pretty raw. I was participating in a live virtual event and ended up being spotlighted and coached for about forty-five minutes as I unpacked some very vulnerable experiences around my visibility. It was SO uncomfortable to be SO publicly vulnerable.

As much as I advocate for women to be more visible, I must acknowledge that visibility is not for the faint of heart. Because being visible requires us to get out of our comfort zones. If you want to be visible for the things you want to be known for, be prepared to wrestle with discomfort as you get out of your comfort zone.

Katrina Adams, the former president and CEO of the United States Tennis Association and chair of the US Open, blazed many trails as a "first." She shared how she takes up space with confidence while operating in many predominantly white spaces: "Although I may be the only black person in a room, I silence any self-doubt. I own the room with confidence, convincing myself that I belong there and acting like it from the moment I enter. At times, it can be tough to pull off, but my parents taught me that I belong wherever I am. Naturally, the discipline and style of play I learned in tennis has carried over into my professional life. At the exclusive level of sports management, I'm often the only black person in a variety of situations, which was similar to my tennis development where I was the only one in the draw. To have presence in these rooms, frequently filled with white men, I rely on my life skills gained through tennis to make a meaningful contribution."[12]

One of my clients, Courtney, came to the stark realization that she had been playing small for years in her corporate role. It had started so subtly that it had crept up on her. She used to be confident and a bit of a disrupter. But in one of her recent roles, she'd worked for a boss that was intimidated by her confidence and her presence—so much so that she would direct her to stay quiet at meetings.

At first, Courtney wasn't concerned, and she went along to get along. But after a couple of years of intentionally shrinking so her boss could feel more competent, playing small started to become her new default way of being. She started to second-guess herself and doubt her opinions more frequently. She didn't take charge in meetings the way she so naturally used to. She started to mute herself and play small, telling herself she was making conscious choices to do so even when she wasn't.

After a few years, even after being promoted into a new position with a new boss, Courtney forgot the truth of who she was. She was no longer comfortable in the spotlight, no longer making her presence felt in meetings, no longer voicing her dissenting opinions. She had become a shrunken version of herself, and she didn't even realize it.

In our work together, she started seeing how she'd adopted a pattern of playing small to make those around her comfortable. She told herself this was the right course of action without noticing the high price she was paying to dim her light. Unfortunately, all the systemic biases she faced as a minority woman in her work environment didn't help either; they only justified her actions.

Courtney's wake-up call came when she finally saw just how far she had gotten from the big bold vision she'd had for her career. This realization was shocking to her. She'd lost momentum and motivation and had been going through the motions, playing it safe, and operating at a level far below her capacity.

With this new awareness, she became determined to make up for the lost years, reimagining a new trajectory that would get her out of the corporate box she'd put herself in and into her own venture where she could leverage ALL her skills, expertise, strengths, and superpowers to elevate other women in similar situations. With that monkey off her back, Courtney had an entirely new energy and persona, one where she brought her FULL brilliance into her workspaces, one where she could advocate strongly for herself and others, and one where she could see her true dreams come to fruition. To be fair, this energy wasn't "new." It was who she was until she'd forgotten herself along the way.

Does Courtney's story resonate with you?

Who are you, sister, in the deepest part of your heart and what have you been called to do? Do you know? Have you spent time with yourself and God to figure that out? What will it take for you to step into the fullness of your power and brilliance? As you read these words right now, think of one small step you can take to get you closer to your heart's long-held vision. Your people need you to show up fully so they can be blessed by your brilliance. They need you, just as you are, to rise.

What will it take for you to play bigger? What is your "for such a time as this" vision that you need to birth now before it's too late? Where can you make the greatest contribution to your company or organization? Where do you want to be in your career five years from now? What do you have to offer that is unique, special, and distinctive that will transform the lives of others? What do you believe is possible for you?

All the trailblazers, changemakers, and disruptors we know didn't get there by being comfortable. They didn't get there by playing it safe. You don't get to be a "trailblazHER" without a healthy dose of courage.

Reshma Saujani, founder of Girls Who Code, writes, "Being afraid to try something new, to boldly ask for what we want, to make mistakes, and yes, maybe even look a bit foolish lead to a lot of wasted brilliance, swallowed ambitions, and regret."[13]

What brilliance are you hiding because you're afraid to be in the spotlight?

What has fear held you back from achieving?

What brave step would you take now if you knew people were counting on you to take that step?

The time is now to be brave and do the things that make our knees buckle and our hearts flutter. The things that make us feel a heck of a lot of discomfort. Because if not now, when?

We're meant to be like stars, shining. But so often we hide our light and let fear and self-doubt dim our luster.

When you shrink back and don't speak your truth, we can't see your light.

When you stay in work environments that are toxic to your well-being, we can't see your light.

When you compare yourself to others and try to be more like them and not you, we can't see your light.

When you listen to that voice in your head that says who are you to dare do what your heart and soul is meant to do, we can't see your light.

We're each meant to make our brilliance evident, to shine fully.

Only when you truly believe that you're uniquely designed for a specific impact will you permit your light to shine so you can bless all those in your sphere.

Your visibility requires your vulnerability and authenticity—your visibility is an act of courage.

Stepping into the spotlight (whatever that looks like from your vantage point) can feel terrifying and derail your confidence. But there are small steps you can take to build up your confidence muscle.

I have a fun challenge for you. Pull together an outfit that is way out of your style comfort zone and calls attention to you. It can be an ensemble with bold, bright colors, patterns, or texture. Or a look with a dramatic flair. Or a look that is so NOT typical for a woman like you that heads turn by default. Be as bold and as daring as you can with this stretch exercise.

Next, step out in the outfit at an event or place where folks will see and look at you. Yes, I know, this is a tough one! But if you can summon the courage and complete this successfully, this exercise will strengthen your confidence muscle for being in the spotlight so that when you really need to be front and center, you will be that much more prepared. (I'd love to hear your feedback on this challenge! Leave your comments here: www.theunveiledway.com/unveiled-blog/visibility-challenge).

Brené Brown says that being seen and known is one of our deepest needs. But it's also one of our greatest terrors because what if we are truly seen and people didn't like us anymore? This ties right into our fear of rejection. No one wants to attract rejection, but elevating our visibility feeds right into that fear.

But don't buy into that fear, ladies. Don't you dare stay stuck and small. With courage, support, and confidence, dare to shine brightly like the star you already are!

Chapter 6

Presence with a Purpose:
Leverage Your Leadership Presence

"I raise up my voice—not so I can shout but so that those without a voice can be heard... We cannot succeed when half of us are held back."

~ Malala Yousafzai

IF YOU DESIRE TO BE an impactful leader, cultivating your leadership presence is critical. Presence—that ability to project a sense of ease, poise, command, or self-assurance—is an energy and an attitude. It can be magnetic. It draws people to you. When it is purposeful, you have created the equivalent of a slam dunk, especially in your professional interactions.

My cat Trinity is terrified of storms. Whenever she hears even one thunder roll, she compresses her body by bearing herself down low, tucking in her tail, slicking back her ears, and bowing her head, running as quickly and as quietly as she can to the basement. What she's doing is taking up as little physical space as she can. She's minimizing her presence because, in her smart kitty brain, that's a survival strategy. Her body is communicating: *Look how small I am. I am not a threat. Don't mind me.*

Trinity knows how to play small when she thinks her survival depends on it. Seeing her play out this scenario recently got me thinking how my playing small shows up when subconsciously I believe my survival or self-preservation depends on it.

Sometimes it's physical, like when I think my Amazonian height is just too much, which makes me bend down to meet the (typically) much shorter person next to me. Often, however, my playing small is how I choose to show up energetically.

Playing small is what a lot of us women do. Often, we take up less space by making ourselves smaller when we feel out of place, inadequate, or insecure. We slouch, keep our head down, draw in our arms and legs, or slump our shoulders. Or we move to the back of the room and speak softer or not at all. We diminish our presence by these behaviors, and when we do, we're also telling ourselves that we don't belong.

Physically minimizing our presence communicates a lack of authority, influence, and power. It conveys doubt about our right to be present and take up space, to be fully seen and visible enough to be acknowledged.

I believe most women truly want to shine. But there are so many reasons why a woman's brilliance gets dulled, diminished, or becomes a barely visible glow. We fear being judged. We are uncomfortable with our own magnificence. We learned to take the backseat to avoid making others uncomfortable. We got used to an inner narrative that said we didn't deserve to be seen or heard because we believed we weren't worthy of attention. We lacked confidence or struggled with our self-esteem. The bottom line is that most of our discomfort with shining has to do with fear—the fear of showing the world who we truly are, what we believe and think, and walking our truth out loud.

At its heart, presence is an inner attitude. It's an energy, an aura of confidence and self-assurance that leaves those around you inspired, engaged, and motivated. To convey presence, you must be comfortable with who you are. True presence, like a solid sense of your signature style, is authentic, transparent, and unapologetic. Your presence is about you, not about those around you and what they may or may not think. Being in your brilliance is about being vulnerable enough to let your guard down so that others get to see you in your full, magnificent, God-given glow!

By now you should realize that most of what hijacks your ability to own your brilliance is your mindset. We've talked about your imposter and the ways it can sabotage every noble intention you have to make an impact, shine in your calling, or serve your sphere in your exceptional gifts and talents. Once you've done the work to silence your imposter and address your insecurities, channeling presence will become effortless because it will flow from the core of who you are and your unique design.

What does leadership presence look like? A woman with presence is memorable and respected. Others automatically view her as a person of authority. As an image consultant, I used to advise women to boost their presence by wearing their power colors, opting for jackets with strong lines so they could convey more authority, and ensuring their visual image was flattering and attractive.

Those things help of course, but what is perhaps more important is communicating that same powerful presence with our behaviors, actions, and speech. And actually being *present*, being there in the moment with your full attention, actively listening and engaging, offering your thoughts, advice, and opinions, and holding space so those you're interacting with also feel seen and heard.

Being fully present in all your richness gives you gravitas as a leader. It's what lets others say, "Wow, she has such leadership presence!"—a compliment that a woman of impact longs to hear.

One of my friends is a young woman with fantastic leadership presence. Even though she's the youngest person in the room by far, no one present would ever know. She speaks with courage, conviction, and authority. She challenges perspectives, thoughts, and opinions. She's smart, yes, but also compassionate and vulnerable.

She shares courageous stories about her struggles and failures. She is transparent and honest from a heart space of awareness and humility. When she shows up authentically, she invites those around her to do the same—to be vulnerable and authentic too so that the whole energy of the room changes because of her presence. She also has the gift of empathy so she can acknowledge others' feelings, making them feel more seen and understood so they're more comfortable speaking their truth.

My young friend fosters greater communication, connection, and courage just by showing up. Call it poise, composure, command skills, or clout. When a woman of significance like her walks into a room, you feel it. When they speak, people lean forward to listen. When they share their ideas, people champion them. When they offer praise, others feel validated. This is what presence is all about!

Leadership presence is a powerful combination of attributes that elicits respect and admiration from others, gives them the confidence to trust you, and motivates them to rally behind your ideas and vision. It's all about how you are perceived by others and the impression you make in your interactions.

Because leadership presence is not a given based on title, smarts, expertise, or leadership skill, it is a quality we need to cultivate and manage. Leveraging your leadership presence requires a solid understanding of the impact of your image on those you lead, an awareness of your body language, poise, and other nonverbal cues, and clarity around your level of emotional intelligence and how effectively you communicate.

In the past, when I gave seminars or workshops on professional presence, I always showed a slide that highlighted groundbreaking findings from sociolinguist Albert Mehrabian. Mehrabian found that over half of first impressions are based on a person's body language. Just under 40 percent are based on someone's voice—their tone, intonation, and volume. The key finding? Just 7 percent of first impressions are based on the literal content of the message communicated. This was my "aha" slide, the slide that made everything else in my presentation on image and professionalism click. The "just 7 percent" was my reason for focusing on the visuals over the verbal.

Mehrabian findings validated the importance of image, body language, and communication in presence. When you are intentional about harnessing the best of yourself in these areas, you elevate your presence. Essentially, your leadership presence has everything to do with:

- Your level of confidence
- Your self-awareness, authenticity, courage, and vulnerability
- Your relational skills (are you compassionate, genuine, and sincere?)
- Your posture and poise
- The way you communicate, including your nonverbal gestures and body language
- Your voice (tone, quality, inflection, and strength)
- Your energy (quiet, calm, hyper, or high)
- Your charisma
- Your appearance and image

For simplicity, I like to boil these elements down into three C's: Command, Communication, and Clothing. Let's explore each of these a bit more.

1. Command

Command and leadership presence go hand in hand. Command is what gives you the clout to inspire and motivate those you lead. It gives weight to your thoughts, ideas, and actions, causing those in your sphere to gravitate toward you. Command is owning your lane and field of expertise, which gives you a credible, influential voice. Command helps you create the culture of your choosing in which your team respects and looks up to you. Command sets you apart as a leader.

Command is an attribute that can be felt immediately when you walk into a room. It is not so much about physicality as it is about how others experience your power energetically. Part of command is your poise—you enter a room, and we notice your presence by your stellar posture; your shoulders are squared, your head is straight, your feet flat on the floor and shoulder-width apart, your pelvis tucked in. It's what yogis refer to as the "Mountain Pose" posture.

The true command I felt when practicing "Mountain Pose" on a beach in Barbados is memorable to me because I felt the energy of the experience so powerfully. As I walked back and forth on that beach affirming myself and standing tall inwardly and outwardly as I practiced Mountain Pose, I summoned the most intense feeling of command that I've ever felt. It was so strong I felt unstoppable and that, if I dared, I could walk out on the water in front of me!

I believe command is something that is easier to feel than to articulate—we can feel it, as I did, in ourselves or from others. When I think of someone in the public eye who had command I think of Barack Obama. His leadership wasn't that forced, egotistical type of energy that some may confuse for command. He brought a quiet, powerful aura with him. It was in his poise, his voice, his body language, his confidence, his communication. I would argue that Obama's command is what ushered him on the fast path to becoming the first Black President of the United States.

In Barack Obama, you can see that command has an aura of authority while also being warm and inviting. His command was grounded in his effective communication, his level of self-control in managing his emotions publicly, and his positive attitude and outlook, as well as his expertise. It was also grounded in his understanding and appreciation of his strengths, talents, and value.

In her book *Executive Presence*, author Sylvia Ann Hewlett writes that the gravitas underpinning command "signals that you have not only depth and heft but also the confidence and credibility to get your point across and create buy-in when the going gets tough."[1] People feel your command as you communicate with authority and interact with them. The confidence and ease that effortlessly flows out of an icon like Barack Obama is dynamic and powerful.

Command and confidence are like fraternal twins—they look alike and are paired together, yet they are distinct from each other. As a confident leader, you are willing to take risks, accept failure, and learn and grow from missteps. You are knowledgeable without being the know-it-all. You are open and curious, so people feel comfortable approaching you, asking questions, and providing feedback.

For you to authentically lead and command attention and respect, your clarity and confidence about who you are and what you bring to the table must be incredibly strong. Identifying and owning your unique value helps you shut down that inner critic and remind you of your worth. This is where partnering with a leadership coach or mentor can be so beneficial. The objective feedback and insights from coaching help strengthen your confidence and give you the tools to manage the areas where you fall short as a leader.

2. Communication

Every interaction you have with another person is an opportunity to make a positive impression that helps you strengthen your presence. Effective communication is essentially about engagement—whether you can connect with your audience, get their attention and respect, and maintain it. Your verbal and nonverbal cues work together to enhance or diminish your communication. But interestingly, as Mehrabian's research shows, the content of your words doesn't drive your communication as much as your nonverbal cues and your communication style.

Let's look at the power of your voice and the words you wield, your ability to actively listen, and how your nonverbal communication impacts the delivery of your message.

Your Words and Voice

Even though the words we speak are not necessarily the first thing people connect with, our choice of words matters greatly. I always had tremendous respect for the veracity of voice, the power of the pen, and how our words wield our truth. Way before I became interested in style and image, I was a truth seeker. I believe we all are to some extent.

What I believe is true, I value. What I value is what I focus on. What I focus on is what I speak into existence. What I speak into existence by a tweet, talk, conversation, or post is my voice—it is my opinion, my expression, or the truth as I see it. My voice and my words leave an indelible print of my time here on Earth.

Mahatma Gandhi advocated for unabashedly speaking one's truth when he said, "Many people, especially ignorant people, want to punish you for speaking the truth, for being correct, for being you. Never apologize for being correct, or for being years ahead of your time. If you're right and you know it, speak your mind. Speak your mind. Even if you are a minority of one, the truth is still the truth."

Your voice reflects your truth. In this era of cancel culture, where others rush to judge our positions or beliefs, our words leave a legacy in the metaverse of our thoughts, beliefs, priorities, and perspectives.

In the past two years, we have witnessed unprecedented tragedy in our country, from the one-million-plus deaths from COVID-19, the politicization of everything from masks to what books kids should read in school, the coup that almost occurred in the country's Capitol on January 6, 2021, continued racial injustice and police brutality against Black men and women, economic hardship for millions, and being on the edge of WWIII with Russia's invasion of Ukraine. In times like these, when the divergence of viewpoints makes us enemies of each other in our own country, how do we choose to use our voice?

We must all fight to find our voice and speak our truth within the context of the events happening around us. Scripture speaks often of using our words to uplift and encourage each other. For example, First Thessalonians 5:11 says: "Therefore encourage one another and build one another up, just as you are doing." What does that look like from your vantage point? How do you comfort, encourage, or embolden others?

Consider the greatest leaders, orators, and champions in our modern world—John F. Kennedy, Martin Luther King Jr., Maya Angelou, Theodore Roosevelt, Mahatma Gandhi. Their words continue to surface decades after they have passed on. Their words leave a legacy unfettered by time. Their voices offer hope, guidance, encouragement, purpose, and motivation. Their words were in sync with their characters and deeply enmeshed with their value systems. JFK said it best when he wrote, "As we express our gratitude, we must never forget that the highest appreciation is not to utter words but to live by them." Vice President Kamala Harris has remarked, "Anyone who claims to be a leader must speak like a leader. That means speaking with integrity and truth."

Your influence and impact will be anemic if you don't leverage the power of your voice. Speaking your truth and communicating your thoughts, beliefs, perspectives, and ideas publicly can arouse your imposter, which is why many of us tend to shy away from the full capacity our voice commands.

We may choose to stay silent, to not risk making waves, to tell ourselves no one wants to hear what we have to say, that our opinions are not valuable. Or maybe we choose to believe that we're meant to be seen but not heard. These lies keep us muted and our views unexpressed.

But your voice plays such an instrumental role in your leadership presence that to not harness its potential is not just timid, it's foolish. Communicating your unapologetic views may mean the difference between being respected or being dismissed.

Listen, changemaker, there is no need to apologize for your voice or to be scared of it, but you do need to discover it, own it, wield it, and use it in all its fullness.

The account of King Edward VI's journey to finding his voice in the movie *The King's Speech* fills me with awe.[2] Here was a leader who struggled with a debilitating stammer, who fought to find a way to communicate to his people with confidence, command, and clarity at a critical juncture in history.

The heart of the movie is the unbreakable bond that develops between the aspiring king and his speech therapist, Lionel Logue. We see how much is at stake. The only way to communicate in real-time with the public in those days was via live radio where voice reigns supreme. The climax of the movie is the new king delivering his first wartime radio broadcast where he announced Britain's declaration of war on Germany in 1939. He did so without a hitch. The king's speech inspired the country and united them in battle while giving the new monarch the confidence he needed to be king.

Most of us will never be a king or president of a country, but we all have platforms to communicate. On social media, we have virtual followers and online friends. Some of us are influencers. We may be leaders in our business or our community. We may pontificate from a pulpit or coach in a classroom.

Regardless of the platform, make no mistake: your words leave a legacy within your sphere of influence. This should give you pause before you speak, tweet, post, or share. Your words can uplift, edify, elevate, or enlighten. Or they can disempower, tear down, vilify, and condemn. Your words can spread joy, pain, love, or hate.

Theodore Roosevelt's quote about the "man in the arena" is now even more famous because Brené Brown derived the title of her bestselling book *Daring Greatly* from that speech. That's the power of voice! Truth begets even more truth. From Teddy Roosevelt's poignant description of courage, we have a book that leaves a legacy urging us all to let go of our facades and show our vulnerabilities because therein lies our strength and courage. We need that message more than ever today.[3]

In these precarious times, will you join me in committing to entering the arena, letting our voices be heard, living authentically from our truth, and using our words for good? In that arena, hopefully, prayerfully, we will leave a legacy worthy of our time spent on earth.

Listening

Everyone wants to be seen and heard. One of the pegs of presence and having an impact is being a good communicator. And being a good communicator starts with being a good listener.

A good listener takes the time to listen in a highly engaged way. A good listener gives the person in front of them their full attention, minimizing distractions (including their phone), mirroring the person's cues, and ensuring both sides are on the same page of understanding. You show you are engaged in a conversation when you use small verbal and nonverbal cues like nodding, eye contact, raised or furrowed eyebrows, appropriate laughter, and sounds like "hmmm."

People feel heard when you can summarize what they've said using some of their exact words and phrases and when you chime in with relevant comments appropriate to what they've shared. When you say phrases like "I hear you," or clarify that you are hearing correctly with, "What I'm hearing you say is… Is that correct?" you connect even more deeply with the speaker and you can observe another's emotions in a conversation. For example, if you pick up hesitation in their response, be curious about that. Ask, "It seems like you have reservations about this. What's that about?" This allows you to elicit even more valuable information than you intended.

As an effective listener, you never make it about yourself, but you stay engaged with the other person's topic of interest. When you hijack a conversation by making it about you, you've not only lost that person's trust, you also lose out on valuable information they may have shared. In the same vein, manage your emotions and watch your triggers. Being detached and remaining nonjudgmental allows you to respond from a place of grace.

These are all techniques great coaches use in a coaching conversation and there's a reason why—it's because this is how we create a safe, trusted container for our clients to share and explore their deepest truths.

Listening allows you to observe important signals which may not be apparent if you're the one talking. Listening enables you to problem-solve more comprehensively by helping you focus on solutions because you're tuned in to everything others are saying. Listening helps you build rapport, camaraderie, and trust.

Another trait that's important to mention here is your ability to read a room. Being able to observe the energy in a room and check in with people's moods using our emotional intelligence (we'll get to that in the next chapter) allows you to discern whether you need to match, level up, or scale down the "vibe," depending on the message you're delivering. If you need people to feel inspired and motivated and your read of the room says their energy has plateaued, you as the speaker will need to adjust your voice, tone, and delivery to bring the energy up. The more successful you are at reading the room, the more effectively you'll be able to connect and engage with others.

Body language

Body language is a significant aspect of communication and presence because our nonverbal cues are louder than our verbal ones. When you speak, people don't just engage with your content. As I mentioned earlier, in your presence, your words matter less. Rather, those you lead are continuously evaluating your expertise, authenticity, integrity, and knowledge as they take in your posture, tone of voice, and gestures. Only when all these components resonate will they care about the actual content of your message.

Therefore, a lot of the information others form about you is through your body language and way of communicating. Poor body language can minimize your presence and detract from your message. Awareness of your body language faux pas can result in immediate improvements.

Later in my career as a market researcher, my body language spoke volumes about how confident I was in myself and my expertise. I would enter predominantly white spaces, with my six-foot frame already commanding attention. But even more, I had started to dress according to my authentic style sensibilities, wearing bold colors and donning a curly, afro-esque hairstyle that made me look bold and fearless. I strode into meetings no longer insecure and self-doubting. My posture, stride, and stance all communicated powerfully that I not only deserved to be there but that the audience needed my perspective.

I remember one instance when I was part of a meeting with about thirty professionals. I was the only Black person in attendance. The chair of the meeting, our client and the meeting's host, was a short man with a huge ego. He asked a question at the beginning of the meeting, and I was the only person to raise my hand in dissent (a pretty badass move, I must say!) That set me apart even more, but I also remember feeling so confident about my opinion that I truly did not care what the other professionals in the room thought.

Later, when a few of us were debriefing after the meeting, I happened to be standing right next to this client. The difference in our height was pretty significant. I'll never forget how, after a few moments, he skittled a few feet away and sat down. I laughed so hard in my mind because I knew he did this out of his discomfort in standing next to me, this tall woman who had her own mind, and who also held the key to the project's success (I was the point person implementing the research). I knew unequivocally at that meeting that my nonverbal cues (and verbal ones) gave me a gravitas even this larger-than-life client had to acknowledge, albeit quietly so.

Ladies, our presence is such a key component of the impact we're able to have in our sphere that I really want you to take this chapter seriously. Presence can make the difference between making a difference or missing the mark.

Review the nonverbal cues below and examine whether any of the following red flags are areas you need to address to level up your presence.

- **Not maintaining eye contact:** When you don't look people in the eyes, it can be perceived as insecurity, nerves, or poor confidence. Eye contact is one of the rules I would demonstrate in the "Dress for Success" seminars I facilitated. When greeting, I maintained eye contact for as long as I could, making note of the color of the other person's eyes while shaking their hand. When you converse with someone, frequent, sustained eye contact helps you come across as engaged, trustworthy, and present, especially when you're in listening mode. When speaking to groups, your ability to maintain eye contact is powerful in helping you to connect, engage, and inspire your audience.

- **Weak handshakes:** A weak handshake tends to signal a lack of authority. In my seminars, I would demonstrate a strong handshake. I coach others to "pump" their palms a couple of times with a firm but not overly aggressive hold while maintaining eye contact. This greeting establishes your presence from the get-go, especially when networking.

- **Folded arms:** In a group context, this stance creates a sense of being closed off to feedback and gives off a negative, judgmental vibe. It can also appear aloof or authoritative. Be mindful of what you're doing with your arms when standing and talking. This posture conveys a lot about your confidence and command.

- **Poor poise/posture:** This one should be a no-brainer. Your posture communicates so much about your confidence and esteem. Bad posture signals to others that you lack confidence, have poor self-esteem, or low energy levels. Poise takes posture a level up and conveys a bit more gravitas. A woman with great poise will always command respect and attention. If one of the compliments you hear frequently is that you look like a dancer, folks are talking about your poise! If you struggle with poise, taking yoga or dance classes can help address this.

- **Looking down:** When speaking to a group, looking down can make you look uncomfortable or self-conscious. It also communicates that you may be disengaged. This weakens your presence.
- **Angling your body away from others:** Taking too much physical distance or not leaning into a conversation shows that you are uncomfortable, distrustful, or disinterested in the person or subject. Again, be mindful of your body and what it's doing when in dialogue with other people.
- **High voice tone:** Raising the pitch of your voice at the end of a sentence as if asking a question when you're making a statement is something many women do. This tendency reeks of insecurity, and it's one of those things that comes up a lot for women, especially younger ones. The way you speak matters—your cadence, tone, and voice. If you want to command attention, you want your voice to land on peoples' ears sounding strong and resonant. We're not all designed to be excellent orators, but we can control how our message is communicated via our voice.
- **Fidgety behavior:** Behaviors like tapping your foot, twirling your hair, playing with jewelry or clothes, or rocking back and forth can highlight hyperactivity, discomfort, or anxiety. These behaviors weaken your presence because they also convey an element of immaturity.
- **Unnecessary qualifiers:** Softening statements by inserting words like "kind of," "maybe," "just," or "actually" weakens your message and diminishes your presence because they suggest doubt or insecurity. Make sure you're pausing when you're thinking about what to say next mid-sentence and not using filler words like "um" or "you know." Pay attention to whether this is one of your issues. You may want to listen to your voice on audio to hear where you fall short. Personally, I had to work on deleting the word "just" from my email communications. I found that I used it ALL the time. Oof! Now it still comes up, but because I'm aware of it, I edit it out immediately.

3. Clothing (& Appearance)

The phrase "a picture paints a thousand words" correlates well with how our image speaks volumes before we even open our mouths. Your appearance matters because it gives those you interact with another way to assess your leadership presence. Your choice of clothing, accessories, the colors you wear, and how you style your hair all impact your appearance and can enhance your leadership presence or minimize it.

Many of today's professional women lack the time and wherewithal to create the polished and pulled-together office outfits they desire to meet the demands of their careers. This is why so many women resort to uninspired "defaults," including the traditional suit; black slacks and a sweater; chinos and a button-down; jeans and a button-down; or some variation of these. In their minds, it is better to blend in and play it safe rather than risk making a wardrobe faux pas.

What's missing in these women's work wardrobes is a happy medium. Heck, what is missing is a big dose of their personalities. These may be women just like you. This might very well be your story too.

If this is you, regrettably, style and presence have gone out the door, and with it, your opportunity to shine—not just in the caliber of your work, but in your visual presentation. Your image is the packaging of YOUR unique brand. If you're dressing in "default" mode, your attire is not going to represent you at your most brilliant. It certainly won't help you look or feel empowered, confident, polished, fresh, modern, or *present*.

Context is so important in determining what is appropriate for you to wear to work. Are you in a corporate or informal environment? Do you own your own business? Do you work from home and primarily interact through Zoom meetings? Does your company have a dress code policy? What type of industry are you in? What is your role? Are you in the public eye? What outfits make you feel most confident? Where do you work? Snazzy boots and skinny jeans may work in a creative office environment in New York City but can be career suicide on the Hill in Washington, DC. The key is to be smart about your career wardrobe, no matter where you work or what you do.

Here are a few wardrobe tips to help you bring the best of your image to your workspace. If you want more, I dedicated a whole chapter to "Wowing at Work" in *Frumpy to Fabulous: Flaunting It.* I even broke down the eight scenarios of wardrobe-challenged professional women for you to understand your own tendencies. I also include illustrations of inspirational ensembles to get you motivated.[4]

Dressing for work is a challenge for many women, so if this is you, don't be disheartened. There are plenty of resources out there to support you, including your copy of my book (wink emoji).

- You've heard this before, but it is worth repeating: Always dress for a higher position than you currently occupy. Dressing for the position you are aspiring to will boost your confidence in your ability to achieve it.
- Invest in quality pieces. Your clothing can be one of your more important career "investments." Look for timeless well-made designs and mix these

up with more stylish accents depending on your personal style. The way you treat yourself is how the rest of the world will treat you. If you dress like a winner and act like a winner, the world will treat you like a winner.

- Pay attention to the accent pieces that make you stand out and where you can express more of your unique élan. Your signature can be shoes, handbags, jewelry, and scarves and how you wear them. Also, the style and cut of your business attire speak loudly about the type of professional you are.
- Fit is a clear divider separating the well-dressed from the wanna-be-well-dressed. Only wear what fits you perfectly. Have your clothing altered by professionals as needed or pay attention to the designers and brands that work well for your figure and proportions. If your $1,500 Calvin Klein suit puckers, pulls, or is too tight or loose, you're better off wearing a cheaper alternative that fits you impeccably.
- Ask yourself what type of image is important for your career. For example, if you are a physician, people have certain expectations about the image of a physician which may include traits like competency, detail-oriented, intelligence, compassion, and authority. If you're in marketing, your image should communicate traits such as creativity, outside-the-box thinking, and strong communication. The context of your job demands certain expectations, so get clear on what you need to communicate (via your image) for your position, corporate culture, and industry.
- Use color strategically. I can never emphasize the importance of this enough. Color strategy is especially important from the waist up, and if most of your meetings happen virtually. Colors convey energy and you need to understand how to use colors in business to achieve different outcomes. Dark colors, like black and navy blue, convey seriousness, "all business," and authority. Brown, while professional, has less authority than black or navy and engenders reliability and security. Pastel colors are soft and convey approachability and femininity. And red, the color of passion, communicates strength, confidence, command, and assertiveness.

While people notice your wardrobe first, remember that your nonverbal cues—your posture, eye contact, confident aura, personality, energy, and more—have as much to do with how you're perceived as your clothing.

Developing your leadership presence is an ongoing and evolving process. While it may look effortless, it's often the result of years of intentional examination, objective feedback, and experience. Every step you take to enhance your presence will have a positive impact on how you're perceived.

Chapter 7

Find Your Best Fit:
Lead with Your Heart

"People are like stained-glass windows. They sparkle and shine when the sun is out, but when the darkness sets in; their true beauty is revealed only if there is a light from within."

~ Elizabeth Kübler-Ross

FIGURE TYPING WAS a transformational aspect of my in-depth image consultations with women. The freedom and empowerment that came when a woman knew how to dress her unique figure and proportions in ways that flattered her was always special to witness.

Many clients came to me thinking their body was wrong. They had bought into the narrative that they had to look a certain way to be attractive. Often these women came frustrated and stuck in their wardrobe choices because they were trying to fit a square peg into a round hole.

A woman would come into my sessions with a beautiful hourglass figure, for example, trying to fit her body in structured, androgynous silhouettes because someone at some point in her life said she had to hide her curves. Or a woman with a triangular or pear shape would try to minimize her heavier hips, butt, and thighs by wearing overlong tops to camouflage, not realizing this tactic made her look frumpy.

We're not readily taught the art of figure flattery, so women have no guide unless they have a natural knack for style and fashion. Nowadays, women have access to YouTube videos and other resources to help them figure some of this out, but 10+ years ago it was hard to get this type of feedback.

I would measure each woman to determine her figure type and her body's proportions. Then, once we were both in alignment with her reality, the next step was showing her how to accentuate the best of her body by drawing attention to those parts while using the optical illusions of lines, tailoring, color, pattern, cut, accessories, and more to balance out the rest.

This was such exciting work because I could see firsthand how a woman's perceptions about her body could change with a bit of education. And once she could embrace her body with a new, positive lens, her possibilities to create the image of her choosing came into view.

Figure typing is never about a woman's body being wrong or unworkable. It was about viewing her body with a possibilities mindset anchored in the reality of her figure and proportions. For example, the client with the inverted triangular figure (wide shoulders, prominent bustline, narrow hips and butt) with the killer, shapely, long legs learned to highlight her assets by opting for fabulous shoes and knee-length or above hemlines on her bottom half while choosing more closed-in necklines (asymmetric, narrow V-neck, etc.), softer contours, and simple lines on her top half.

Just as every star has a unique brilliance, you too have a figure, size, and proportion that's unique to you. There are many templates you can follow to help you dress in a way that best flatters you. What many of these templates don't discuss is the importance of proportion as well. This was something I learned in my image consulting certification that made me understand how to dress my tall frame more effectively. I have an EXTREMELY long rise. When low-rise jeans were the trend, I was screwed! With the current high-rise trend still on the rise (ha!), I am making sure I take advantage of all the jeans and slacks with this feature because it is so much more flattering (and comfortable) on my frame and figure.

My mantra in my work was that every woman had the makings to look fabulous once she knew what she was working with. "How can you Flaunt what you don't even know you have?" I would say as I helped women work *with* their body, rather than fight *against* it.

Men are really good about focusing on their assets and downplaying where their body needs work. I can't tell you how many times I've been on dating sites where a man describes himself as athletic, who from his photos is a good 20+ pounds overweight. Women do the opposite. We fixate on our perceived flaws and shortcomings, deeming ourselves undatable when, in reality, we're just dealing with the same stuff everyone else deals with around midlife—graying hairlines, saggy skin, a few more wrinkles around the eyes.

I'm the last person to advise against trying to improve where we can. I'm all about the serums and the weight training now that I see my skin sagging more readily toward the floor! What I'm not about for myself and women is beating ourselves up for how we think we fail image-wise.

Our bodies are unique and special, so too are the TAGS we bring to the table. We are fearfully and wonderfully made by a Creator who intentionally designed the very strands of hair on our heads for His specific purposes.

Just as I encouraged women to embrace their body's best assets and features, so too I implore you to acknowledge your brilliance. I believe that each of us has been uniquely made with a purpose we are uniquely designed to fulfill. When I talk about purpose, I'm talking about what you can do to make an impact in the lives of others. I'm talking about leaving your mark so that the world is better off because you're in it. I'm talking about that sense of calling you hear deep in the recesses of your heart—the thing you know you're made for, your best fit in life.

As I'm writing this section, the news about Rihanna's *Vogue* cover and photo shoot where she proudly flaunts her pregnant body is making headlines. In her third trimester of pregnancy, Rihanna is using her body's changes to display that we can look and feel fabulous in every season of life. In the cover feature, she shares, "When I found out I was pregnant, I thought to myself, there's no way I'm going to go shopping in no maternity aisle. I'm sorry—it's too much fun to get dressed up. I'm not going to let that part disappear because my body is changing."

Rihanna hopes her pregnancy clothing choices of midriff-baring looks and sheer belly exposing dresses will inspire and empower other expectant moms to embrace their bodies. She says, "I'm hoping that we were able to redefine what's considered 'decent' for pregnant women. My body is doing incredible things right now, and I'm not going to be ashamed of that. This time should feel celebratory. Because why should you be hiding your pregnancy?"[1]

You go, girl! This is what body consciousness is all about! While you may not agree with Rihanna's clothing choices, you can respect her confidence and agency to go against societal norms that imply women must camouflage and mask their burgeoning pregnant bellies to make those around them feel comfortable.

Many women have been indoctrinated to believe that they must be perfect, pretty, and pleasing so they can fit in. This indoctrination locks us into gender stereotypes that keep us playing small, muting ourselves, and never bringing our full, authentic selves to the arena.

This chapter will inspire and encourage you to cultivate the best version of yourself. You'll learn to lean on your innate traits, strengths, and attributes as a woman—traits like empathy and authenticity, which allow you to be a more heart-centric and empathic leader.

Creating Connection

Brené Brown writes, "Love and belonging are irreducible needs for all people… Belonging is a practice that requires us to be vulnerable, get uncomfortable, and learn how to be present with people without sacrificing who we are."[2] As human beings, we are designed to be social and relational.

If you care about your impact, understanding how to connect with others in an authentic, vulnerable, and confident way will determine your effectiveness. You won't be able to do meaningful, transformational work if your connection skills are weak.

Leadership is highly relational, which is why cultivating high Emotional Intelligence or EQ is an area most leaders need to grow into. The relational nature of leadership is what begets genuine engagement and trust. This is what forges that strong connection between a leader and her people.

You can be a powerful speaker and you can have the smartest ideas, but without the ability to connect with your people, your impact is diminished. Leaders who can form strong bonds with others are perceived as more relatable and down to earth, which creates greater trust and loyalty.

In their CliftonStrengths Assessment, Gallup describes people with the "Relator" talent as possessing the ability to, "form genuine and mutually rewarding one-on-one relationships."[3] Those with "Relator" strength can authentically build close enduring connections that foster trust and confidence.

One of my clients, Amanda has "Relator" in her top strengths. She's come to see how this trait is what differentiates her brand as a leader. She knew she had a relational superpower because she had a natural knack for finding common ground among people, especially people who looked and thought differently than she did. As a Black woman, she had access to exclusive spaces where she was often the only minority and/or woman present. Yet being a minority was never an obstacle for her.

Her gift of forging authentic connections with others was greater than any perceived differences. Her presence created harmony, camaraderie, and inclusivity, which were critical because she sat on several corporate boards where her voice and opinion mattered. Her connection-creating ability made her an impactful and transformative leader whose opinions and ideas were heard, seen, and valued to the benefit of all.

Amanda is so good at creating connection that she sees this ability as a "permeability superpower." She can so effortlessly navigate her way through spaces and groups that, on the surface, would be particularly challenging for her to access, let alone have a voice in.

Brené Brown defines connection as "the energy that exists between people when they feel seen, heard, and valued; when they can give and receive without judgment; and when they derive sustenance and strength from the relationship."[4]

Authentic connection is empathy, caring, integrity, curiosity, and effective interpersonal communication in action. It's tough to connect if you're blind and oblivious to those around you. Understanding how your energy, mood, and aura impact those around increases self-aware, a critical component of EQ.

If we see our interactions with others as relational versus transactional, this changes how we show up. When we put people first, seeing our shared humanity rather than looking at others as pawns to achieve our agenda, we signal that we value people over our priorities.

By being brave enough to ask for help or acknowledging when we don't have the answer, we model vulnerability as a desired trait, which creates a positive ripple effect in our sphere.

Let's go a little deeper into what EQ is all about.

It's Not About Your IQ but Your EQ

Your impact and effectiveness as a professional and leader require more than just your diligence, performance, and good ideas. You need all that plus strong Emotional Intelligence. EQ matters because it's important that you understand, inspire, and motivate those around you and those whom you lead.

A strong EQ means you can be aware of, control, and express your emotions, as well as handle your professional relationships empathetically. EQ involves recognizing, understanding, and choosing how you think, feel, and act. Your level of EQ shapes your interactions with others and your understanding of yourself—it defines how and what you learn, allows you to set priorities, and determines your responses to situations.

Enhancing your professional relationships and ensuring the personal well-being of the individuals you lead are all key outcomes of developing emotional intelligence.

As our worlds upturned with the COVID-19 pandemic, many leaders started to question, redefine, and reflect on the ways they lead. Talk about leading in uncertainty!

The Institute of Coaching (IOC) conducted a qualitative study in 2021 that examined how leaders navigated the workplace consequences of the pandemic.

A few of the quotes pulled from the report particularly resonated with me. These quotes highlight the importance of leaders cultivating high EQ, especially during the challenging times we've all been through in the past few years.

"I always felt the real secret to leadership goes back to more adaptive leadership styles, which is connecting with people, bringing out who they are, bringing psychological safety into every conversation, showing empathy, building teamwork, where people can show up and be vulnerable."

Another leader talked about how the pandemic revealed weaknesses in leaders:

"The real secret to leadership goes back to showing empathy, building safety, building teamwork, where people can show up and be vulnerable. The pandemic really exposed leaders who were uncomfortable doing that because if you hid behind numbers, if you hid behind management, if you were uncomfortable creating safe spaces for people to truly open up… it exposed cultures that were based on fear."[5]

A positive result of the pandemic was that leaders saw the need for, and had to lean into, the more human-centered skills at work. Simon Sinek calls attributes like listening, empathy, authenticity, compassion, transparent communication, and trust-building "human skills."

Some of these skills arguably come more naturally to women than men. But because there are no systems or metrics set up in organizations to recognize and reward these skills, organizations often overlook their best internal leaders because they don't place enough value on these crucial qualities.

Individuals who possess "hard skills" that can be objectively measured (technical knowledge, strategic thinking, financial expertise, marketing prowess, etc.) are the ones typically selected for leadership roles because these skills drive performance.

But leadership is about people, and when individuals who don't possess human and interpersonal skills get put into leadership roles, they are ill-equipped to manage people, especially during crises like the pandemic. This ill fit can lead to unproductive teams and organizations where low morale, toxic work cultures, dissatisfaction, and unhealthy striving become the norm.

In the current uncertain and constantly changing environment, leading with empathy is foundational. We're stressed out and anxious. Mental health statistics highlight grim realities: Burnout is on the rise and people are resigning from their roles, leading to the Great Resignation. According to the US Bureau of Labor Statistics, 4 million Americans quit their jobs in July 2021, with a record-breaking 10.9 million open jobs at the end of that July. The trend has not stopped in the beginning weeks of 2022.

This Great Resignation trend points to how the pandemic has overturned our expectations of what career and life satisfaction looks like and the cost of teetering on the brink of exhaustion or burnout. Many people are drawing a solid boundary around their mental, emotional, and physical health and reimagining what they want.

The pandemic helped us see and understand at a deeper level that without a sense of purpose, our work cannot fulfill us and make the impact we long for.

So many of my clients are already planning their exits from their current roles to launch their own bold endeavors. Often this transition involves embracing long-held passions and dreams they all but gave up on that now seem possible! They are reinventing, reimagining, and redesigning work that draws from their innate gifts and talents, their passions, their sense of purpose. There is a new urgency of "If not now, when?"

All these paradigm shifts point to models where compassionate leadership is at the core. In the IOC report, leaders talked about the ability to bring one's "full self" to work, along with exhibiting emotional empathy. They saw these abilities as crucial in COVID-19.

A 2019 study on compassionate leadership discovered that "compassionate leaders set themselves apart and come from a place of integrity and presence. This allowed them to be acutely aware of the impact of their actions on others."[6] This heightened sense of empathy and understanding for coworkers is a posture leaders can continue beyond the pandemic as empathy fosters a trusting, safe, and authentic work culture. More than being just a "nice to have," leading from empathy and compassion creates the resiliency that we value in each other.

Academically, EQ is broken into four quadrants: Self-Awareness, Self-Management, Social Awareness, and Relationship Management. Self-Awareness is what it sounds like—having a keen sense of who you are, your strengths, limits, competencies, and confidence. Self-Management has to do with your self-control and how well you regulate your emotions. This quadrant centers itself on transparency, adaptability, optimism, and other positive traits that make those around you feel safe and supported. Social Awareness has empathy at its core. Relationship Management relies on competencies such as influence, inspiration, conflict management, mentoring, and effective team building.

The world needs more heart-centered leaders these days! While some people are naturally gifted with EQ, it can be cultivated with intentionality and practice.

The guidelines for communicating with others in emotionally connecting ways include these components:

- **Emotional understanding:** Understanding the problem through the other person's point of view. The ability to accurately read another's emotions and connect with your own.
- **Respect:** The recognition and full acceptance of the other person as a human being.
- **Authenticity:** Being transparent, vulnerable, and showing up in a real and relatable way.
- **Mirroring:** The ability to identify and reiterate the other person's words and feelings.
- **Active listening:** In coaching, we refer to this as listening at Level 3— where we hear not just what someone says but also what remains unsaid as well—the other person's emotional state.
- **Understanding:** Seeing the other person's perspective and being able to put yourself in their shoes. Respecting another's feelings on a topic speaks volumes about a person's EQ.

With your emotional intelligence skills honed, you'll be better equipped to navigate, strategize, and adapt to any circumstance, situation, or interaction to benefit yourself and those around you.

Empathy: A Leadership Superpower

I believe empathy is the bedrock of EQ. Many women can tap into empathy and use it as a superpower at work. In addition, empathy is increasingly recognized and lauded as a foundational leadership skill.

In her latest bestseller, *Atlas of the Heart,* author Brené Brown unpacks the essence of compassion and empathy and how they are distinct but also connected. She defines compassion as "the daily practice of recognizing and accepting our shared humanity so that we treat ourselves and others with loving-kindness, and we take action in the face of suffering."

Brown defines empathy as "the most powerful tool of compassion… An emotional skill set that allows us to understand what someone is experiencing and to reflect back that understanding."[7]

In a recent Forbes piece, author Tracy Brower posits that empathy is the most important leadership trait because research has found that empathetic leadership leads to more innovation, engagement, retention, inclusivity, and work-life balance.

The article highlighted that empathy in action at work looks like "understanding an employee's struggles and offering to help. It is appreciating a person's point of view and engaging in a healthy debate that builds to a better solution. It is considering a team member's perspectives and making a new recommendation that helps achieve greater success."[8]

In *Atlas of the Heart*, Brown says researchers agree that empathy has two components: cognitive empathy and affective empathy. "Cognitive empathy, sometimes called perspective taking or mentalizing, is the ability to recognize and understand another person's emotions. Affective empathy, often called experience sharing, is one's own emotional attunement with another's person's experience."

She makes the important distinction that cognitive empathy (coupled with compassion) drives meaningful connection because it entails understanding what someone is feeling rather than feeling it for them.[9]

Many of us have encountered people described as "bleeding hearts"—the ones that feel so much about other people's experiences that they get so wrapped up in their situation that they end up carrying that person's burden. As benevolent as this may seem on the surface, it is so damaging, draining, and depletive for that empath.

For our empathy to be a true strength, it must be strong enough that we understand another's dilemma or situation but not so strong that we feel all the feelings for them. When our empathy is healthy, we can use our understanding to support that person we empathize with in constructive ways that don't leave us depleted and ineffective.

Undoubtedly, empathy is key to developing high EQ. But it's important to remember the difference between sympathy and empathy, as the two are often confused. Empathy is *feeling with* and sympathy is *feeling for*. Big difference. Empathy sounds like, "I get it, I've been there, I feel for you." Sympathy sounds like, "I'm sorry for you, you poor thing." One leads to connection; the other to disconnection because it comes across as judgmental and aloof.

Empathy is about connection. In contrast to *being* something, empathy is something that is offered, a connection at an emotional level that is deeply felt.

Being able to identify and label your emotions is a key and pivotal element to building emotional intelligence and empathy. The more specific you can be with your emotions, the better you can communicate and understand others.

In our fragmented, disconnected, divisive culture, I believe embracing empathy is the key to authentic connection and effective leadership.

When your leadership brand is anchored in empathy, your ability to connect with your audience in authentic, resonant ways puts the focus on building meaningful experiences with them. As a leader, having empathy lead your brand identity shows you care deeply about your people, and demonstrate this by aligning your actions and behavior with this truth.

Jo Saxton writes, "Don't devalue the vulnerability you feel when you lead. Don't dismiss your vulnerability, your emotions, your tears as a sign of incompetence and disqualify yourself. Your voice doesn't need to be polished; it needs to be real, raw, and brave."[10]

President Biden is a leader with a high empathy quotient. It is the single most associated attribute with his brand. In a speech in 2021 acknowledging the 500,000+ milestone of people who died of COVID-19, Biden made a single gesture that demonstrated empathy.

He pulled a card out of his jacket pocket—which he said he keeps with him wherever he goes—and read off the exact, up-to-date number of Americans who had died from the coronavirus. (That number at the time was more than 527,000.) Yes, of course, Biden did that for dramatic effect. But it worked. And it drove home the idea that this is a leader who keeps those who have died from the pandemic close to his heart.

If you're a naturally empathetic woman, you're able to easily put yourself in another's shoes and respond out of compassion and kindness. You also sense others' emotions readily so you can address and express your concern, allowing them to have a space where they feel seen and understood.

Maya Angelou famously said, "I've learned that people will forget what you said, people will forget what you did, but people will never forget how you made them feel," which speaks directly to how traits like empathy help us show our care for each other.

Empathy & Boundaries Must Unite

When leading with empathy, it is crucial to have healthy boundaries. Boundaries are the guard rails that protect you from overextending yourself. I've seen empathy gone rogue, leading to toxic relationships, overworking, and unhealthy work-life balance.

One of my friends, a physical therapist with high empathy, was recently sharing with me how she found herself trapped in an unhealthy relationship with a woman who'd been a client because she started lending her money. "Genine, that's crazy," I said to her. "How long has this been going on?" "It's almost a year now," Genine said. "I know I have to stop but I don't know how. She really needs help because she has a child that she cares for." As I went on to explain to Genine how her empathy was way out of bounds and this situation could spiral into something disastrous for both of them, I realized that she did not know how to protect herself with boundaries. She had always been that person with a soft heart who would care so much for others that she sometimes forgot to channel that same care to herself.

She's not alone. Many women struggle with this type of behavior because of their empathy or because they've been taught that their needs, wants, and desires should come last. They become proverbial doormats or victims of narcissists and other toxic people. Your empathy is a gift. But for it to be the gem that it is in bringing care, kindness, and civility into your sphere, you must establish boundaries.

When you're an empath, you have to learn how to set healthy, strong boundaries to protect yourself from over-extending. It's about learning to prioritize being free over being liked and needed.

As I explained in chapter two, our boundaries define us and help others understand where we draw the line. Our boundaries declare who we are and who we are not, what we like and what we do not. They dictate the responsibilities we choose to take on and those we don't.

In their bestselling book, *Boundaries*, authors Henry Cloud and John Townsend put it this way: "Knowing what I am to own and take responsibility for gives me freedom. If I know where my yard begins and ends, I am free to do with it what I like. Taking responsibility for my life opens up many different options. However, if I do not 'own' my life, my choices and options become very limited."[11]

You are the only one who can set your boundaries, so you must take full ownership of them. When you are whole and empowered, you are free to establish clear, healthy boundaries about what behavior is and isn't tolerable to you.

Your boundaries are like fences and not like walls that prevent anyone from getting into "your yard." Instead, boundaries say, "You can come up to this line in my yard but no further." But you must take ownership of the parameters of your boundaries.

Prentis Hemphill sums up boundaries this way: "Boundaries are the distance at which I can love you and me simultaneously."

Setting boundaries serves us in several ways. With boundaries in place for ourselves and others:

- People won't have to guess where they stand with us, and we don't have to guess where we stand with them.
- We set the stage for clear and direct communication about our expectations in relationships.
- We lessen the chance of misunderstandings. Often resentment is caused by unclear or weak boundaries which have been violated. When we own the lack of clarity, we can then strengthen our boundaries so those abuses don't reoccur.
- There's clarity on what's needed for us to occupy space in the lives of others and vice versa.
- We understand how others want to be treated and they know how we want to be treated.
- We invite communication and curiosity, which help us learn more about each other.
- We feel safe to communicate our boundaries with each other.

When you start setting and honoring your boundaries, those who knew you before may need an adjustment period to get used to your new and improved way of relating. There may be times when people will hear you and still challenge you to go against what you've said, reminding you of what you used to tolerate. Expect pushback from those who liked your old way of engaging better, when your unspoken boundaries were violated because this served their needs but dishonored yours.

Boundary setting is transformational work, and with every transformation there is a transition process. You will feel uncomfortable saying no and not feeling guilty about it.

For my friend Genine, just the idea of not lending her past client money seemed unimaginable. She felt guilt and a responsibility to this woman that was not hers to own. She had allowed this woman to violate her client/professional relationship but was now so caught up that the healthy choice seemed unkind.

Getting to a place of emotional and mental clarity around our boundaries is part of the adjustment and transformation process.

For Genine, it was helpful to have a conversation with her client, validating her reality while giving a clear explanation of why the behavior must change for both sides. It mattered that she showed she cared and understood how difficult it could be for her client to adjust to the new normal. A mindset shift she had to practice was removing herself as the problem solver/fixer for her clients' challenges, even while allowing herself to empathize with their situations. A healthier approach than giving her old client a stipend each month was sharing established resources that are set up to help people in her client's situation.

As Genine exercises her boundary-setting muscle in ALL areas of her life, she will need to continue to assert and remind herself why the boundaries are there in the first place. When people challenge or try to break her boundaries, she will need to think of the personal cost of allowing those violations to continue without consequences.

While boundary setting can be challenging for women, especially those like Genine who really empathize and sincerely want to help others, the freedom that comes from not taking on others' responsibilities is a game-changer. The more Genine and others like her assert their authority in this way, the more the new behavior normalizes. And Genine will see that she has more energy and capacity to take on responsibilities that are right smack in her career domain and personal life. And THAT is where the transformation takes root.

Authenticity Creates Trust

It is our true, authentic self that our employees, followers, clients, and constituents are inspired by, engage with, and ultimately trust. Authenticity is one of the cornerstones of being an effective leader.

Authenticity has at its Latin root the word "author." Think of this in terms of authorship of your life or your career. With this understanding, being authentic is about crafting our words and actions and authoring our values, beliefs, and principles.

Psychologist and author of *The Little Book on Authenticity*, Nina Burrowes puts it this way: "Authenticity is… not about revealing something, it's about building something, and that something is 'you.'" She explains that in the context of leadership, "embracing your authenticity is the only way to become 'you' and being 'you' is the greatest asset you have when it comes to being a leader."[12]

During our early years, many of us learn how to compartmentalize ourselves to fit in with our surroundings. This is especially true for women of color who excel at what's called "code-switching." We shift our personas to conform to the perceived acceptable societal norms. But by doing this we only become someone else's version of who we are, rather than our true selves.

The larger the gap between our "work persona" and our "home persona," the more alienated we feel from ourselves. According to an article in *Insead*, "This self-alienation increases the pressure and anxiety we feel to perform and makes it difficult to make decisions that align with our values."[13]

Oscar Wilde said, "Be yourself; everyone else is already taken!" Authenticity demands that we fully integrate ourselves and act in alignment with our core values, beliefs, and true desires, regardless of the context. This true self is the hallmark of our unique signature style as trailblazing women who care about making a difference.

Authenticity is bringing all of you to the table, fully faceted. Each part of our being has value. Collectively, all our multifaceted uniqueness is what gives us our competitive advantage.

In our authenticity, we form deeper connections versus transactional ones. In our authenticity, we can be bold, unapologetic, and fearless in the pursuit of our vision. In our authenticity, we can be the change we want to see and impact the sphere we're designed to transform.

Authenticity can be scary. But it's necessary if you truly care about serving your people.

Research shows that acting authentically promotes personal well-being and overall fulfillment, higher self-esteem, and enhanced work performance and leads to stronger interpersonal relationships.

The reason so many of us don't bring our full authentic selves to our workspaces is that we worry that our true selves are inadequate or unacceptable. So we hide our opinions, mask our personality, and conform to fit in.

But going against our authentic being by forcing ourselves to conform is exhausting, confining, and limiting, and it hinders our ability to perform at our brilliant best. In contrast, in our authenticity, we are free to leverage our assets, talents, and strengths and bring our unique contributions, perspectives, and superpowers to work. This integrated approach optimizes our mental and emotional energy so we can excel and thrive in our arenas.

When we try to imitate another leader or another brand, we are doomed to fail because we cannot sustain connection with others if we are inauthentic. Our words and actions as a leader will ring hollow if they are not sourced from the true desires of our hearts. The more we "be," the greater the impact of our "do." When we imitate, mute, or mask ourselves, we can never be in our full brilliance.

Authenticity is at the heart of every powerful, impactful, and influential leader. Only when our actions and words are congruent with our beliefs and values, and we are showing up fully as ourselves, are we leading authentically.

In my professional life, showing up in my full brilliance involves embracing my Trinidadian roots. From the moment someone hears me speak, they hear my accent, and they invariably ask about it. I cannot tell you how many times this seemingly inconsequential disclosure about my heritage has led to tangential side conversations that *seem* to have no bearing on the business at hand. And yet it has everything to do with it.

To harness the power of your authenticity, you can start from where you stand right now, no matter your vocation. As Jo Miller so perfectly put it, "Becoming a leader isn't about changing yourself. It's about becoming yourself."[14] This advice holds true whether we lead in a corporate environment, a classroom, a church, or on Capitol Hill.

When you authentically display your true self, without the pressure to appear flawless or perfect, you can transparently admit and address your weaknesses, missteps, or mistakes and be open and humble enough to appreciate and learn from others. In this way, you engender trust and inspire those you lead to feel safe enough to authentically connect to those around them.

In the professional arena, if we look at our interactions as transactional, we miss out on opportunities to form deeper connections, which can only happen when we show up authentically. By letting our guards down and stepping into our authentic selves, we can start to unveil the human beings we truly are behind the labels, masks, and armor we attach to ourselves and others.

By intentionally cultivating connection as a woman of influence, you'll build the trust of those you lead and gain their respect, thereby deepening your relationships with them. Perhaps even more importantly, you'll be able to get their buy-in on your vision and mission, which increases the likelihood of making your impact.

Chapter 8

Are you a Louboutin or Choo?
Build a Brand Based on Your Brilliance

"Sometimes you can't see yourself clearly until you see yourself through the eyes of others."

~ Ellen DeGeneres

W HEN MICHELLE OBAMA became first lady, her sense of style evolved and became bolder and more creative. I remember blogging about her fashion choices in 2008. Michelle is a very tall woman with a similar body type to mine, so I was always intrigued by her choices.

When she first started becoming visible as the potential FLOTUS, her style was noteworthy because it was down-to-earth and relatable. She wore simple shift dresses in bold colors or patterns. As she settled into her role as FLOTUS, she started accessorizing more and would cinch her waist with her signature wide-width belts. Over time, her look got even bolder, and she shocked the pundits when she emerged on the 2009 special edition cover of *Life Magazine* with a sleeveless black dress showing off her toned arms.

Later she became known for choosing obscure designers, such as Naeem Khan, who then skyrocketed to fame. She charmed women across the country because she would just as readily show up to interviews in an Ann Taylor dress as she would in a dress from Jason Wu. Her choice to mix high-end luxury designs with mass-market ones was lauded, and Michelle soon became a fashion icon.

But her rise to glamor goddess did not take away from her impact as FLOTUS; it magnified it. Michelle Obama worked to end obesity and encouraged healthy food choices by creating a vegetable garden at The White House. She championed veterans, and elevated those whose invisibility needed a platform. Her work was well received and successful. Every time she showed up at an event, we paid attention.

What I truly admire about Michelle Obama is how her sense of style reinforced her brand image. Her authenticity, relatability, confidence, savvy, and charm showed up in her wardrobe and her work. She became our Forever First Lady because of her inside and outside persona. Her fashion choices captivated us, and her heart for the underserved connected her with us. Her personable, smart, relatable, accessible personality shines through everything she does, says, and shows to the world, whether as FLOTUS or as an author and podcast host. Her authenticity is one of her most prominent leadership brand attributes.

As a strong Black woman in the public eye, Mrs. Obama could so easily have been ostracized, criticized, and maligned, but with every challenge, she rose even higher in the public's estimation because she remained genuine and true to herself and her values.

Few women have had to navigate the variety of spaces and contexts Michelle Obama has, but she's mastered the art of being relevant, relatable, and down-to-earth when rallying crowds on the campaign trail, singing along with James Corden's carpool karaoke, planting gardens, engaging with families at the Obama's Annual White House Easter Monday event, or promoting her memoir, *Becoming*, on one of the many national mega venue events.

Michelle Obama is an excellent example of a compelling, effective, enduring personal brand. Unfortunately, many professionals don't take the time to consider how they are positioning one of their most powerful assets—their brand's identity.

Several years ago, I gave a presentation on personal branding to a group of young professionals. As part of the workshop, I challenged them to consider how they wanted to be perceived as a brand. Specifically, I asked what they wanted people to know about them when meeting them for the first time. The responses were as diverse and creative as the attendees, and they underscored the importance of thinking strategically about one's brand persona. In one of the more interactive aspects of the workshop, I worked with one of the professionals to help him flesh out his brand story. I queried him on his skills, interests, values, personality, experience, and more—anything that could potentially have a bearing on his brand promise. It was a rich exchange.

Before long it became clear that he valued people and that this was a deep core value for him. It informed his work ethic, management style, the type of purpose he felt called to fulfill in his role, and his relationships with colleagues. Valuing people even influenced the way he showed up dressed for work. He was the perfect example of what personal branding is about—getting clear on your unique value proposition, your special points of differentiation from others in the professional arena.

We all have a brand, whether we leverage it or not, tout it or not. We are communicating messages all the time about who we are, what we stand for, and what we bring to the table. Yet so many professionals, entrepreneurs, and solopreneurs do not intentionally craft their brand personas. Instead, they leave their brand up to the whim of others to define for them. That approach leads to a weak, ineffective, inauthentic brand. Why let others define who you are?

Think of the trademarked red soles of Christian Louboutin pumps and how that feature sets them apart from other high-end pumps. This feature is the highlight of Christian Louboutin's pumps' unique value proposition as a brand. Women splurge just for the "wow" factor of owning those branded shoes. Many people also spend way more money on an iPhone than another brand and choose to pay more on Under Armour leggings versus a standard pair from Old Navy.

I pay extra money to have a specific shade of MAC lipstick that costs twice as much as the typical drugstore brand. We pay extra for what we believe a consumer brand offers us—the unique value proposition that is at the heart of every solid brand. Often, we can't even articulate the difference between one brand versus another, but for whatever reason, we put aside our coins to invest in our preferred brands because we believe in the promise those brands market to us.

Personal brands are no different than consumer brands. Strong public personal brands—including Michelle Obama, Oprah, Kim Kardashian, Beyoncé, and Martha Stewart—all have a unique expression that makes them distinct from anyone else. These women are household names worldwide because of their differentiated talent/expertise/platform, but also because of how distinctly they present themselves. Therein lies the power of personal branding.

As a leader on the rise or rising, your personal brand highlights the skills, qualities, and strengths which define what makes you different from the next professional, just like a consumer brand. Personal branding is important because it is a way for you to establish and consistently reinforce who you are and what you offer in the workplace.

Your personal brand can strategically position you so that the most salient aspects of your brand identity become front and center, making it obvious to your peers, clients, managers, customers, or coworkers.

Your personal brand is part of your identity—it is a way to communicate who you are and what you stand for in your professional circle. It is your unique value and reputation in the marketplace. What it is not is a facade or persona you put on to impress. What makes a personal brand personal is how authentic it must be to be effective. It MUST be about you—your skills, your values, your experience, your interests, your points of differentiation.

Jeff Bezos famously says, "Branding is what people say about you when you're not in the room." And he's right. Personal branding is every detail about you and how you manage others' perceptions. It is what differentiates you from other people in your sphere of influence so that your authenticity and originality shine through. It's a promise of what others can expect from your performance as a leader.

We each are our own walking advertisements, our own personal brand that markets and conveys information about our credibility, competence, intelligence, self-image, and confidence.

Personal branding is built upon establishing a reputation for yourself, standing up for what you believe in, showcasing what differentiates you from others, and consistently performing above par regardless of what you do.

An effective personal brand helps you:

- Establish yourself as an expert in your field
- Reinforce a clear, enduring, and powerful brand message
- Establish credibility for what you do
- Engender trust and loyalty with your potential clients/audience
- Present a more authentic image of yourself to others
- Differentiate yourself as a leader
- Exert your influence (your point of view, message, etc.) with those around you

As a professional, executive, or entrepreneur, every aspect of your brand needs to communicate your overall brand value. This includes:

- Your image
- The way you communicate (verbal, phone, written)
- The way you relate to people (approachability, likeability, trustworthiness, etc.)

- The level/type of service you offer to clients or customers
- Your mission and vision
- Your values
- Your online identity: website, e-newsletters, blogs, online profiles, social networking sites, message board posts, and so on

Remember that personal branding is personal. Just as Christian Louboutin pumps are differentiated from other designer shoes by their red soles, we each have our own unique brand identity based on the unique value proposition or distinctiveness we bring to the game. Personal branding is your secret weapon you can wield to express who you are and the message you want the world to know about you.

Your brand is aligned with your reputation in the workplace or marketplace. As a professional or entrepreneurial woman called to make a difference, your brand is your promise of what customers or clients can expect from you. Take the time to build a solid foundation, to shape it in a way that propels you forward and helps you achieve your professional aspirations.

Developing Your Personal Brand

You have the choice and the authority to craft a strong, healthy, vibrant brand that engages, inspires, and performs. Developing your personal brand starts with getting clear. It starts with intent.

As a foundational step in building a strong brand, write out six or seven attributes that you want to be associated with you. Think intentionally about each attribute to ensure it resonates with you.

These descriptors will be the runway from which you start to create a fabulous narrative for your brand. Your narrative includes everything about you as a professional; all the salient experiences, interests, skills, and aptitudes you possess, anchored by your values, beliefs, and character. Identifying these descriptors is where you will do the heavy lifting defining and shaping your brand so it is positioned for success.

Getting clear on how you wish to be perceived gets you thinking critically about the messages you have inadvertently been communicating. For instance, in one personal branding workshop, a young man described one of his attributes as "creative," yet he had difficulty articulating how he expressed this trait professionally. He certainly did not "look" creative—in fact, he looked very conservative!

Nothing in his appearance or demeanor gave the impression that he had a creative bone in his body. Yet he wanted to be perceived as creative.

When your appearance or communication is at odds with your desired brand identity, how do you reconcile them? The simplest way is to project the desired trait so it becomes an integral part of your persona. In this young man's case, I asked a few probing questions: Did he share creative ideas at work? Did he come up with creative ways to solve problems? Was he creative in the pursuit of his career goals? Did he manifest creativity in other ways?

With some digging, we found quite a few creative kernels in his professional life. Because he now had a renewed awareness of how important this attribute was to him, he vowed to make it a more vital part of his professional reality.

To ensure you cultivate a brand that powerfully represents the best of who you are as a leader, reflect on the following success tips I've curated for my branding clients.

Get Clear on Your Who and Your Do

To build a personal brand that accurately reflects your personal and professional identity, you need to be clear about your points of differentiation. A wonderful place to start is by examining your strengths, which we discussed in chapter three.

Go back to chapter three and revisit the questions when considering how you're innately wired. As a professional, business owner, coach, or leader, your brand represents your Who and your Do. When those two aspects are fully integrated into your brand, the result is transformative and magnificent because it will represent the best of who you are and what you bring to the table.

Your Who includes qualities like your character, values, persona, strengths, and distinctiveness. A few of the attributes that distinguish me from other coaches include my culture as a Black woman with Caribbean heritage, my relational and strategic strengths that are dominant in my CliftonStrengths Assessment, my personality as an INFJ type with high empathy, my core beliefs as a Christian and a woman driven by a desire to make a transformational impact, and my long history learning and growing personally and professionally through therapy, self-help books, and more. All these things define my posture as a coach, even without looking at my many Dos.

What are the Dos? They include all your As: your accomplishments, awards, accolades, and achievements. They include your expertise, your career journey, your role, your education, and certifications—all the things you do that make you exceptional.

My Do includes my three business degrees (and one a full scholarship to Cambridge University, for bragging privileges), my 15+ career as a market researcher, my role as a vice president leading a team, my journey into entrepreneurship as an image consultant, all my image consulting training, my expertise working with hundreds of women, my achievement as the author of an Amazon best-selling inspirational and style book, my coaching certifications, my Strengths Champion certification, my work as a career coach, and more. I'm proud of my *As*! But my *As* alone won't get me above the fray as a Career Transitions Strategist and Leadership Coach.

The secret is that it's the intersection of your Who and your Do that will distinguish you as a brand. That is your secret sauce, your exceptionality, your unique value proposition. When you overlay your Who and Dos with each other, you will be able to distinguish yourself and begin to harness what I like to refer to as your Woo.

All those abilities and accomplishments I listed above are integrated into the package of my personal and professional brand as a business owner. They enable me to set myself apart. I'm not like any other career coach or leadership coach.

Clarity around your Who and your Do informs your Woo. And your Woo is what is the key to your brand differentiation and your impact.

Define Your Niche

Who are you expecting to respond to your brand? Are you vying for a position at another company and looking to capture the attention of recruiters or HR managers? Are you on track to secure a coveted fellowship or grant and need to ensure your brand is on point? Are you in a visible leadership role at your company and need to attract key stakeholders to your project or initiative?

The answers to these questions will determine for whom you craft your brand narrative. The sooner you define your niche, the easier it will be to shape your brand narrative.

As a business owner, your niche has to do with your ideal client or customer. Who are you serving? What are their demographics, such as age, gender, ethnicity, education, geographic location, etc.? How do they behave, buy, shop, relax, etc.? How do they make decisions? Identifying your ideal customer is foundational in branding a business because until you do, your marketing efforts will be misdirected.

Identify Your Specialized Area of Expertise

As a seasoned professional woman, you have years of expertise in your area of knowledge to draw upon which makes you a subject matter expert (SME). What specialized lane differentiates you? What do you already know that you can share within your sphere of influence? What subjects in your field do you want to learn more about? What does your company or organization need more of? The more niched your expertise, the more differentiated you are and the more powerful your unique value proposition.

As a professional or executive, find a way to verbally engage in staff meetings, events, launch events, or conferences. If you don't say anything or ask anything in a meeting, others simply won't notice you. Speaking raises your profile among fellow colleagues and amplifies your brand as an SME.

As a business owner the same principle applies. Whatever your product or service, you want to ensure that you own a space in that arena where you can stand out.

There are many leadership coaches out here. But each of us must differentiate ourselves else how would the people looking for leadership coaching know who to hire? My niche is high-achieving women in career transition who are passionate about making an impact. Because I've had a career as an employee and leapt into entrepreneurship many years ago and built a solid brand, this also distinguishes me and my brand in my business now. It helps too that I also have specialized experience in image, presence, and dressing for success for women. My experience, expertise, and passions have all informed my niche and the folks who can readily connect with my brand and offerings.

Again, with branding it's about examining the aspects of your career, knowledge, experience, and strengths and how these come together to differentiate your brand in the marketplace.

Create a Personal Brand Manifesto

The Great Resignation and COVID-19 have upended how we do everything. Women are leaving their jobs in droves. Entrepreneurship is on the rise. Freelance consulting is a new normal.

Like many of my clients, it may be time for you to rethink your unique value proposition and ensure your resume reflects your brilliance.

Have you ever heard of a functional resume? If you haven't, you're not alone. Most folks assume their resume must follow a chronological format but that's not always the best way to highlight one's experience. The functional format allows you to craft a resume based on your key strengths and core competencies, so the focus is more on you as a brand.

I believe the functional format is often the better option for game-changing women of impact and purpose because this format lets you focus on your brilliance and gifts, not your titles and responsibilities. It highlights you, not the companies you worked for.

One of my clients was thrilled after we rebranded her resume following the functional structure. Before this, she always felt her resume never truly reflected her or her abilities. She had tremendous extensive experience, but her brilliance was lost in the chronological formatting. With her rebranded resume she was finally excited to share her resume with key influencers in her circle so she could build her thought leader brand leveraging the best of her brilliance regardless of where she'd acquired it. This is the beauty of the functional resume.

I have worked and interacted with so many professionals who are not walking in their full gifting. They minimize their accomplishments and shrink back from commanding positions of visibility, completely unaware of the true value they add to their organization, company, or institution. Because of this, they've resigned themselves to positions that do not inspire, challenge, or energize them. They think that's just the way it is.

But it doesn't have to be that way. We are all born with unique gifts and have tremendously valuable experiences—if only we dare own and market them accordingly. You *can* strategically pursue your unique calling with your qualifications, talents, passions, and expertise and get that career, position, or role you desire. My vision for you is that your skills, experience, ideas, and strengths are communicated authentically, powerfully, and persuasively.

If you view your resume as a personal brand manifesto, you'll see why rebranding your resume may be one of your most important first steps in building your personal brand.

It makes sense to rebrand your resume if:

- You're at a career crossroads
- Your resume is needed for more than just applying for a job
- You need a way to highlight your brilliance and unique value proposition
- You want to highlight YOU and not your job titles
- You want to change the narrative of what makes you qualified in your arena

- You want a personal branding tool to leverage as a leader, consultant, entrepreneur, creative, or influencer
- You're an innovator, disrupter, a "color outside the liner"
- There are gaps or perceived inconsistencies in your work history

We're not just employees. We're personal brands. Your personal brand manifesto helps you display your unique brilliance. The functional resume format will help you document your skills, strengths, and superpowers in a way that truly makes you shine.

If you need a resume that gets you excited when YOU see it, and one that touts the many ways you bring your brilliance to the table, you may want to explore the functional resume.

Prepare an Elevator Pitch

Named for the type of quick, succinct conversation you may have while riding an elevator, an elevator pitch summarizes your background and experience in a way that showcases the best of what you have to offer. A well-crafted elevator pitch is also extremely helpful when you're networking and people ask about you and what you do.

In *How Women Rise*, Sally Helgesen and Marshall Goldsmith talk about an experience that Dong Lao, an executive at a global financial firm, shared at a women's conference. In Lao's words, "Having a clear, concise statement ready to deliver at any moment—one that says what you do now but emphasizes what you want to do in the future and why you're qualified to do it—gives you a huge advantage in terms of visibility and positioning. It sets you apart from the pack and enables you to make the case for yourself at the highest level when the chance presents itself. In my experience, great careers are to be often built on chance encounters. It always pays to be prepared."[1] #Facts.

Your elevator pitch should be a 30 to 60-second story about who you are and your area of expertise and differentiation. In short, your pitch is a way to share your brand quickly and effectively with people you're just meeting. When done well, your pitch ensures you are focused and specific in your personal brand messaging.

It's smart to think about stories that spotlight your top strengths in action to help people conceptualize your distinctiveness. Things to include in your pitch are your current role, where you're headed professionally, your strengths, and your areas of specialization.

Here are a few more guidelines to help you craft your elevator pitch:

- **Make it a mic drop.** Your elevator pitch needs to be punchy and compelling. It needs to be powerful enough to engage the listener so they want to know more about you. Use action verbs and persuasive descriptors.
- **Be aspirational.** You do need to mention your current role or title but don't stay there. Make sure the listener has a sense of where you're going. For instance, you might say, "a visible role in DE&I," or "an opportunity to apply my strategic skills creatively," or "to lead a small team of self-starters." If you're an entrepreneur, make sure you mention your vision even if you're not quite there yet. For example, "I'm looking for investors to help me develop a self-care retreat center for women."
- **Showcase your brilliance.** Make sure you highlight your signature strengths and key achievements. If there is one time when you want to amplify your accomplishments confidently, this is it. So go for it! Let them know what makes you amazing!
- **Customize your pitch to your audience.** Before you pitch, try to get as much info as you can about your audience so you can tailor it accordingly. If you're talking to investors, you want to focus on casting your vision. If you're talking to industry leaders, you want to show how you can add value to their enterprises. If you're talking to an influencer, you need to show them why they should get behind your idea/product/service. If you're talking to a recruiter, keep your pitch simple and focused but make sure they are clear on your points of differentiation.

Network

Yes, I know, networking can feel like a grind, but you won't be able to elevate your brand unless you're out and about and visible to others. It's important to network regularly to grow your professional circle and to attract potential advocates, sponsors, clients, or customers.

Since COVID-19 entered our lives, there are now more virtual events than ever. This includes virtual networking events and mixers which, for introverts like me, can often be more comfortable than in-person events.

Engage in both online and offline communities. Serve on boards. Engage with other industry leaders and influencers. Join relevant groups and make connections.

Another way to shape your professional reputation is to participate in projects, roles, or initiatives that strengthen your desired identity. Think about where you want to be in a few years, then consider which specific activities will help you build the personal brand you need to reach that goal. Actively seek out and volunteer for high-profile roles and assignments where you can demonstrate your new brand in action.

Internal networking and relationship-building are critical to constructing your personal brand. Networking is how you build allies, advocates, and sponsors. Raising your visibility among colleagues also makes you more promotable. People promote the people they know, like, and trust who they see stretching outside their comfort zone. Interacting with other teams makes your name known and creates new opportunities.

The more authentic connections you make, the more you elevate your personal brand.

Manage Your Online and Offline Presence

Like it or not, it's not just your in-person presence that matters. Your online presence matters too. In fact, for many professional women, their online brand may be more powerful than their offline one if they have the knack for influencing, speaking, or writing. In your online efforts, if you can become associated with an issue, cause, or platform, you're well on your way to becoming a thought leader—a known and respected voice on those matters.

Consider the channels that may make sense for your brand, such as:

- Customer or employee interactions
- Social media
- Blog posts
- Podcasts
- Vlogs
- TEDx talks
- Books
- Speaking engagements
- Events
- Networking
- Partnerships with other businesses
- Workshops, webinars, and seminars

Being the featured speaker, either in front of fellow colleagues within your company or other professionals at a larger industry conference, can be an incredibly powerful way to build your professional reputation and reinforce your credibility as an expert.

I talk a lot about the "eyes up" strategy in *Frumpy to Fabulous: Flaunting It* because it is so powerful. Eyes up is about making sure your presence from the waist up is on point, via the use of color, accessories, hair, makeup, and accents from the waist up. When you want folks to listen to you, your image from the waist up should draw our focus to your face. This means the colors you wear, the accessories you choose, the way you style your hair and use makeup—all these play a role in drawing our attention to your face.

This is vitally important when attending virtual meetings or events, especially if you're the speaker or facilitator. In a Zoom meeting, make sure you stand out more than your Zoom background. In a crowded, 100+ Zoom event, your little square should pop out over the others.

I recently attended a 100+ person Zoom networking event and I found myself noting the people whose squares stood out. The attendees in these squares wore a strong color like red. Or their hair caught my eye. Or they were smiling and engaged. In a crowded Zoom event where you want to be visible, using "eyes up" matters.

One evening I had a one-on-one Zoom session with a client, and from the moment her camera turned on, something was off—she just didn't look like her attractive, stylish self. She was wearing a tan jacket over a fitted black dress, no lipstick like she usually does, and minimal jewelry. The tan jacket was working against her—it was not a flattering color or silhouette. And while her dress was cute, her boxy jacket swallowed up all its pizazz.

When I asked her what made her select the ensemble, she admitted she rushed out the door that morning and threw on the jacket over the dress to be more conservative—she hadn't paid attention to whether the color of the jacket was complimentary to her or not. She then showed me her shoes, which were a pair of black and white polka dot pumps. The shoes were fabulous, but over Zoom, this was lost because no one would see them.

That whole day, especially over Zoom, my client wouldn't have been strengthening her brand via her image because her ensemble lacked power and presence, particularly from the waist up. Even though her shoes were fab, they would have drawn attention away from her face, which is the opposite of the "eyes up" technique.

As a leader and influencer, whether you're working in an office, networking, or presenting, your visual brand must always be working for you to reinforce the attributes you want to be known for. Because my client cares about her impact and wants to set a powerful example for those she leads and influences, her presence matters because it impacts her brand as a confident, relational leader.

After my feedback on her Zoom presence, my client shared with me that she ditched the tan jacket once she got home. She agreed that it was not doing her any favors because wearing it took her look down several notches.

As leaders and influencers, we always want to project authority, presence, and stay on brand. As you build your presence, make sure your personal brand stays consistent and authentic, both online and offline. You must demonstrate consistency across your communication channels for your brand to get traction.

Take the time to design a strong foundation for your brand, one that uses authenticity, credibility, expertise, and reputation, just to name a few. Once you have established your brand, make every effort to reinforce its message in everything you say and do. Remember that every interaction a person has with you is an opportunity to build or undermine your brand message and strength.

Cultivating a Leadership Brand True to Your Who

Who you are is how you lead. Your values, your persona, your character, your faith, personality, strengths, weaknesses—all these components inform how you lead others.

In addition, all the distinctive, crazy, or challenging aspects of your journey to leadership shape how you lead. If you're an immigrant like I am, perhaps you'll lead with a broader perspective, more inclusivity, greater resilience, more adaptability. If you've had incredibly tough life challenges, this too will inform your leadership style—you may lead with more kindness, compassion, generosity, and heart.

Cultivating a leadership style aligned with the very best of who you are is based on your Who.

I firmly believe that leaning into your specific style of leadership is critical in cultivating your leadership brand. This is why I created the "What is Your Leadership Brand" assessment, to give you a jumpstart in discovering your brand of leadership. You can download it for free at www.theunveiledway.com/what-is-your-leadership-brand.

I created this assessment to help you harness your points of distinction as a leader and see how they inform how you lead. It is a quick, fun assessment you can complete in about five minutes, and it gives you a template for designing and cultivating your leadership brand.

When you complete the assessment, you will be given your top matched type based on your responses and a summary of how that type typically operates in leadership. The eight leadership brand types in the assessment are:

- Developer
- Implementer
- Strategist
- Heart-Centered
- Visionary
- Commander
- Analytic
- Disruptor

Each of the eight style types above are distinct, differentiated, and impactful. Your most matched type result gives you just a glimpse of how you can assert your leadership in your arena. Your leadership style is your own. Use the result from the assessment as a guide. Let it be one of the guides you build your leadership brand on.

While your work as a leader is fundamental, what often becomes more enduring is your leadership style and brand. Hillary Clinton achieved many accolades throughout her career and yet she is not revered as her achievements may indicate. Her leadership brand never quite connected with people—she was seen as unemotional, unsympathetic, too tough, too stoic, and perhaps too resilient. She rarely showed her "softer side" publicly and this weakened her brand. From her Netflix special, *Hillary*, it appears that with time and reflection, there are things she'd do and handle differently if she could.

I think the same may be true for Vice President Kamala Harris. Sometimes it seems she can't win on either side. A lot of this has to do with her assertiveness as a woman of color, something I understand far too well. And let's face it, most men cannot handle an overly confident woman, which Harris is. She was primed to get backlash, and she's getting it. But her track record shows her toughness and resilience. She will get past this and evolve her style and brand as she navigates the often rocky political leadership career path.

There is such a fuzzy, thin line we must navigate as female leaders, one that shows our authority, gravitas, and effectiveness while still showing our vulnerability, transparency, and humility. These are unique challenges for women in leadership who are also often daughters, sisters, wives, and mothers—roles that call for very different strengths than the ones we tend to use as leaders.

It can be tough to get it all right in the beginning. But it's important we look to those who've come ahead of us for clues, warning signs, and red flags as well as inspiration, encouragement and hope. Use this chapter and the type most matched with you from my "What is Your Leadership Style" assessment to inspire and inform you and position yourself for success.

Personal branding takes time, effort, and energy. But investing your energy to selectively engage with specific projects, conferences, meetings, relationships, and influencers can help you build a focused reputation. If you don't, you may be leaving yourself open to being labeled in ways that don't align with the type of professional you want to be.

With all the strategies in this chapter, your brand will grow, gain respect, and stand out from the pack. Whatever your future career aspirations, your reputation will precede you, giving you the flexibility and the confidence to be the brilliant leader you are in the spaces of your choosing.

Hello, trailblazing superstar!

GLOW

"Nothing can dim the light that shines from within."

~ Maya Angelou

Chapter 9

Wear Your Power Colors:
Become Your Own Best Champion

"Don't compromise yourself. You're all you've got."

~ Janis Joplin

I N MY IMAGE CONSULTATION sessions, I loved teaching women how to determine their power colors. It was one of my favorite things: the breathtaking visual transformation when a woman wore her best colors. But more than that was seeing how her self-perception changed after she understood which colors made her pop and which flopped. The truth in the phrase "seeing is believing" rang true when a woman verified her colors in my sessions.

If I had to guess, I'd say about one of every two women I worked with had no idea which colors enhanced her appearance. One of my colleagues was a strawberry blonde woman with freckles who only wore moss green, black, and yellow because her mother had told her those were the only colors that worked for her. Holy fashion cannoli, she looked frumpy in those colors, but it took the heavens parting for her to see she could expand her color palette to include rich blues, warm greens, and red hues.

While not all image consultants had the gift of helping clients find their power colors, I had that gift in spades. With one look I could usually tell if a woman had a warm or cool color palette. Sometimes, upon meeting a client for the first time,

I could go a step further and classify her as an "autumn," "spring," "summer," or "winter," the typical seasonal classification used to categorize the color palettes.

I was enthusiastic about helping women understand their power colors because I knew if that was the only thing they changed about their image, they would experience an instant transformation. I would often say that it cost the same price to buy a dress in a flattering color versus an unflattering one to prove that shopping with a personalized color palette could change how good a woman felt and looked.

You could be wearing the most figure-flattering ensemble, but if the colors don't work for you, you won't just blend in with the crowd, you might look more unattractive for it. In short, you can't have an image makeover without changing the colors you wear.

When a woman owned her power colors and worked them for maximum impact in her wardrobe, I'd get excited. She'd start to elevate her style game with authority! A woman would go from drab to fab just by wearing her right colors.

Style magazines often touted the benefit of having an LBD (Little Black Dress) on hand for special occasions, but the truth is that not everyone looks good in black. Some women look better in brown or gray, just as some look better in gold rather than silver. The power of color has everything to do with your makeup— how your skin tone, eye color, and hair interact with the full spectrum of colors.

When a client learned her power colors, it was like she discovered a secret weapon she could wield in her image arsenal. Wearing your best hues makes your skin, eyes, and hair vibrate on a higher frequency, and you feel more attractive, confident, and secure.

For example, in business, a woman could choose to wear *her* "super-hero red" jacket to that important client meeting to have a greater chance of winning them over. Alternatively, in her personal life, she could opt for a rich magenta dress that makes her brown eyes sparkle, her chocolate skin luminous, and her black hair glisten so much that everyone is wowed by her.

Once, I attended a networking event in one of my favorite red dresses because I knew it would make me feel more confident. As I mixed and mingled with folks, I noticed how much attention I was getting. People seemed so excited to meet me, and everywhere I went, I was making solid connections. *Wow,* I thought, *I must be getting better at networking because I'm killing it at this event.*

The icing on the cake was when I turned around and a handsome gentleman looked at me and said, "I've been trying to get your attention all afternoon, but every time I tried to get close to you, someone would beat me to it. My name is Maurice. Can I just say you are really wearing that red dress?" As I blushed and introduced myself, it hit me that wearing my red dress to the event was my ace in the hole. That particular hue of red not only made me feel confident but it had the effect of a gravitational pull toward me. It made me magnetic!

Wearing your power colors, my friend, is like giving yourself the gift of advocacy. When you choose to dress in ways that flatter and enhance your visual presentation, it positively impacts how you feel about yourself and shapes how others perceive you. Choosing to wear colors that make you visible and noticed, ones that truly enhance your image, is an act of advocacy!

It's such a simple thing, right? But I've encountered so many women who choose not to advocate for themselves this way, who dress so they blend in. By making this choice, they're playing small, opting to not stand out, and minimizing their presence.

Because we women have so much to contend with just to have parity with men in the workplace, our self-advocacy is important. It matters. If we don't advocate for ourselves, why should we expect others to advocate for us? If we show up looking like we are not bringing our "A-game" in any way, then is it any wonder why some of us fail to have the impact we desire to have at work?

Just as you have the authority, capability, and agency to wear your power colors and use them to your advantage, you have that same ability to advocate for yourself in your work life. But it is a choice.

Why Advocacy Matters

When I was about ten years old, my music teacher heard that I had some vocal talent and decided that I should try out as a soloist for the biannual countrywide music festival. I don't remember how I felt before the audition in front of my whole class, but I surely remember how it felt to be on stage by myself, my music teacher in the wings and the pianist behind me. I was petrified!

As I looked out at all the expectant faces of my classmates waiting to hear me sing, I realized perhaps for the first time what it felt like to be in the spotlight. Let's just say it didn't work out too well for me. I opened my mouth and no sound came out except this squeaky voice—not the one my music teacher heard during the earlier trials. I was mortified that I failed so miserably in front of everyone. I knew I could sing, but I just couldn't get the sounds out. I was summarily dismissed as a soloist and given a spot in the choir instead where I could just blend in.

I think that experience, along with others, informed how I shied away from the spotlight for decades. For years I would not speak up in class and would do everything in my power to avoid attention. I couldn't control the fact that I was a tall woman, but I could be quiet, not share what I felt, and not speak up for myself. I tried to take up as little space as possible.

In giving away my personal power back then, I gave away my ability to stand up for myself, to self-advocate, and to make myself be seen, known, and understood.

This is why I am such a champion of self-advocacy today. For many women, the toughest voice to elevate is their own. Advocating for others is important and necessary, especially if you have the authority and influence to do so. But no one can advocate for you as much as you can for yourself.

Self-advocacy is about letting people see the full expanse of who you are and how you contribute to creating good in your sphere of influence. When you self-advocate, you're confident enough to articulate the scope of your leadership and influence. It is not arrogant, braggadocious, or prideful to let people know of your successes and wins. In fact, this is the essence of self-promotion, a habit every purpose-driven woman should be actively engaging in.

A woman who self-advocates doesn't shrink in the presence of others or devalue her worth. She doesn't edit the excellence of her accomplishments because she's worried that folks will think she's bragging. She doesn't hide how amazing she is and all the gifts, talents, and expertise she brings to the table. She plays big. She speaks her heart. She unapologetically asks for what she needs. She sets hard boundaries to respect her time, energy, and resources. She makes her presence felt, seen, and known because she knows she's worth it!

My friend's five-year-old daughter Violet is already showing signs of being a force to reckon with. Recently she showed me a picture she had just colored. Looking at me directly with a look of self-satisfaction, she announced, "Look at how good my picture is. I'm really good at coloring." "Wow, yes, that's really pretty Vi," I replied, quietly marveling at her strong self-assurance. Violet has not yet learned the cultural context of being a woman in a patriarchal society. She is comfortable in her skin and abilities. She owns and celebrates her brilliance. I pray she never loses that.

Savvy female leaders play an active role in their own advocacy because, through self-advocacy, they unveil the amazing gifts of freedom, dignity, visibility, and agency.

In my past, I have been a woman who minimized my skills, downplayed my intellect, and hid my talents so that I would not call too much attention to myself, wouldn't offend others, and wouldn't invite criticism or rejection. I know I'm not alone in that. Many of my clients tell me similar stories. For women of color, a lack of self-advocacy is almost the norm.

But here's the thing. We gotta push through the voices in our heads that keep telling us to stand back, don't speak up, don't rock the boat, and leave well enough alone. Those voices make us play small.

When we act in ways that diminish or dismiss our abilities, we can never live in our true purpose. Instead, we end up boxing ourselves into ill-fitting roles, cramping ourselves in a corner so we don't take up space, and edging ourselves out of our leadership potential.

Even worse, we are acting in ways that are misaligned with who we truly are, and that sets up forces of resistance within us. That resistance can cost us and show up as illness, burnout, depression, addictive behavior, numbing, and more.

It's not too late for us to start playing bigger and allow our full selves to be seen and experienced. Using the tools in this chapter and in this book, we can build new muscles. We can reclaim our power to speak up for ourselves and advocate for others, especially those who don't have the authority, agency, or privilege that we do.

In a recent post, therapist Brittney Cobb wrote about taking our power back this way:

We take our power back when:

- We practice accepting people for who they are (and) choose relationships that align with our values (and) needs.
- We stop attaching our self-worth to another person's choice.
- We stop asking for permission to do what contributes to our happiness.
- We learn to trust our decisions—despite who doesn't approve.
- We stop reaching for understanding (and) validation from people who refuse to give it because of their own insecurities, lack of emotional availability, (and) unresolved trauma.[1]

We have the power to choose what is right for us, the type of role that is aligned with our brilliance and gives us the most fulfillment.

Yes, it can be SO challenging to believe in yourself. But what's worse is not self-advocating and staying in roles and organizations where people don't appreciate you, celebrate you, or even acknowledge you. What's worse is never becoming who you are meant to be.

You can choose to speak up to create space, play bigger, feel seen and heard, and get your needs met. Or you can choose to stay silent and continue to be misunderstood, frustrated, and resentful.

If you're tired of feeling ill-equipped to speak up, set healthy boundaries, or stand up to those who have the power to dictate your career satisfaction, it's time to use your self-advocacy.

If you're a woman who was silenced so much early on that muting yourself became the norm, self-advocacy is crucial.

When I observe a client backing off from advocating for herself, I challenge her with a question like, "Who are you becoming if you continue to put up with disrespectful behavior?" or "What's the downside of you not sharing how you truly feel?" or "How important is it for you to retain your dignity in the face of opposition?"

Questions like these shift a woman's focus from worrying about what people may think to honoring her dignity and self-respect. It becomes clear to her at that moment how much she may have abandoned herself for the sake of pleasing or not offending another. Typically, a paradigm shift takes place that allows her to move forward strengthened and emboldened to bring her full, amazing self into her workspace.

For all the times we women have tolerated bad behavior, disrespect, and unfair treatment and regretted staying silent, use the tools here to become your own best and powerful champion.

My Career Advocacy Journey

My first serious job was with a small team of predominantly female market researchers based in New York City. I had completed my MBA and had an MPhil in Finance, so I thought I could command a decent salary. But I had no idea how negotiations worked or what to expect, so I naively said my expected salary in my interview with the group's team leader, assuming because I did so it would materialize as such. What a disappointment when I received my acceptance letter a few days later with a salary offer of a solid $10,000 below what I had asked for. I was confused and crushed. Did he misunderstand what I'd said?

As a newly divorced immigrant in the US, the first and only one in my family to have this privilege, I had no one I could turn to for advice. And because I was tired of interviewing and really needed a job, I accepted it after a feeble attempt at negotiating a sign-on bonus which ended up being a measly $1,000.

This was the start of my fifteen-year journey with this company. All the market researchers in the office were white, but I was used to being "the only" in these types of environments, so that didn't faze me. Plus, they were kind, smart, industrious women with a true desire to see me succeed.

They were still in the process of expanding the office space, so I had to work from the conference room for my first few months. That wasn't ideal, but I also didn't think much about it, especially when another woman my age was hired a month later as another project director and shared the space with me.

But things got awkward for me when the first available office cubicle space was given to her. That made no sense. She was hired at the same level a month after me. Why wasn't I given first dibs on the space? I never knew because I never asked. Again, my primary goal in that first year was to hold onto this job, micro-aggressions aside. I had learned through all my college experiences to keep my head down, my mouth quiet, and not make waves. So again, I did not advocate for myself. I didn't know how.

Later on, this woman, Nicole, and I became very close friends. I learned that in her first few months she had had issues with anger, so much so that the team leader had her take anger management classes. I had no idea this had happened. From my vantage point, she was treated like a rising star and given prime project assignments and the privilege of working directly with the team leader. He clearly was her advocate and offered her the protections, mentoring, and allyship so needed early in our careers.

As the sole Black researcher not just on the New York team but across the whole company of 200+ employees, I didn't get that privilege. The office assistant / administrative assistant to the team leader was an older Black woman and, God bless her heart, she was especially kind to me. Sometimes she would share insights with me to help me understand the office dynamics. But she had no authority and was not a researcher, so her help and advocacy could only go so far.

Nicole was eventually promoted to senior project director way before I was, anger issues in tow. I was happy for her but realized then that I'd have to start figuring out how to get my needs known and addressed. Waiting for someone to advocate for me was not going to happen without my effort.

A few years in, my confidence steadily grew as I got more comfortable with my performance. Amazingly, even though I was still dealing with the aftermath of my divorce in my personal life, I was doing well in my career and my annual reviews proved that. I started being given the responsibility of mentoring new hires.

Around the five-year mark, my boss, who had played a large role in training me, was doing my review and she asked me a pivotal question. Almost as an afterthought, she said, "Natalie, I'm not sure you're interested in this, but you know you could be a senior researcher now. You could choose the research director or research manager track."

I was stunned. All this time I hadn't given my career trajectory much thought. I was working hard, and I cared about the quality of my work, but I had been playing a short-term game the whole time. When she posed the question to me, I realized for perhaps the first time that I needed to start thinking of this as my career. *What did I want?* I wasn't even sure. My boss was a research manager, and I wasn't crazy about that role, but the research director track was less about managing people and more about getting in on more high-profile engagements. *Did I have what it took to do that?*

The imposter in me had always won out before, but this time something shifted. After a few minutes, I surprised myself by saying, "Karen, I am interested, yes. Let me think about it some more and get back to you." The look on her face told me she was as surprised by my response as I was. "Sure, think on it. I almost didn't bring it up because you seemed content where you are."

I don't fault Karen for those remarks. She was right. I hadn't let on that I was ambitious or cared about how far I got in the company. I had never shared with any of my peers what I wanted for myself. I didn't have a mentor to help me think through these types of decisions. And I hadn't yet learned how to use my voice in a corporate setting. But from that point on, I decided to be my own champion. I was good at my job. I got great reviews. My clients were loyal, kept renewing their contracts with our company, and liked working with me. This Black girl from Trinidad deserved to finally get her coins!

When we don't advocate for ourselves and find ways to speak about the value we bring to an organization, when we don't mention our career aspirations, we send an unconscious signal that we don't put much value on ourselves. By not speaking up, we unintentionally communicate that we may be ambivalent about getting ahead. This was the exact scenario I'd found myself in, but thank God Karen probed deeper so I could evaluate what I truly wanted from my career.

I became a research director, and it was a smart decision—it put me on a faster career track than the research manager role. I grew in confidence and started to feel like I belonged and deserved to get the best the company had to offer.

As the years went by, I reinvented myself many times, taking on new roles with new teams, which meant new challenges. But what I discovered about myself during this period was that I was an excellent strategic thinker. Once I started advocating for myself, I realized I was good at it! When I moved from New York to Maryland, I advocated for being the research director for a newly formed internet research team with one of my NY coworkers. She knew the caliber of my work and did not hesitate to bring me on board this virtual team, ideal for my move.

When the team disbanded a couple of years later and I was left without a team, I advocated for being the research director on the Grand Rapids team with a senior researcher, Maureen, with whom I'd only previously partnered on one project. I argued my case for adding me to her team and she took me on, which started a years-long relationship with her in different roles in the company.

A year or so later I became the group team lead for the Midwest team, a merging of the Grand Rapids, Chicago, and Cincinnati teams. Our entire company eventually merged with a much larger research company and all our teams disbanded, but I made sure I kept close to Maureen, who was partnering with my old team lead from the New York office, Bill. I knew Maureen would support me because I'd become indispensable to her.

My last shindig was as a senior research director for the financial services vertical of the company led by Maureen and Bill. After a couple of years, I got promoted to Vice President of Research for that team—a title I'd had my eye on as a goal for a few years (more on that story in the next chapter!). When I became VP, I felt I'd come full circle. I was now an expert in not only advocating for myself but others who needed my voice so they could be seen and acknowledged.

I share this part of my career history to shine light on a few pieces of self-advocacy wisdom:

1. The importance of self-advocacy in our careers cannot be overstated. It is vital if we are to be the leaders we are designed to be.
2. Having others advocate for you can make or break your career trajectory. Because I lacked mentors and sponsors—not knowing at the time that I needed them or how to get their support—my rise up the ladder was slower than it needed to be. Part of owning your brilliance and having an impact is having the support of what I call a Success Squad. We'll visit that topic in more detail in the next chapter.
3. Self-advocacy starts with believing in our worth and value and having the confidence to ask for what we know we deserve.
4. Finally, when we learn how to advocate for ourselves, only then will we be able to advocate for others and pay it forward.

Putting a Pause on People-Pleasing Behaviors

One of the signs that you may not be advocating for yourself is if you find yourself routinely engaging in people-pleasing behavior.

- Do you say yes to tasks or jobs that you know will eat up your time and bring little joy or benefit to you?
- Do you spend an inordinate amount of time in the company of people who drain you?
- Does it matter to you what others think so much that you try to win their stamp of approval by what you say and do?
- Do you have little time or energy for yourself because you're too busy taking care of the people around you at work and in your personal life?
- Do you tolerate toxic or unhealthy people and find that they tend to cling to you?
- In short, are you sacrificing your well-being in the name of serving others?

Let's slay this dragon once and for all.

People-pleasers undermine their ability to operate in their brilliance because they waste valuable energy and time trying to make everyone happy, often at the cost of their own well-being. The hard truth that people-pleasers need to understand at their core is that they do not have the power to make others happy, and it's not their responsibility to try to do so!

In their book *How Women Rise*, authors Sally Helgesen and Marshall Goldsmith describe the career-limiting impact of people-pleasing like this: "It can rob you of the capacity to act with authority, for fear of disappointing others or making them even temporarily unhappy. It can make you an unreliable advocate or ally because you are so easily swayed. It can distract you from your purpose, squander your time and talents, and contribute to your general stuckness."[2]

People-pleasing is not often talked about, but it is so pervasive among women because it stems from the gender-biased narratives we subconsciously absorb from an early age. The ones that say good girls should be seen but not heard. The ones that say if a woman asserts herself she will be negatively perceived. The ones that say we need to placate people, not advocate for ourselves. The ones that insist we modify who we are so that we conform to agreeable gender stereotypes.

In her book *The Most Powerful You*, author and executive coach Kathy Caprino writes, "In a patriarchal society like the one we live in, people are still uncomfortable and even frightened to see assertive women asking for more because they have been taught that this behavior is just not right or 'appropriate' for women."[3]

In this age of #MeToo and Time's Up, where women have been empowered to march and advocate for themselves, this type of thinking may seem outdated, but it isn't. Gender bias is real and the backlash against strong, assertive, confident women who use their voices to elevate others is fierce. This is the paradox of the double bind; when women act in ways that make us seem soft, nurturing, or likable, we get dismissed and unacknowledged because those qualities aren't seen as leadership attributes.

But when we adopt more "masculine" traits and act more assertively, when we're confident and speak our truth, then we're also dismissed—in this case dismissed as aggressive, too emotional, or too high-strung. We're damned if we do and damned if we don't—the double bind.

In a recent *Chief* article, Lindsey Galloway shared, "Women in leadership roles all too often encounter unrealistic double standards when it comes to being "too much," "too loud," or "too aggressive," even when using the same exact language or tone as a man in an equivalent position. And nonwhite women face even harsher penalties for expressing strong emotions like anger in the workplace."[4]

At the end of the day, whether we're seen as "too much" or not enough, we need to honor our values, preferences, and goals, and respond in a way that serves us. This is the heart of self-advocacy.

When women eschew the narratives that tell us to shrink because others are uncomfortable with some aspect of our presence, we can bring our full brilliance to our work arena.

But these narratives are embedded deep into the ethos of our culture. As children, many women were taught that asserting themselves by challenging their parents' rules or judgments was disrespectful and inappropriate, and they carry this baggage into adulthood in their workplaces, homes, and social circles.

How many of us have been taught to be accommodating and overly humble and to put others' needs ahead of ours in order to be accepted in society? When we internalize these mindsets, we learn to resist self-advocacy of every kind, to deny ourselves the things we deserve or have earned because we don't want to risk coming off as arrogant, assertive, aggressive, or ambitious.

In this regard, I was more fortunate than most. I spent much of my teenage years challenging my father and we argued a lot! He was extremely strict, but somehow I had the gumption as a teenager to challenge him without fear. How many times did I barrage him with questions like, "Why can't I go to X place?" or "Why are you treating me like a child?" or "What is the worst that would happen if I go out with person Z?"

I see now that my father must have respected my views because he never belittled me for standing up to him. Instead, he listened, and even though I did not win many of those battles, it never stopped me from going up against him. Through these arguments, I gained confidence in my decisions and the courage to go against authority. It grew in me a spirit to believe in my ideas, opinions, and perspectives in the face of opposition.

This is one of the things that enables me to be an advocate not just for myself but for many women today. Yes, I had my self-advocacy evolutions in my career, but I had seeds planted deep in me that I drew from when the opportunity to advocate presented itself. Because of those seeds, I could evolve into greater and greater self-advocacy.

In her book *The Gifts of Imperfection*, Brené Brown talks about the importance of showing up authentically, even in a culture that may want us to "fit in" or "people-please." She cites a quote from E. E. Cummings which highlights the challenge we face in cultivating authenticity: "To be nobody-but-yourself in a world which is doing its best night and day to make you everybody but yourself—means to fight the hardest battle which any human can fight—and never stop fighting."

Brown goes on to admit that there is a cost to authenticity, a risk in putting your true self out in the world. But she asserts, "There's even more risk in hiding yourself and your gifts from the world. Our unexpressed ideas, opinions, and contributions don't just go away. They are likely to fester and eat away at our worthiness."[5]

People-pleasing, being inauthentic, and hiding who we are to avoid feedback, criticism, or rejection is not worth it, and it ultimately hurts us because we'll never get what we truly want. And this is particularly damaging in our careers.

A January 2022 episode of the McKinsey Global Institute's Forward Thinking podcast featured Dr. Hayaatun Sillem, the CEO of the UK's Royal Academy of Engineering—the first woman and the first person of color to serve in that role. She shared how, as a woman of color in a male-dominated sector, she struggled to fit in. For years, she engaged in people-pleasing behavior by minimizing aspects of her identity and behaving in ways she thought would make other people feel comfortable. But later she came to see that she had been "knocking the corners off" herself.[6]

I resonate with that phrasing "knocking the corners off." It reminds me of the saying, "Trying to fit a square peg into a round hole," which speaks to how we sometimes try to make ourselves "round" by chopping off our "corners," our edges, the things that make us distinct, different, differentiated, or even disruptive!

People-pleasing behaviors can be challenging to address because they can serve us at the beginning of our career. That early reward from people-pleasing makes it hard to let go of. We think it's how things should flow. But when we step into the higher echelons of leadership, when we are directors and executives, our people-pleasing skills hurt us and those we lead.

One of the most obvious signs of this is difficulty delegating. People-pleasers can be afraid to trust their teams to do as good a job as they can. Because they hate the notion of letting others down, they tend to take on all the responsibilities in their role by piling more work onto their plate. The unfortunate consequence is that they groom people with no authority or initiative because they're always coming to their rescue.

As a people-pleasing leader, what you're essentially doing is training your team to rely on you for everything. At some point, this structure falls apart, leaving you wondering what went wrong.

People-pleasing will limit your impact, satisfaction, and success in your arena, so finding healthier ways to function is crucial. Here are three ways you can start to nip these tendencies in the bud.

1. Establish Clear, Healthy Boundaries

Women are natural nurturers and givers—it's in our DNA. This gives us a greater capacity for being more helpful, service-oriented, and empathic than our male counterparts. These attributes are strengths until our need for being liked and useful supersede other considerations and make us doormats, constantly ridden with guilt if we dare say no to anyone or anything.

People-pleaser, meet Boundaries. I've already tackled this subject in earlier chapters, so I won't repeat it except to emphasize this: The biggest truth about boundaries is that you cannot force someone else to establish them. You can only establish boundaries for yourself. Learning to set boundaries is one of the first steps in self-care and advocacy.

This can feel difficult at first because it requires you to change behaviors that have been hardwired into your neural pathways. You will need to rumble with discomfort for a while as you learn to say no and choose yourself first before others. It will also take some time for the people who are used to you saying yes to everything to respect and honor your boundaries.

Leaders need to have clear boundaries and manage their teams by setting expectations for what's required. Start getting clear about what is yours to own at work and what's not. What aspects of your role actually need to be completed by you? What can you realistically delegate? What behaviors will you refuse to tolerate? Reflect on these questions as you start establishing clear boundaries.

2. Nourish to Flourish

Your self-care should be your top priority. If you cannot be there for yourself, then how can you be there for your family, work, business, or friends?

Time for yourself needs to be as nonnegotiable as the other important priorities in your life. Put your self-care or me-time on your calendar just like you would put down a meeting with your boss or colleague. Except it's a meeting with yourself.

For one of my clients, this was the only way she could start prioritizing time for herself to decompress during the day, process things, ideate, and just have the space to strategize rather than jumping from meeting to meeting or task to task. At first, she inserted time for herself in two, thirty-minute increments throughout her workday, but what invariably happened was that she would bump it off and put another meeting in the slot.

We talked about ways she could give her me-time in the day more priority. Her highest priority items were color-coded, but her appointments with herself were not. Only when she elevated her time so that there was a clear boundary to honor this time for herself and those she shared her calendar with did this calendar method start to work. But it was a process for her, because she would so easily default to putting meetings with others over her time for herself, even with the color-coded system in place.

To put a stop to people-pleasing and focus instead on giving back to themselves is one of the hardest hurdles for women to overcome. But only when you put yourself first are you then able to give to others unconditionally and feel fulfilled, not depleted.

It's time women stop seeing self-care as selfish. It's a beautiful act of kindness, grace, and compassion to give to others, but only from a place of overflow, not self-sacrifice. Your time spent in self-caring activities is not just good for you—it's good for all the people you're meant to serve (more on this later!).

3. Remove Toxicity from Your Life

Once it's clear to you what is your responsibility and what is not, you are free to start letting go of the people, situations, environments, relationships, and even jobs that do not serve you and seek out the ones that do.

Permit yourself to let go of any responsibilities that do not belong to you. It's not your baggage. You can only be responsible for your stuff.

Just as we must put on our oxygen mask first before putting it on our child in an airplane, we have to pour into ourselves first before we can pour into others. Putting yourself first allows you to have the margin and bandwidth to do good, be of service from a healthy place, and impact the people you're meant to from a full well.

Toxic people will push back when you stop allowing them to control your life and choices. But remember that it's not your job to enable unhealthy people and take care of their messes. Instead, focus on all the positive allies, colleagues, and peers that are truly there for you. In shifting your focus, you'll experience a whole new type of freedom. And you'll discover you can move forward and upward faster without everyone else's baggage weighing you down.

Women of Color and Self-Advocacy

Self-advocacy is especially important for Black women and women of color (WOC). Many of us share similar experiences like mine, where there are no mentors or sponsors to advocate for us and where microaggressions at work because of our ethnicity and cultural differences make work harder than it has to be.

An article by *Harvard Business Review* in early 2022 addressed the issue of women of color and negotiation. The article talks about how WOC are especially discouraged from advocating for themselves in a work context, often going along to get along "particularly when it comes to grasping greater power and resources or saying no to undervalued work."

According to the article, WOC tend to be overly humble and grateful for what they do have so they stay silent to avoid any backlash. But with this thinking, they don't leverage the power they hold in their hands.

To make matters worse, many women think negotiation is about hardball manipulation tactics to get what one wants, which is why they may resist the idea of self-advocacy. The article provides many useful examples of how it's helpful to look at effective negotiation as a means of "asking for what you want and deserve, bending norms to break open new paths, and shaping new ways of working," which is a win-win proposition for both parties.[7]

But part of the challenge for WOC is that when we advance through corporate ranks, we don't have models and examples "tailored toward the unique spaces (we) occupy." Plus, WOC must always wrestle with "standing out while also being marginalized," so it's difficult for us to take action that may draw unwanted attention to ourselves.

Not to mention that we often bear the brunt of the "invisible work," like the DEI initiatives that companies say they value but do not acknowledge or consider leadership responsibilities.

When advocacy is viewed from the lens of reimagining asks as opportunities and a way to get creative with available options, it won't seem as intimidating. So in the case of a company wanting a WOC to take on extra work supporting its DEI initiatives, before saying yes, the WOC can ask a question like, "If I lead this initiative, how will it be measured for my annual review?" or, "Help me understand how this would make sense for me to take on now, given my other priorities?"

Questions like these open the dialogue and put the woman who is negotiating in a place of power and agency to turn the request down or get added compensation for the extra work.

But often we can't figure this out on our own—which is why the support of a mentor, sponsor, or coach becomes invaluable in helping us reframe our perspectives around self-advocacy.

An article in *Fortune* magazine on Judge Ketanji Brown Jackson's confirmation hearings clearly articulated why these realities are forcing more women of color in senior executive positions to jump ship and leap into entrepreneurship where they get to call their own shots and create cultures where women like them are supported.[8]

A 2021 *Forbes* piece shared research data showing that one in three women of color was considering leaving her job—an alarming statistic.[9]

The *Fortune* piece mentioned that WOC face a challenge known as "inclusion delusion," which they explain as the "conundrum of being highly visible as the first or only woman of color at their organization and at the same time never feeling like they belong, are respected, or have power."

Moreover, "inclusion delusion" gives WOC the illusion when they are first hired into their positions that they are accepted and embraced and have the authority to create real organizational change. But the reality they soon experience is that they're merely being asked to fit into the existing corporate structure and leave it as is.

These hires placate the people in power (predominantly white men) to believe they are advancing diversity, equity, and inclusion, but in truth, it's more about the optics of adding women of color to a few visible roles that sound lofty on paper than it is about cultural transformation.

Today, where diverse cultures are the norm and not the exception, companies need leaders who have the lived experiences to understand and bridge the current gaps—and women of color have the capacity and cultural competency to fill these gaps. Companies need us. And it's up to us to band together, voice our truth, and advocate for what is fair and just in these work environments.

It starts with us valuing our worth enough to demand equitable compensation and benefits. Many of my clients who are women of color in senior roles are evaluating whether all the stress, undervaluation, and inequitable treatment are worth fighting against or whether they are better off just charting a new course for themselves.

As their coach, champion, and fellow WOC, I consider it part of my role, if not my charge, to help them advocate for the best scenario for their skills, expertise, and quality of life. If that means leaving their roles, it's the company's loss, not theirs.

Celebrating Your Wins and Advocacy Go Hand in Hand

As a high-achieving, purpose-driven woman, one with a vision to positively impact the lives of others in my work, I, like many of you, suck at celebrating my successes. Let's face it, many of us have no modeling or training on how to do this, so the notion of celebrating our success can feel self-absorbed, silly, or worse, braggadocious.

But celebrating your successes is part of self-advocacy. It's an important aspect of how you become your own best champion. You must be as excited and pumped up by your wins as anyone else, if not more so. You alone truly know the challenges, setbacks, or obstacles that were in the path of your win, so you are the one who can celebrate it fully.

Imagine you are driving to a desired destination along a gorgeous, scenic route. Instead of taking in the scenery, you are preoccupied with what you'll do when you get there. Three hours later you arrive having missed the opportunity to revel in the beauty along the way. You not only missed the view, you also missed the chance to boost your mood while driving. Instead of mindfully leaning into the moment, your scattered thoughts likely left you more impatient and discontent upon your arrival. You've also possibly lost out on the opportunity to be inspired by what you would have observed had you taken the time to be present.

This is not unlike what happens when you go from goal to goal, project to project, without taking the time to stop and cheer yourself on. You lose out on giving yourself a boost in serotonin and dopamine (the "happy hormones"). If you miss the many moments of your wins, then when trials come, as they surely will, you have no margin to draw from within you because you have not allowed yourself to be your own best champion. Not celebrating your successes hurts you, so finding ways to do so makes sense to foster greater success and is the self-caring, loving way to honor your achievements as well.

When I coach women who are looking to elevate their career profile or personal brand around celebrating their wins, they admittedly struggle at first. It can be hard to acknowledge the importance of this seemingly insignificant practice.

Below are ten truths I've uncovered from my own experience and in my work with ambitious women who desire to make a greater impact in their career or business endeavor. When you start to make these truths a part of your practice, you'll begin reaping the power of celebration and be spurred on to even greater heights.

1. **Find a way to celebrate that excites you so much it motivates you to achieve your goal.** For me, treating myself to a gift I've wanted but felt too guilty to indulge is so motivating that it assuages any guilt I feel because now I have a perfect reason to indulge. My latest thrill is buying pieces of art to mark new achievements. I love art but never really invested in it. Now I have an "excuse" to do so, and I'm loving it.

2. **Celebrate the small wins along the way too.** Very often the big wins are only accomplished through small achievements, so it is important to honor those too. If you land a huge new client, that's cause for a big celebration, like treating yourself and your loved one to an upscale dinner or planning a mini-vacay somewhere awesome. In celebrating achieving all your "to-dos" in a given week, the scale of that celebration can be much smaller. Your acknowledgment doesn't have to be on a grand scale. Sometimes doing a private victory dance is enough for your brain to get the message. Other small gestures are sending yourself a congratulatory card, treating yourself to a new pair of shoes (or whatever your guilty pleasure is), or permitting yourself to a midweek binge of your favorite TV series while kicking your feet up on your couch. The treat does not matter to anyone else but you. So do you, friend.

3. **Mark your progress toward your goal with a reward.** Your goal achievement carries with it all the hard work, commitment, and dedication you put into it and these steps deserve to be recognized too. Celebrate the fact that you are getting closer to your end goal and on track to achieve it. For example, if you're looking for a promotion and you've just completed

a big project that brings you new visibility, celebrate that win because it gets you that much closer to your promotion and keeps your momentum going strong.

4. **Be strategic in planning the celebration of your wins.** When you have a major project or task to complete, brainstorm the type of incentive that would help you more easily accomplish the goal. This increases the likelihood that you'll achieve the success you want.

5. Visualize **yourself achieving your goal, reaching that milestone, or performing that special task with excellence.** As part of envisioning, imagine how you'd like to celebrate when you are successful—who are you celebrating with, what are you doing, how are you feeling, where are you celebrating? With the vision clear, you can then plan your celebration before you even begin the task, as a motivation.

6. **Try to pair your celebration with self-caring activities.** Spa packages including massages, facials, or bodywork are all amazing ways to treat yourself with compassion. So is taking a day off to just exhale or partake in that hobby you never make time for anymore. One of my coaching clients is a crafter and her soul was crying out to her (through aches and pains) because she hadn't made time for this nurturing activity in months. Just talking about the joy she feels when crafting brought her nearly to tears because she realized she'd been denying herself this outlet. Use your wins to connect to the deepest part of your being.

7. **Celebrating forces you to concentrate on the positive rather than the negative.** Running your business or rising through the ranks in your career can be stressful. It's easy to get put off by the many things that don't go your way. But when you acknowledge the things you are doing well, and take a moment to experience gratitude, you start to focus more on what's working. Before long, this attitude of gratitude pays off big time. Your thoughts, mindset, and perspectives shift positively and give you more margin to attract even more positivity into your life, which is a prime ground for even more successes to bear fruit.

8. **Savor it.** Taking the time to soak up your accomplishments, cheer yourself on, and pat yourself on the back helps you to savor the moment. This

time also helps you reflect on what went well or what you would do differently so you can be in a state of continuous improvement as you strive toward the completion of your greatest career goal.

9. **When you give yourself credit for your accomplishments, you're also boosting your confidence in your ability to realize your vision.** By celebrating, you are validating yourself, your unique strengths, your growing expertise, and your core competencies. As a woman serious about making an impact, you'll want to do this routinely so you continually fortify your confidence in your work or business. The strengthened sense of self you attain will attract even more opportunities for you to achieve even loftier goals in the future.

10. **Taking time to acknowledge your wins allows you to dream even bigger.** Every major win opens the door to pondering what you can do next to achieve your ultimate goal. Perhaps you've finally published that book. After you have celebrated that major milestone, you can start envisioning speaking at events to promote your book and perhaps zero in on one venue that will amplify your accomplishments even more. After all, once you know what you're capable of, don't just camp out there. Stretch yourself and aim for even greater heights because, my friend, you've got what it takes!

Advocacy = Asking

Asking for what you want involves strengthening a muscle you may not realize you have, so it takes time to get proficient in self-advocacy. You may not know how to ask for what you want, or you may be afraid of rejection. Regardless, as a woman with the power and agency to speak her truth (yes, Ma'am!) it is up to you to clearly and confidently communicate your needs and truths.

The first step to self-advocacy is becoming aware of your own limitations and preferences, and the things that help you to thrive. This takes introspection and reflection. I highly recommend journaling around a few basic questions, to get the clarity you need to begin self-advocating, including:

- What do I need to adjust in my work environment, so it works best for me?
- What support do I need to succeed in my role?
- What learning opportunities would help me in my career trajectory?

As you start to speak up for yourself, be realistic. Just because you ask for it doesn't mean you'll get it. You will be disappointed and let down some of the time. But in the ask itself you gain, even if you don't get what you want.

First, your confidence grows because, by exercising the muscle of asking, you'll get better at it. Second, by articulating what you need or what is true for you, you will build more authentic connections with others because they'll know how you feel and what you need, whether they oblige you or not. This has the ripple-effect of making you feel more seen, heard, and understood—this, in turn, will bring a huge boost to your self-esteem. Third, by asking you may actually get the thing you want, or something close to it. Asking allows you to meet your needs, negotiate, compromise, or decide to walk away. Finally, when you communicate your desires, it allows you to get out of your head—no more assuming, second-guessing, or judging. You've made it clear what you need and want, and even if you don't get the result you want, others will respect you and take you more seriously for it.

Use your voice. Your self-advocacy matters. And the more we as women self-advocate, the more we ALL benefit.

Chapter 10

Love the Skin You're In:
Give Yourself the Gift of Self-Care

"The Hummingbird always moves most fast when standing most still."

~ Beryl MacBurnie

AS AN IMAGE CONSULTANT, I used to give workshops to teens on image and self-esteem. I called the workshops "Dare to be Brilliant," and I gave these young ladies a space to embrace healthier self-esteem. For one of the exercises I facilitated, I had each of them name five aspects of themselves that they *absolutely* loved. It could be anything—their fingernails, voice, hair, or smile. The point was to make the girls aware of the positive attributes they could embrace.

The exercise started with the girl saying her name and then listing the things she loved about herself. As in, "My name is Mina. And I love my bustline, my eyelashes, my belly button, my eyebrows, and my upper lip." Then the whole group would clap and affirm Mina, with lots of "yeses" and "You go, girl!" and "You're gorgeous" from around the room.

What was so heartwarming to observe was how instantaneously comfortable and affirmed this exercise made them feel. As each girl stood up to claim her positive attributes, sometimes she started shy and uncertain, but by the end she would be smiling and looking that much more confident. Something substantial shifted in her. Her self-esteem soared and solidified more deeply within her. The gift in the exercise was daring to name it and claim it!

I share this experience to underscore the importance of healthy self-esteem and the power we each hold to bring it forth. Self-esteem describes a person's overall sense of self-worth or personal value. It plays a role in every thought we think about ourselves, our sense of identity, the yardstick against which we measure ourselves and determine how we let others treat us. Self-esteem dictates our level of success in life.

In *Frumpy to Fabulous, Flaunting It*, I devoted a chapter to "Beauty From The Inside Out" because I understood that no matter how a woman packaged herself on the outside, what truly mattered was her inner mental game. I wrote, "We radiate outwards what we believe about ourselves deep inside. No amount of window dressing can create true transformation if you don't like the person you see reflected at you. The externals, as important as they are, merely enhance and refine what's going on inside. Beauty truly comes from the inside, out."[1]

As much as the book was about "Flaunting It," I wanted readers to understand that they couldn't flaunt what they didn't feel or believe to be true about themselves.

This chapter's title, "Love the Skin You're in," is from the well-known Oil of Olay slogan. The skincare brand produced that tagline over twenty years ago because their advertising research showed that women needed to be engaged at a deeper, more emotional level. The new ad campaign they launched in 2001 communicates that women don't need to look like models to love themselves or their skin. They understood that women had to embrace self-love and self-love started with loving our bodies, not some idealized version of what we sometimes dream of looking like.

Similarly, Dove's groundbreaking campaign, "The Real Truth About Beauty," delved into young women's self-esteem, body image, and body confidence issues and uncovered the difficulty women and girls have in recognizing their real beauty. A startling statistic from the campaign found that six in ten girls will stop doing something they love because they feel bad about the way they look. If that's the case of low self-esteem in girlhood, consider the implications of poor self-esteem on women's career choices, educational achievement, relationships, and lifestyle.

As our culture becomes more technologically sophisticated, the rate at which we are bombarded by images that erode and negatively impact our self-esteem increases. How do we move the needle in the other direction? How do we stop ourselves from increasingly striving toward unrealistic perfection? How do we reverse a visually hungry, socially competitive generation who can never attain the impossibly lofty standards we set for ourselves?

We get back to basics. We relearn ways to honor and uphold the absolute best of ourselves as the unique individuals we are. We feed and encourage healthy self-image habits in ourselves and those we parent or mentor.

More than ever in today's culture, ideas of beauty, success, achievement, and creativity are converging around a "one size fits all" paradigm that snuffs the very life out of our brilliance. Every human being has a fundamental need to belong. To foster inclusiveness, without sacrificing uniqueness, we need a great measure of patience, humility, and tolerance.

What does that mean for you reading this? It means being true to yourself in a more embracive way than you may have allowed yourself to be in the past. It means being bold and unapologetically expressive. It means being fearless in sharing your perspective of a given situation. It means being graciously honest with your feedback. It means lovingly encouraging those under your charge.

Nurture your passions. Hone your skills. Be insatiably curious. Discover your purpose and challenge your beliefs. Trust in your innate excellence. Love from the inside out. Love your God. Love yourself. Love your brothers and sisters. Isn't this our ultimate call?

We've only just begun to tap into the incredible abundance available to us. Our love is a resource we need to be using all the time. It is free, unlimited, and cumulative, and it starts with our love for ourselves and our esteem for ourselves.

Self-Care Isn't Selfish

Loving the skin you're in has a lot to do with self-care. We often think that self-care is about taking a spa day, but it's so much more than that. Our self-care includes the physical, emotional, mental, and spiritual practices we use to care for our FULL self. You can't truly show up for others unless you show up for yourself first. Others treat us how we show them to.

The heart of healthy self-care centers on establishing boundaries (yes, boundaries again!). Boundaries in this case mean saying no to something or someone in order to say yes to yourself and your well-being. Our boundaries help us maintain healthy and safe connections with others and ourselves.

What does it mean to REALLY show up for yourself? It could look like making commitments to yourself, such as:

- Only saying "yes" to projects, tasks, and work aligned with your purpose, values, and passions
- Not taking on any more tasks when you know you need a break
- Deciding to return calls and texts when you have the margin and time to do so
- Not making yourself vulnerable to someone who has shown themselves to be untrustworthy or unsafe

There is no more important relationship you have in your life than the one you have with yourself. Loving yourself well isn't selfish; it's a form of self-care!

Loving yourself could look like:

- Setting a recurring time on your calendar for the things that nourish you and bring you joy
- Saying no to something you don't want to do
- Picking up an old hobby you've long set aside, or finding a new one
- Acknowledging the unique life, gifts, talents, and strengths you bring to the table
- Investing in your emotional and mental wellness in new ways
- Celebrating the small and big wins you achieve every single day

When you show up for yourself, you can also fully show up for others. As a high-achieving woman, this self-focus may be difficult for you at first because you're so used to putting others' needs above your own.

If you're feeling drained, exhausted, or downright unhappy, those feelings are cues for you to start changing the ways you show up for YOU.

Maya Angelou said, "My mission in life is not merely to survive, but to thrive; and to do so with some passion, some compassion, some humor, and some style." Take a page out of Maya's playbook and start taking the actions to thrive. But know that thriving starts with honoring your needs, setting boundaries, and learning how to love yourself.

Take The Time to Savor Your Successes

If you haven't figured it out yet, this chapter is all about focusing on your *being* so you're set up to make your impact. Hang in there with me in this section because you'll soon start tracking with the truths I share and discover new ways to show up that will help you to thrive.

Most of you reading this book can probably relate to being a high achiever. High-achieving women are hyper-focused on accomplishing, achieving, and attaining. They're all about what I call the Do. They are naturally hardwired to work hard.

High achievers want stuff to fall into place NOW so they can get to the steps they need to get busy with their Do.

They willingly devote hours and energy to their role and take satisfaction in being productive. Just the act of completing tasks fulfills them. Their inner drive to achieve propels them forward and gives them momentum to keep going when others would stop or give up.

Yet they often move from project to project, achievement to achievement, without taking the time to appreciate and own what they've done. These are hard-working, high-performing, goal-oriented women who often struggle with some level of perfectionism. They are all about the Do. But even when they achieve a goal, they move on to the next milestone without giving a second thought to what they've attained.

As a coach working with high-achieving women and leaders, I have learned that as much as they Do, these leaders are woefully inadequate in acknowledging it.

Let me explain. Theresa is a multi-talented seasoned leader who has been managing her own company for over a decade after leaving a successful corporate career in Tech. She has written books, launched new initiatives, developed programs, and is currently helping a leading online platform level up so they can more effectively service the millions of subscribers in their network. She is killing it!

Yet when asked about the things she's accomplished, she just shrugs her shoulders nonchalantly and says, "It's no big deal. I'm just doing my work." Yes, that is true, but the magnitude of her many accomplishments escapes her. When I pressed her on this, she acknowledged that she has a hard time taking in her successes. She loves a challenge, but with every challenge she conquers, she moves right on to the next one, not taking time to savor her success.

When I encounter women like Theresa, I suggest we spend time focusing on her brilliance, because I know the truth of the matter is that she has no clue how exceptional she is. I know it because I was like this too. When I look back on the past twenty years of my professional life, I can't believe all I've accomplished. I impress myself! But as I was in the midst of my many successes, I had no idea how valuable, exceptional, and distinctive my gifts and talents were. I would have shrugged my shoulders too, just like Theresa, thinking, *doesn't everyone have these abilities?* No, they don't.

I learned a long time ago that it's vital for me to remember to put people over priorities. It's a mantra I still must repeat to remind me that my life is not about moving from milestone to milestone. As driven as I can be, what truly matters to me is how I show up for the important people in my life. But left to my own devices, I could just keep going, forgetting, and sometimes missing the moments, memories, and meaningful interactions that feed my soul.

Truth be told, so many of us high achievers look like we're doing "fine" on the outside, but inside we have fears, limiting beliefs, and insecurities that block us from making needed changes. These fears keep us playing smaller than we're meant to.

Additionally, our identity and sense of worth cannot be attached to our work. If it is, we must work on our Who to get to our true identity.

Learning how to press pause is a habit every high-achieving woman needs to include in her life in order to savor her successes, reflect on her journey, and manage her self-care. In the last chapter, I shared many strategies for celebrating our wins. Part of making this a habit is that it forces you to take a moment to take it all in. To PAUSE.

As a high-achiever, I continue to learn new ways of internalizing my successes, because my default is still to over-deliver, over-work, and add value, which means it's not yet normalized for me to take a beat, to internally check in, or to savor the good moments.

I had a huge AHA just recently which I feel compelled to share so this point really lands for you, dear reader. I had taken part in a two-day intensive training experience called "Sacred Rhythms" that is taught by the phenomenal leader and trainer Joanna Lindenbaum, grounded in understanding the natural cycles of life and how we can best honor and lean into the different phases of our lives.

I was lit! Going deeper in learning anything I'm passionate about is my love language. But what was even more amazing were the takeaways for me.

One of the biggest ones was how I never celebrated and embraced all I accomplished when I built my image consulting company Elan Image Management.

Let me explain. The seasonal cycles of life mirror the seasons in nature, and in fall, the harvest season, we are to reap the harvest of all we sowed in the spring, and what grew in summer.

With Elan Image Management I had built a successful business and brand from scratch. I had no road map, model, or mentors, yet I accomplished in a few years what should have taken many more.

I *should* have been celebrating the gains as I went along. I should have been awed and humbled at the doors God opened for me and the impact I had upon hundreds and hundreds of women from my transformative work with them.

I *should* have been thrilled about the many things I achieved outside my comfort zone—being featured as an image expert on TV multiple times; creating seminars and workshops that I delivered singlehandedly for universities, associations, and corporations; being asked to write articles for high-profile magazines; participating in fashion events in my region, and so much more.

Yet upon reflection during the training, it hit me like a ton of bricks that I never truly harvested what I'd sown. I did like many high-achievers are prone to do—I went from task to task, initiative after initiative, created, built, wrote, innovated, and so on, without taking time to savor what was happening in the present moment.

With every achievement, milestone, and win, I'm sure I did a mental "Yes!" but then I would have moved on to the next thing in front of me without really *savoring* the win.

The harvest periods in our lives are about celebrating what we've done, taking pleasure in what we've accomplished, reflecting on our growth and expansion, pausing to take it all in, and being grateful for the fruits of our labor.

I realized that with Elan Image Management, what I'd done was create, build, grow, and let go, over and over, but I never *harvested*.

This mattered because when the business came to its unfortunate end, because I hadn't properly harvested the fruits of my labor, I told myself I had failed. Failed!!

All those years of building, creating, and transforming lives one wardrobe at a time never registered in my mind when it was time to end. All I felt and understood was a failure. I had not savored my many wins. I had not internalized how much I had done in a short period of time. I was just going, going, going trying to hit the next milestone in front of me.

This had disastrous consequences when I had to let the business go. Because that message of failure that rang loudly in my heart, mind, and spirit led to a depressive episode.

All those years of creating a business, having a following, and truly impacting the lives of so many women, never registered in a deep way in my mind/body/spirit. What remained at the end was just the grief from my business ending and that sense of failure that I carried with me for YEARS!

I know this may sound crazy, but it's all true. Even though I'm the coach now who champions and roots for her clients and reminds them to celebrate their many wins (and celebrate with them!) and I have learned to prioritize my own self-care WAY better than I used to, I realized I still had not fully processed my last business experience until the Sacred Rhythms training!

This is the unfortunate consequence of not honoring the seasons and cycles in our lives. There are four phases in any cycle, just like the seasons, and these four phases can be applied to so many aspects of life, like our relationships, careers, projects, and businesses. All these things have a Spring, a beginning/initiation a time of excitement and energy; a Summer, a time for growing/nurturing where we patiently let the seeds we have sown grow; an Autumn, a time to harvest/celebrate/acknowledge where we savor and take pleasure in the fruits of our labor; and a Winter, a time of letting go/shedding/regenerating where we quiet and prepare for the next cycle.

Because of our cultural norms and conditioning, most of us are taught to conform to patriarchal structures and narratives. We're not taught to value and honor these natural cycles and rhythms of life. As Joanna taught, our society and culture have placed so much emphasis on creating and producing that we have lost the art of receiving and harvesting. This was my reality.

But the good news is that I learned that it's never too late to harvest. And recently, even before the training, life was giving me experiences that made me harvest that period of my life in many ways.

Like writing this book, which has woven in so many aspects of my past career and experiences. Writing this book has given me a deeper gratification and appreciation for all that I learned, built, and accomplished as an image consultant. For me personally, writing this book has invited me to savor so much of the fruits of my labor from the past.

I have been harvesting as I write and reflect and share with you, dear reader, and it's been a gift.

The part of the training that strongly resonated with me is the archetype of the autumn season—the Sovereign or Queen. Picture a visual of a queen (you!) sitting on her throne, resting on her laurels, taking in the view of how she's transformed lives and made an impact. Imagine breathing in the gratification and pleasure of knowing you did good, really good, with all your hard work.

To be able to channel that energy, you would have to *own* your brilliance, right? You'd have to be aware of your achievements and influence, you'd have to have processed and savored all the work that got you to this point—seeing the fruits of your labor.

One of the homework assignments Joanna gave me after I shared my huge takeaway was to sit and write out all the things I accomplished as the founder of Elan Image Management and take the time to celebrate them. When I did the exercise, I wrote three pages of bullets—all wins/achievements/successes/accomplishments. My jaw dropped as I stopped to take in what I'd written—it was a lot!

My invitation to you is to do similar homework with yourself. To take a moment to internalize and integrate ALL that you've gotten done and how you've grown to get you to the present moment. This reflection and integration is an act of self-care, of nourishing your soul.

As you introspect and reflect, channel YOUR inner Sovereign. Imagine yourself sitting on a throne especially designed for you. What are you wearing? What do you see? How do you feel? Now ask yourself some key questions:

- How can I celebrate?
- What have I learned?
- How have I grown?
- Have I truly harvested all the good that has been the fruit of my labor?
- What do I still need to harvest?
- What am I now ready to fully own?

When I did this visualization in the training with my partner Staci, it was powerful. As Staci guided me through embodying my Queen/Sovereign, I envisioned myself sitting on a beautiful throne-like wicker chair that my parents purchased for me when I was about sixteen years old. I used to sit in that chair in my purple-accented bedroom and look out my window which faced mountains, dreaming of who I'd become someday.

In the visualization, I was sitting in my wicker chair ON a mountain, taking in the view down below. I FELT that Queen energy rising in me. I was wearing an off-the-shoulder, vibrant red gown, my hair full and long and my seated posture fully Sovereign-like. When Staci asked me what my Sovereign wanted me to know, the words that came out my mouth were, "My impact will be known and felt."

Like I said, the experience was powerful for both of us. Just spending a few minutes in that energy reminded me of how I felt when I was strutting on that Barbadian beach years ago practicing Mountain Pose.

For many of us, that Queen is in hiding, invisible, unknown, and underutilized. But if only we *DARED* embrace her truth and power, we would be truly unstoppable.

Our inner Queen is rich with wisdom, presence, capacity, and benevolence. She stands solidly in the truth of all the fruit of her labor, and she is gratified by her impact in her sphere.

She exudes light and love.

She is confident without being arrogant, empowered without wanting to be in control, steadfast, principled, content, and free.

She knows she's phenomenal, but she does not need our awe or attention. She marches to the beat of her drum with purposeful intention, committed to leaving the world a better place through her labors.

She is not distracted by what her peers are doing or have done. Her gratification resides in her care and compassion for those she serves.

Her beauty shines from the inside out, and she embodies the fullness of her magnificence with ease and humility.

She reigns Supreme. And this is not from her but *through* her. Because she knows she is the vessel for the One who created her for His purposes. And she delights in seeing the manifestation of it by her faithful obedience to her call.

Sitting gracefully on her throne resting on her laurels brings her peace because she knows she has finished well.

When her time reaches its fulfillment, she'll be ready to move on, passing the baton to those ready and waiting in the wings to bring their brilliance to bear to bless others.

This is powerful stuff, ladies! It is time for ALL of us to reclaim that Queen power and energy that lies within us.

Harvesting or celebrating is important because when we do it, we create space, expansiveness, and joy inside ourselves. When we are filled with the joy, gratification, and fulfillment from our accomplishments and achievements, we internally light up. This light that shines inside us emanates outwardly too and can be an inspiration, beacon, and draw for others.

When we truly harvest, we're giving ourselves the fuel we need to keep going—to keep achieving, accomplishing, and attaining what's there FOR us.

Outcomes Trump Outputs

No one is wired to go, go, go. We all need to replenish our inner resources in ways that have nothing to do with efforting and accomplishing. The downside of continual high achievement is burnout. This is a huge cost to pay, and it is more prevalent now than ever. We have to stop being all about the Do. After all, we are human (BE)ings, not human (DO)ings.

Many brilliant professional women bog themselves down with completing never-ending to-do lists, losing sight of the big picture impact that is at the heart of their Why. They become so busy doing mind-numbing busy work that they never get their leadership influence off its training wheels. They essentially hijack their leadership development because they become known for this busy work and not their high-level, more strategic, outcomes-focused vision.

These women may be driven by the stress and sense of accomplishment from meeting goals while missing the point of why they are working in the first place. And often all this hard work leads them nowhere—just doing more hard work.

You must take a step back and evaluate what's your why, your purpose, your calling. If the hard work you are doing does not align with your calling, it's time to move on! Here's the thing: on its own, work does not have value. This goes back to the point I made in chapter five, "Flaunt It," about engaging in non-promotable work, which does nothing to advance your career.

All the demanding work you're engaging in that's exhausting you may not be worth it if you mistakenly believe that visionless hustling and grinding is valuable. It is not. The work you do is only valuable if it lines up with your calling and the priorities and initiatives that help you make your impact. Otherwise, you're just laboring to make a buck. I know that's not what you want.

Your completed tasks are not the measure of your effectiveness. The truth is you won't get to the next notch up the career ladder without making a significant mindset shift from "doing" to "leading."

The tasks you complete, your outputs, do not highlight the value or impact of your services to your organization. Neither are they the work that will get you recognized as a leader. It's the outcomes that matter at the end of the day. It's the Why not the What or even the How, and certainly not just the Do.

The key to getting your leadership mojo on track is shifting from tactician to strategist, from tasks to goals, from outputs to outcomes, from doer to leader. And this transition from doer to leader happens mostly in your mind.

One of my clients struggled with this a lot, so one of the things we worked on was having her redefine what "productive" looked like. "Productive" to her was checking off the items on her to-do list. In reality, her new leadership role required her to cast and deliver a vision to her teams, lean on her strategic strengths, and cultivate trusted relationships with key stakeholders. All her "doing" wasn't getting her far in achieving these new goals. She had to shift her focus to the bigger vision of her role and map out a game plan for success.

Here is a breakdown of the difference between outputs and outcomes:

Outputs	Outcomes
Project/task-focused	Purpose-focused
Checking off to-do lists	Planning and goal setting
Transactional	Relational
Short-term horizon	Long-term horizon
Low-impact results	High-impact results
About What/How	About the Why

You likely climbed the rungs of the corporate ladder because of your particular expertise—for your outputs. So you assume that to keep moving up requires you to keep doing, producing, and outputting. But that's not true.

A shift needs to happen the higher up you get because the skills you need to keep moving up change from project completion to project vision. It's not so much about what you can do at the higher rungs but about who you can be.

In my "Unveil Your Brilliance" work, I've found that hyper-focusing on the Do won't help my clients achieve their goals unless they do the deeper work needed to shift their mindset—things like opening their thinking to new possibilities, reframing the way they see their reality, addressing their limiting beliefs, and embodying the posture and heart of Who they are becoming.

The truth is that most change is an inner game—it's the work on the Who. Most of us must work on the Who before we can achieve our God-ordained Do. This transformation takes place by harnessing the power of our "Woo." As a gentle reminder, your Woo is what I refer to as your secret sauce, superpowers, and sizzle—all the special and unique things that make you shine and differentiated from the next leader.

Your impact only comes to fruition when you are ready and available for the new version of yourself needed to achieve your appointed mission. That mission can look like finding another job, getting a promotion, launching a new business, writing a book, building a platform, or scaling up in whatever role you're currently in. The mission is the thing your heart knows it's meant to do, but the why, how, and what aren't fleshed out yet.

If you try to move too fast to hit the milestones required on your mission, you're going to miss out on your true impact or veer off course. And the mission of the to-do that's in front of you may look like the real deal, but it's not—it's a mirage of the real deal.

I'm sorry, ladies, but to get to your ordained purpose and mission, you need to first do the work required on your Who, which is what the first peg of this book, "Know," was all about. You can resist the work, try to navigate around it, be in denial about it, or downright avoid it, but none of those things make it go away. They only postpone the inevitable work that needs to get done before you can move forward in your anointed and appointed purpose.

The Who work impacts not only your career but your life! It's transformative, powerful work that will get you to a whole new level of your destiny. And it doesn't have to take a long time if you're willing to yield, surrender, and commit to doing the work you need to do.

My approach with each client is different because each woman is at a different starting point with a different destination. She is coming to me with her unique brilliance, personality, desires, blocks, etc. How I'm called to unveil her brilliance is going to be different because she is a unique star with a particular shine, which is not like anyone else's.

As a leader, you will need to work on your Who and see your work from a new perspective. In addition to all the reflections from the Know peg, I recommend setting aside time to get more specific to your role and career aspirations, given the greater clarity you have about your strengths and limitations from reading the book thus far. Here are a few reflection questions to get you started. Schedule 30-45 minutes to reflect on these questions:

---

1. What does success in my role look like now?

   _____

   _____

2. How do I see myself as a leader?

   _____

   _____

3. What do I need to start doing more of? What do I need to stop doing?

   _____

   _____

---

4. In what ways am I overly attached to who I've been? How is it preventing me from becoming who I need to be?

_____

_____

5. Who do I need to become to be effective in my role?

_____

_____

6. How am I living my life in my comfort zone?

_____

_____

7. How do I need to show up to gain the respect of my colleagues and teammates?

_____

_____

8. How do I become more purpose-driven versus task-driven as a leader?

_____

_____

9. How can I lean into my relational strengths to command the influence I desire?

_____

_____

10. Where do I need to grow personally?

_____

_____

Reflect deeply on the questions above to see in what ways you can shift and focus on your *being*, where you need to grow, and what support you may need as you evolve into the impactful, purpose-driven woman you're designed to be.

You Can't Rise Without Failing Forward

As leaders, if we are going to embark on a new venture, confront a challenge, learn something new, or do something differently, failure is par for the course. But we cannot let failure get the best of us; we have to let it refine us. And we can't be so scared of failing that we don't face our fears head on.

I believe many women don't seek sought-after leadership positions because we're afraid to fail, we're afraid we don't have what it takes, or we're afraid that we're just not qualified enough. Unfortunately, I have seen and experienced that sometimes the reason women are underrepresented in leadership spaces is due to their own fears and insecurities.

Consider the experiences you said no to because you were afraid. Or the innovative ideas you never shared because you felt they would be rejected. Or the opportunities to fast-track your career that you dismissed because you didn't think you were good enough.

Most of us have been there and done that at some point in our careers. I know I have.

There is a story about a young chess master that I just love. It's the story of a ten-year-old, newly titled (as of 2021) chess master, Tanitoluwa Adewumi. His attitude about winning and losing perfectly encapsulates a growth mindset, which no doubt is at least partially responsible for his amazing achievements in his life despite incredible odds.

Tanitoluwa's family migrated to the US from Nigeria after fleeing religious persecution and were living in a homeless shelter when he began playing chess at seven years old.

Fast-forward three years later and he has become the newest US national chess master and author of a book about his beliefs which may be produced into a Trevor Noah movie.

His mindset sheds light on his amazing triumph in his young life. When asked who he most loved playing, he answered, "I guess Hikaru Nakamura... He's a grandmaster, a very strong one." Even though young Tanitoluwa lost that match, he was not intimidated and saw his failure as an opportunity to learn: "I say to myself that I never lose, that I only learn. Because when you lose, you have to make a mistake to lose that game. So you learn from that mistake, and so you learn [overall]. So losing is the way of winning for yourself."[2]

Out of the mouth of babes, right? As leaders, professionals, executives, and business owners wishing to succeed, we can take a page out of Tanitoluwa's playbook.

I've addressed the issue of a fixed versus a growth mindset in chapter two, but the concept bears repeating. People with a fixed mindset tend to give up quickly in the face of life's obstacles and challenges because they do not believe they have what it takes to overcome. People with the growth mindset, however, believe that any area of their lives can be improved with hard work, application, and learning. As a result, they tend to persevere in the face of challenges, difficulties, and failure.

Tanitoluwa's attitude is the epitome of a growth mindset. It is about being "in the learning zone versus the performance zone," a phrase I co-opted from a peer coach colleague, Chris.

Chris noticed I would fumble in my coaching whenever I was in the hot seat during class, then beat myself up for all the mistakes I made. I can be such an overachiever that even when I'm learning a new skill, as I was as a coach, I still try to perform and do well, leaving little room for mistakes.

But he was right of course. As a student I was there to learn—I needed to be in the learning zone or the growth mindset zone. When I made mistakes as a coach in training, I did not have to feel like a failure. I could instead use those mistakes as a launching pad for improvement. When I allowed myself to do this, as opposed to trying to be the perfect coach student, my growth as a coach took off.

So many women beat themselves up for making mistakes or experiencing what they see as failure. You must know that you are not your last bad result or outcome. No leader is immune to losses, failure, oversight, or missteps. Mistakes are part of the leading game, part of showing up, part of figuring it out.

Regardless of outcomes, what matters is how you learn from failure and use it to improve. Do not let one loss hijack your identity and hold you hostage forever.

Fear of failure shows up in different ways for us. Let's go through some common ones.

1. Fear of Being in Unfamiliar Territory

When we are navigating new terrain, it's not going to feel solid. It's going to feel unfamiliar and unfamiliarity breeds discomfort. The same is true when we are in spaces that are new to us. We may experience trepidation, anxiety, or angst not knowing how things will turn out. We haven't been there and done that before, so it's scary. Understood. But here's the rub: we don't know how it will be and we may fail. We have to accept that reality, even as it makes us extremely uncomfortable. No one wants to fail. But changemakers and trailblazers have to find the courage to take the fearless steps needed to make their impact, even knowing they may risk failure. Courage is not the absence of fear—courage is feeling fear and moving forward anyway.

My friend, you can't let your fear of failure in uncharted territory derail your dreams. Perhaps it is useful to reframe what you imagine as failure in your situation. What if your perceived failure isn't a failure at all but simply an opportunity to learn? This is precisely what I had to embrace as a coach in training. When you're doing something new, especially something that hasn't been done before, you have to find your way. That may mean bumping into obstacles that might *feel* like failures. But they really aren't failures, are they?

There is story after story of leaders and innovators enduring failure after failure before they finally achieved their desired success. Their "fails" were just experiences along the way that gave them the knowledge, data, or information to position them for their inevitable win. Leader, author, and innovator, Arianna Huffington has these wise words for you: "We need to accept that we won't always make the right decisions, that we'll screw up royally sometimes—understanding that failure is not the opposite of success, it's part of success."

Failure doesn't have to be your worst-case scenario. If you can let go of this fear and see it in a new light, then you can move forward with confidence.

2. Believing You Have a Track Record of Failing and Will Fail Again

Sometimes we have a milestone experience in our past that ends up defining who we think we are. But know this: your mistakes are not meant to define you; they're meant to refine you and help you grow and mature.

When I was seventeen years old, I couldn't wait to drive. My father had been patiently taking me out on the major roadways and I felt like I had it under control. Moreover, my sister had passed her driving test a month earlier (she is younger but also an overachiever), and from my perspective, she was not as adept a driver as I was.

I went to my driving test nervous, yes, but confident I would pass. I'll never forget how the instructor intimidated me from the start. He yelled at all of us about to be tested with his three instant fails. I don't remember the first two but the last one was, "and if I tell you to reverse again, DO NOT go in this box," he shouted as he pointed to a square on the ground. In my mind I thought, "Natalie, you know how to reverse, so don't worry about it. Box noted."

I sat in the driver's seat when it was my turn and looked at the scowling tester, my nerves amping up. The first task was reversing, and I started out OK, but my nerves soon got in the way. I kept pressing the brakes creating this stop/go type of effect. It sucked. The instructor sighed impatiently and boomed, "Do it over!" I exhaled and without thinking headed into the exact box which he had just told us ten minutes ago would result in a failed test.

Pulling the handbrake up he stopped me dead in my tracks with the words, "Miss, you've failed." I was speechless. *No, No, No, I can't fail. I can drive. Give me another chance!* I could not verbalize my thoughts. I was in shock. *This is it? It's over? I didn't even really start!*

I meekly got out of the car and walked over to where my boyfriend was waiting for me and started balling. I had failed! I was humiliated! And I could not live that down. That failure defined me and driving for years! I refused to do it; I refused to take the test again, and when challenged on that decision, I was adamantly immoveable—I was not meant to be a driver. That's what I told myself. I'd forgotten how much I wanted the freedom of being able to take my parent's car and go where I pleased. I completely shut down the notion of driving.

It wasn't until decades later that I finally drove. Do you hear what I just said? DECADES later. I let the failure define me, and I projected that failure onto other things I perceived I couldn't do well. Let's just say I wish someone had given me the advice I'm giving you now.

Many of us have things in our past that we wish we could do over. But it's life. Just because you didn't win X number of times in Y number of situations, that doesn't mean you're doomed to fail. That thought, "I'm just going to fail again," is just your fear talking and it's a lie. It's a narrative you've allowed yourself to believe. The truth? We all fail at some things. But failure is not a destiny, it's just a pit stop along the way. Embrace that truth and keep on moving.

3. Telling Yourself If You Don't Try, You Won't Risk Failing

This, in a nutshell, is a cop-out. This thought has more to do with the fear of succeeding than the fear of failure. When Marianne Williamson says in her famous quote, "Our deepest fear is not that we're inadequate. Our deepest fear is that we're powerful beyond measure. It's our light, not our darkness, that most frightens us," she is speaking to this point.

Sometimes we are scared to win! Because with winning comes greater visibility, greater responsibility, and greater expectations, and the imposter in our mind tells us we aren't qualified for any of it. So we don't take the step, we don't do the thing we're scared of, we don't try, or we convince ourselves that we're not good enough—all of which masquerades as fear of failure. But it's really about fear of succeeding.

If this sounds like you, ask yourself what you genuinely want. Do you care more about your comfort and staying in your safe zone, or do you care more about the impact you can make and the lives you can change if you move out of that zone? What are you going to let win? Comfort or impact? You get to choose, and I hope you choose to continue taking the steps that position you for your impact.

Another #realtalk point here is that we will wrestle with discomfort in our lives because there will always be new things to try or do, uncomfortable spaces to be in, or tough issues to confront. And as the purpose-driven woman you are, you have goals to accomplish that can only get done by risking defeat, embarrassment, or vulnerability.

With every mountain you summit, make sure you go all out and celebrate your win because, trust me, before you have a chance to bask in the accomplishment, you'll be faced with yet another mountain to climb, and this time it will be bigger.

You may even come to see that what you thought was the mountain you just climbed was merely a foothill at the bottom of the real mountain ahead. This is because with every challenge we overcome, every goal or milestone we achieve, we open up to a greater capacity to do that much more the next time. There is always more or greater ahead of us.

I'll be the first to admit that failing isn't fun. I still hate it and resist it! But in my own life, I've come to see the gifts of failing. If we open ourselves up to grow and learn from failure, we permit ourselves to be a better version of ourselves because of it.

Here are a few ways you can reframe failure:

- Failure is an opportunity to learn.
- Failure means I risked something and stepped out of the safe and familiar.
- Failure means I'm growing.
- Failure means I'm living fully, holding nothing back.
- Failure means I was courageous enough to try.
- Failure means I'm human.

When was the last time you failed at something? What can you learn from your experience?

For me, the most recent failure I experienced was submitting a book proposal to two publishers and getting rejected. The healthy growth mindset perspective? I have to rethink the angle for my book. The unhealthy fixed mindset perspective? I'm not supposed to write another book. Thank God I'm in a healthier frame of mind than in times past and can act from the wisdom of a growth mindset, otherwise you wouldn't be reading this book in your hands right now!

What new thing can you push yourself to do that triggers your fear of failure?

What has fear held you back from achieving?

What brave step would you take now if you knew people were counting on you to do it?

The time is now to be brave and do the things that make our knees buckle and our hearts flutter. The things that make us feel a heck of a lot of discomfort. Because if not now, when? Simone Biles, the most decorated U.S. women's gymnast ever has these words of encouragement for you, "I'd rather regret the risks that didn't work out than the chances I didn't take at all."

Bust Burnout

Make no mistake. Burnout is real.

You want to contribute, you want to bring your full self to your role, but something is getting in your way. You desperately want to use your strengths and do your part to make an impact. But there's a chasm, and you can't figure out why you can't cross it and achieve your goals. You're being underutilized, and it's not only unfulfilling, it's exhausting too.

I can't tell you how many times women say they want to bring their A-game to their work. But when they're just going through the motions at work, it easily leads to burnout.

In these uncertain, chaotic, and constantly shifting times, if you find yourself feeling unmotivated, blah, unable to focus, frequently tired, or more uptight than usual, it's wise to check in with yourself to see if you're edging into burnout.

There is a term, "languishing," that the American Psychological Association (APA) coined to describe a state of being after they analyzed the results of a study on the COVID-19 pandemic's long-term impact on mental health. Signs of languishing include:

- An overall baseline "meh" mood that isn't happy or sad per se
- Loss of motivation
- A feeling of unsettledness but not quite full-on anxiety
- A feeling of detachment or disconnectedness from life and people
- Fatigue
- Loss of interest in hobbies

If you ask me, those signs sound a lot like low-grade depression, and I'm sure that's the warning flag the APA meant it to be.[3]

Never in my adult life have I witnessed so many collective stressors in our society and world. Sometimes I fear looking at the morning headlines! We're jumping from crisis to crisis as a country, and as an empath, I can feel a heavier weight on all our shoulders.

Many of us are working longer hours but are actually less productive than before the pandemic. Working from home has its perks, but a huge downside is the blurry line of when to "officially" unplug. The tension of navigating all the shifting paradigms is exhausting, isn't it?

One of the upsides of quarantining is that women have had more space to ask themselves, "Is this really what I want to be doing?" In response, some decided to work fewer hours or with a more flexible, work-from-home schedule so they could create more time for family or hobbies.

Whether the result of pandemic stress or the desire to have greater career satisfaction, burnout was the main reason that a study found that three out of four women in senior-level positions thought about downshifting or leaving their careers. If you're feeling burned out, you likely are.

A Deloitte survey found that "senior leaders are struggling under the strain of living and working under pandemic conditions. Rising workloads, longer hours, and the desire to ensure the well-being of staff are all contributing to higher levels of work." All these factors and stressors impact our well-being and mental health. How can we love the skin we're in and partake in self-care when we are flat-out exhausted?[4]

The same study showed that:

- 82% of senior leaders regularly finish work feeling mentally and/or physically exhausted
- 68% of senior leaders reported that the top stressor was an increase in work volume
- 63% of senior leaders said they didn't make time for their well-being

- 59% of senior leaders are unable to relax or pause activity
- 49% of senior leaders have difficulty sleeping
- 43% of senior leaders report increased irritability
- 38% of senior leaders have reduced energy or emotional changes

All of these are indicators of burnout. Maybe you feel these symptoms yourself.

As founder of Girls Who Code Reshma Saujani puts it, "The era of burnout as a badge of honor is over… workaholism is out and wellness is in."[5]

Dr. Laurie Weingart's research discovered that, at one firm, women consultants were working two hundred more hours than their male colleagues. Among the senior women she surveyed, most of that extra time was coming from their personal lives, and "they were working longer hours, and they were putting in a month of extra work above male colleagues." This type of culture is a surefire path to burnout.[6]

McKinsey's "Women in the Workplace" report found that 42 percent of women are "often" or "almost always" feeling burned out. Meanwhile, one in three women said they're considering "downshifting" their careers. And four in ten women say they're ready to update their resume or leave the workforce altogether.[7]

If this is all sounding way too familiar, there are a few questions you can ask yourself to evaluate whether burnout is a root cause of your career frustration from the Mayo Clinic's website:

- "Have you become cynical or critical at work?
- Do you drag yourself to work and have trouble getting started?
- Have you become irritable or impatient with co-workers, customers, or clients?
- Do you lack the energy to be consistently productive?
- Do you find it hard to concentrate?
- Do you lack satisfaction from your achievements?
- Do you feel disillusioned about your job?
- Are you using food, drugs, or alcohol to feel better or to simply not feel?
- Have your sleep habits changed?
- Are you troubled by unexplained headaches, stomach or bowel problems, or other physical complaints?"[8]

If you answer yes to any of these, burnout may be the culprit. If these signs have been occurring for a while, you may want to check in with your doctor or therapist because many of these symptoms are also related to depression. But if you're just flat out tired, there are steps you can take before making a big life decision like quitting your job.

Many of my clients are so purpose-driven that they can be oblivious to the fact that they're grinding at work way more than is healthy. When you start feeling increased tension in your neck and shoulders, have poorer quality sleep, or are just tired and irritable, it can be so easy to dismiss these and keep moving. But that's how burnout starts.

In a webinar Dr. Jacinta M. Jiménez gave to the Institute of Coaching on busting burnout, based on her book *The Burnout Fix*, she talked about the three Rs of Resilience to combat the adverse effects of burnout: Recognize, Respond, and Replenish.[9/10]

First, **recognize** what may be happening. Burnout is insidious and creeps up on us before we realize what's happening. It builds up slowly and invisibly until it starts to impair performance. Only when our functioning is impacted do we begin to pay attention to what is going on. To prevent being taken off guard by burnout, Jiménez recommends we consistently monitor and track our well-being.

She has observed that burnout tends to occur at the intersection of exhaustion (emotional/mental/cognitive), cynicism (low levels of job engagement), and inefficacy (lack of productivity and feelings of incompetence).

When these things occur, it can sound like this:

- "I feel used up at the end of the day."
- "I'm not enthusiastic about my work. I just want to do my job and not be bothered."
- "I don't feel confident that I'm contributing."
- "I'm just not good at my work."

These cues help us recognize when burnout may be at play. Make a habit of checking in with yourself every month to take a pulse on your mental state.

So how do we **respond**?

Jiménez notes that burnout is not just exhaustion from overwork. It's way more complex than that. We are human beings, not computers or machines. We have to give ourselves the grace not to be perfect, grind endlessly, or over-perform. This quote from Michael Gungor makes this point: "Burnout is what happens when you try to avoid being human for too long." Jiménez says, "When you stress you must rest."

Responding is about choosing to act in ways that don't stress us out and make us prone to burnout. It's about self-regulation and the management of our emotions so that we are, more often than not, in a more balanced emotional posture. Responding is about pressing pause and resting so that we can recharge, renew, and release.

Nowadays, the word "resilience" is used a lot as the antidote for burnout. And there's good reason for this. It's in the struggle, the hardships, the storms where resiliency is birthed. Often, we are most enthralled by the beauty of what we see above the ground from a tree—its flowers, leaves, fruit, or buds. But what makes that tree sturdy is the growth below the surface, its roots, and the source of its resilience.

Think of the sequoia tree, one of three species of Redwoods. It is among the world's largest and most enduring trees. It can grow to 300 feet in height, weigh over 2.5 million pounds, and live for 3,000 years.

Though their height and longevity are amazing, the more interesting fact about these trees is their very shallow roots—just six to twelve feet deep. These statuesque trees would not be able to remain standing with such a shallow foundation, but these roots form an intricate structure spreading over as much as an acre of land.

The secret to their strength is that their roots spread far outward from the trunk, intertwining, and sometimes fusing with other Redwoods to create an underground network of powerful connections. This elaborate root system is what enables the tree to survive and thrive, sustaining and grounding its towering height and astonishing weight. A sequoia is built for survival.

These trees amplify the heart of resilience. Resilience is formed and shaped through trial and hardship, fortified and strengthened by a solid foundation and community. I love this anonymous quote which says, "The sturdiest tree is not found in the shelter of the forest but high upon some rocky crag, where its daily battle with the elements shapes it into a thing of beauty."

Resilience is about not giving up, no matter what, because of your commitment to your calling. We will all fail at something. Life will throw us curveballs. We may be forced to contend with a pandemic and its consequences. Tragedy or illness may come upon us or our loved ones. Without the certainty of what the future may look like and how our lives may change, it is important to have that grit to power through.

Resilience is essential for living a life *on* purpose *in* your purpose.

However you feel called to serve your sphere, however you desire to lead, however you envision impacting your people, you are going to need a healthy dose of resilience for your journey.

Resilience, faith, and community go hand in hand as well. The sequoias' hefty, robust root systems help them thrive and stand tall despite their daily battle with the elements. Their roots anchor them and bind them with each other.

We also need our faith to keep us rooted in who God is and who He says we are and know that we are never without His presence. We need to remember that being rooted in the love of God is what gives us His power and strength to endure. God's love is wider, higher, deeper, and longer than *anything* we can fathom.

God created Eve as a companion for Adam because God said, "It is not good for man to be alone" (Gen 2:18). Community can encourage us, spur us on, and inspire us. Those we surround ourselves with can give us perspective we may not get on our own.

Going back to Dr Jimenez's framework, she believes to **replenish** we need to cultivate tiny habits that build resilience over time. Resilience-building rituals can look like:

- Connecting with friends
- Meditating
- Sleeping
- Playing
- Spending time with kids
- Taking long baths
- Living with pets
- Practicing gratitude
- Eating healthily
- Cooking
- Taking twenty-minute naps during the workday
- Journaling
- Listening to energizing music
- Aromatherapy
- Indulging in spa treatments routinely, including massages, facials, mani/pedis, etc.
- Taking walks outdoors (my personal favorite!)[10]

For me, walking is one of those things I intentionally put on my calendar because it is a way for me to refresh, recharge, unwind, process my day, get my exercise in, be outdoors, and listen to music. Yeah, I bundle all types of perks in my walking so that even on days when I'm tired, I'm motivated to do it. See how you can use that hack for yourself too.

There is no cookie-cutter approach here. It all depends on what activities are soul-nourishing and life-giving for you. Schedule these activities into your calendar to pour back into yourself. Yes, as women we tend to want to give, give, give, but at some point, we have to give back to ourselves too.

Consider the type of work that drains you and the type that sustains you. Your energy is one of your greatest assets to manage. Prioritize the work that energizes you. Schedule low risk, low intensity matters for the times when your energy wanes. Save critical work for the times when your energy is at its peak.

Consider the "big rocks first" rule. If you put the big rocks in a jar first, you can then get the little pebbles in, then the sand, and then the liquid. But if you put the pebbles and sand in first, the big rocks won't fit.

Your time is just like that. What are the key priorities that matter to you to achieve your goals? These deserve your utmost attention. But you must make sure you assign them a time and place so they truly get done. If you don't intentionally schedule them in the calendar, they will get squeezed out by the more urgent, time-sensitive tasks (which are typically not the most important ones). The key is to focus on what's important first, not necessarily what's most urgent.

Today, consider what changes you need to make to get back to a place of stability—at least the kind you can control. To start, what does a healthier balance of food, exercise, sleep, play, family, and work look like for you? What steps can you take this week to nourish your body, mind, and spirit?

And when you need to remind yourself of why these things are important to help you become the unstoppable leader you're meant to be, read this quote from Reshma Saujani, a high achiever who has learned the value of rest and replenishment: "There's no way you will have the stamina to take risks if you feel like you're out of gas. It's damn near impossible to muster the courage to say no or to try something scary and new when your energy is depleted, and your brain is fried."[11]

Chapter 11

Build your Wardrobe's Backbone:
Secure Your Success Squad

*"Lots of people want to ride with you in the limo,
but what you want is someone who will take
the bus with you when the limo breaks down."*

~ Oprah Winfrey

W HEN I DID WORK IN a woman's closet back in the day, one of my goals was to get her to understand what aspects of her "wardrobe's backbone" were missing. Identifying these gaps allowed her to see why getting dressed each day was such a challenge (and why she hired me in the first place!).

As I wrote in *Frumpy to Fabulous*, every wardrobe functions optimally when its backbone pieces are intact. These items help a woman pull her look together, express her style, and dress effortlessly with panache. However, without these items, a woman's closet is just a hodgepodge of clothing that had no strategy or intention behind them.

You know what I'm talking about. You have a major meeting coming up, and you must pull together an outfit that showcases your command, confidence, and composure. You want to stand out, feel comfortable, and look professional. You don't want to wear the same old tired suit, but you can't figure out what will work.

Time is ticking, and you've tried on your black slacks with your favorite, emerald-green blouse, but you need a jacket to pull it together, and none of the ones you have work. As you change outfits for the fourth time, the clock's run out. You grab your navy-blue skirt suit in frustration (the one you seem to wear every time you're in this situation) and pair it with a pink shirt. While it will suffice, it's not the look you wanted at all. The outfit screams "boring!" but you've got to roll with it. You make a note to yourself that you must go shopping soon to get some more outfits.

Have you been there?

The fix in this situation is not another shopping trip. The only way to create a closet of clothing you love is to have a true strategy that incorporates:

- Your personal style
- A clear understanding of your figure and how to dress to flatter it
- Knowledge of your power colors
- An understanding of how to pull outfits together
- The right items to fortify your wardrobe's backbone so you *can* pull a myriad of outfits together in a pinch
- Your clear image intention

When I helped women with their closets, we did that work *before* a shopping trip. The work in the closet was eliminating the clothing that didn't work (no longer fitting, no longer appropriate, questionable, etc.). Then we would identify the gaps, the key pieces that were missing that made getting dressed a royal pain in the behind. Once we accomplished that, we could then itemize a list of items needed and shop from that list.

The wardrobe's backbone items are a list of thirteen foundational pieces that help a woman's wardrobe work so that dressing becomes effortless. In my book, I outlined the reasons why each item was essential and how to shop so that the item worked specifically for a woman's body type. This was one of the most practical chapters of the book. Shoot, that chapter could have been its own little book, it's that useful!

So why am I talking about the wardrobe backbone in *this* chapter? Because it demonstrates the heart of what building a Success Squad is all about.

If you're looking to expand your scope of influence, you must build a strong network of champions who trust you and can get behind your ideas and vision. This type of support strengthens a leader's foundation—their backbone.

No leader can lead effectively in isolation. We are a social species. We need each other to survive. We need community. When leaders don't seek out help, feedback, or support, they can never be as impactful as they envision.

Having outside support and objective perspectives from folks who aren't attached to the outcomes of your leadership (other than their care for you as a leader) is the way you grow and mature as a leader. It takes a village, or more specifically a group of supporters who can help you soar to the heights of greatest impact on your people.

Individuals in your Success Squad are those who inspire, challenge, or motivate you in your career and leadership. Their support helps you refuel, develop, stay motivated, and navigate obstacles or setbacks. Your Success Squad can help protect you from your worst instincts, narrow perspectives, or unconscious biases.

These individuals in your Squad are also the ones who cheer you on to make bold, fearless moves. They can remind you of your Why and encourage you when the going gets hard, as it surely will. In your Squad will be those who have walked a similar path but are ahead of you. Because of their vantage point, they can share their experiences and wisdom with you so you can avoid their pitfalls.

Your Squad can open doors of opportunity for you and advocate for you in roles or positions you may have never seen yourself in. In short, your Success Squad helps you make a greater impact than you can make on your own.

When you look at the lives of successful, impactful leaders, you'll see that they had a team supporting them in their success. We all stand on the shoulders of the movers, shakers, and change-makers who've come before us.

One of the shows I routinely watch is *The View*. Whoopi Goldberg is so highly respected by the other women at the table—she's seen as a mentor to them. Whoopi has been part of *The View* for years. But she wouldn't have been there now as the anchor, facilitator, and mentor without the support and encouragement of her mentor and sponsor, Barbara Walters, the visionary behind the show.

In the same way, mentors and sponsors are critical members of our Success Squad.

We All Need Advocates

Over the past two years, we all know and have experienced the pressures of working in a pandemic environment where the very nature of how we work changed before our eyes. Coupled with a polarized political landscape and increasing racial tensions, the focus on DEI work in corporations became the new trend.

This trend is mostly a good thing. However, like any new initiative that requires deep foundational work, much of the work on diversity, equity, and inclusion got thrown onto a corporate checklist. Sure, companies care about the work, but many aren't willing to put *in* the work and have resorted to activities designed to placate people of color and their allies but don't truly move the needle.

In McKinsey & Company's report, they documented the importance of ally-ship among women within this context. They found that women were the ones who bore the brunt of DEI work but weren't getting the credit or recognition for it. The report also found that women leaders were more active allies to women of color. These leaders were "more likely than men to educate themselves about the challenges that women of color face at work, to speak out against discrimination, and to mentor or sponsor women of color."[1]

Allies

Allies matter not just for DEI initiatives but in all our career overall. These are our colleagues and peers who support and encourage one another. Allies listen to our challenges, provide advice, and remind us we're not alone.

Allies are the backbone of your Success Squad. They celebrate your wins with you and they are there when the going gets tough.

Allies can be your colleagues at work or your friends. Or they can be people you meet at networking events, associations, alumni groups, church, or any other organizations where you connect with those who you can both agree to check in with each other regularly. You want your allies to be a diverse group of people, because the more perspectives you can garner for feedback or inform your decisions, the better.

Mentors

Mentors are like our big sisters. They share their experiences, lessons learned, and wisdom to help us navigate our journey. They are our guides. They can help us imagine a vision for ourselves that otherwise might seem unattainable. As one of my WOC clients says, "It's hard to be what we don't see." As a leader and high achiever, you need these outside voices to provide emotional support, advice, feedback, and encouragement so you can evolve in your leadership.

I've had mentors pop in and out of my career journey. What they've had in common is that they encouraged me along my path and provided a space to get feedback and ask questions. More importantly, they modeled what was possible for a woman with my qualifications. They expanded my vision for myself and how far I thought I could go.

While I had a few successful, independent white women mentor me unofficially, what I lacked was female mentors of color. What a difference this would have made for me! It is why I reach out to younger women of color who catch my eye with their potential and provide a space for them to learn from me.

A quote from a Black leader in the McKinsey report summarizes my stance: "In my industry, there's not a lot of women. And most definitely in leadership roles, there are not a lot of women of color. So, I've always been intentional to try to give back and do what I could to inspire and encourage and motivate those who need an advocate."[Ibid]

The wisdom mentors can offer you is undeniable. And their validation and support can make a world of difference in how you navigate your career. When seeking out a mentor, look for someone whose work ethic, success, and values are ones you have or aspire to. While your mentors don't have to look like you, it's helpful to have at least one mentor who shares your ethnicity and gender. And notice I'm using the plural version of the word. You should aim to have more than one mentor to benefit from a variety of perspectives and experiences.

Sponsors

Sponsors go a bit further than mentors because they leverage their network and influence to propel you forward in ways you can't on your own. Sponsors have a seat at the proverbial table and can throw your name in the ring for coveted assignments. They can also spot strengths in you that you aren't aware of and prepare you for future opportunities.

Because of their advocacy, sponsors are crucial in helping you reach your next level of leadership. People often confuse sponsorship with mentoring. But even though a mentor can be a sponsor, sponsors typically go above and beyond the support of a mentor.

A study by Catalyst found that while mentoring is essential for leadership development, it is insufficient for advancing to top levels. The study showed that when women use their influence to help other women forward, the impact of their sponsorship on closing the gender advancement gap is huge.

This is why sponsorship is essential and seeking out sponsors is a significant part of solidifying your Success Squad. According to the report, compared to a mentor, "a sponsor goes far beyond giving general career feedback and advice; a sponsor can propel a protégé to the top of a list or pile of candidates or even eliminate the list itself."[2]

The report also highlighted that because sponsors have privilege and power by recommending employees for special assignments, unique opportunities, or promotions, "they leverage their own power and reputational capital." Sponsors, therefore, have far more at stake than mentors because they're putting their reputation on the line in moving a high achiever forward. When sponsorship works, it gives the sponsee the freedom to take more risk, which increases their likelihood of success because they're protected by the sponsor.

I recently saw a post on LinkedIn that articulated the impact of sponsors versus mentors:

- **Mentors give you perspective. Sponsors give you opportunities.**
- **Mentors talk with you. Sponsors talk about you.**
- **Mentors show you the ropes. Sponsors help you climb them.**
- **Mentors help you skill up. Sponsors help you move up.**

For women and particularly women of color, having sponsors at work promotes well-being, improves job satisfaction, reduces burnout, and decreases the likelihood of resigning.

A few of my coaching clients have shared with me how important sponsors have been in their careers. One client who's been at the same company for decades knows that the company's CEO is her sponsor because she's always been offered new opportunities to reinvent herself in the company. She didn't have to seek those opportunities out—her sponsor presented them to her.

Another client shared how a role was created specifically for her in a government organization because her sponsor, the governor of her state, recognized her talents, contributions, and expertise and wanted to give her the chance to shine in her brilliance. Another client has changed employers and moved to another state because her sponsor invited her to apply for a new position that utilizes the best of her superpowers. And her sponsor continues to support her—she was recently nominated to be part of an elite group of individuals who get to spend a year in a highly competitive, company-funded professional development program.

These examples highlight why a sponsor is arguably the most important person in your Squad. Be open to discovering who that person is for you, whether you're employed in a company or own your own business. We need the influence of those door openers, opportunity providers, champions, and connectors.

For high-achieving women to reach the greatest levels in their careers that command the highest salaries and influence, they need an inner circle of allies and supporters, and they need this most from other women. Sponsorship can be a game-changing career intervention.

Sponsorship in Action

This was true for my client Maria, who worked at a top management consulting firm whose sponsor helped propel her into an entirely new arena. Maria had started in a communications role and expected that to be her career path. Her sponsor, however, recognized her strategic strengths and assigned her to projects where she could build and leverage those skill sets.

Maria, a high achiever and hard worker, thrived with that support because it made her feel seen and validated. On her own, she would not have pursued that path or pushed herself to excel as much as she did. But because she knew her sponsor was championing her success, she couldn't let her down. With her sponsor's advocacy, Maria got promoted each year, positioning her to leave the firm at a higher salary and with a proven record in a field she wouldn't even have known existed for her.

Maria is now a highly sought-out strategic planner with her own boutique consulting firm where she specializes in strategic planning and change management for other companies. And her first major consulting client came from her sponsor too.

This is the beauty of having a sponsor. Because another woman saw Maria's potential and stretched her outside her comfort zone, Maria discovered and refined skills and strengths she then leveraged as a consultant.

Maria's story demonstrates how transformative it is to have the support of a woman in a senior position with the authority and clout to direct your career. When successful, sponsorship can accelerate a woman's career trajectory because it gives her access to resources and networks that would otherwise be unavailable to her.

This reality is why it was disappointing for me to read in McKinsey's 2021 "Woman in the Workplace" report that allyship from colleagues with privilege wasn't backed up with consistent actions like stepping up as mentors or advocates for women of color. This was true even as the proportion of white employees who considered themselves allies of women of color increased from the prior year's report. The report noted, "There is a notable disconnect between the allyship actions that women of color say are most meaningful and the actions white employees prioritize."[3]

My friend Chioma's story about her experience with sponsorship is an example that demonstrates how powerful having a sponsor can be in providing access to key decision makers during the interview process.

Brenda had become Chioma's mentor when Chioma worked for her. Chioma had always operated with a "work hard and deliver" ethic which made her respected and admired by her colleagues, reports, and leaders. Brenda saw Chioma as a top-performer and took her under her wing as a mentee, something she was intentional about doing when she saw potential.

Their relationship blossomed from mentorship to friendship to sponsorship. Brenda was the type of leader that valued relationships, so she got to know Chioma not just from a work perspective but from a personal one as well.

Even after Brenda left the organization four years after they met, she was intentional about staying in touch with Chioma—they became Facebook friends, she sent her cards and gifts on her birthdays, and she made sure they met up for a lunch throughout the year.

This intentionality is what kept Chioma top of mind so that when opportunities arose that aligned with Chioma's expertise and her preferences at different life stages, Brenda could advocate for her. Brenda's advocacy resulted in new positions not just one time but four different times!

Brenda had an incredible network which she willingly tapped into to open doors for those she advocated for. Because of her gravitas as a well-respected leader, her recommendation alone was enough to guarantee Chioma interviews.

My friend is humbled as she reflects on the fact that Brenda was singularly responsible for getting her all four of her subsequent roles since they met. Chioma interviewed for and snagged every new position because it was never just about the role or her expertise—it was about what Brenda believed aligned with Chioma's ethic based on the work environment, commute, salary, leadership role—everything that Chioma needed to thrive and continue to rise up the corporate ladder.

Without her sponsor's advocacy throughout her career, Chioma believes she would have needed to step backward because she wouldn't have had the access to the hiring managers to even present herself in these interviews.

A case in point is the last role she had. She applied for the role on her own but that never garnered her a response. Until, that is, her sponsor dropped her name and qualifications to the hiring team.

The hiring process at many companies will weed out even good candidates to manage the volume of applicants. But Chioma's sponsor knew she had what it took to land the role and got her resume in front of the hiring manager, who, despite the earlier, system-generated rejection, agreed that Chioma's background was perfect for the role!

This speaks SO much to what becomes available to a sponsee from sponsorship and advocacy—access, opportunity, and shared privilege.

Securing a sponsor is arguably one of the most important things you need to do as you advance in your career, to ensure that you continually reach the professional heights you have the capacity to reach.

Securing Sponsorship

I would argue that because of systemic inequality, women of color need sponsors more than any other demographic. When I look back on my career, I didn't have a sponsor. I learned to be a strong advocate for myself throughout my various careers. But what a gift it would have been to have a sponsor. What a blessing it would have been to have an influential individual believe in me so strongly that they used their influence to help me reach a space I could not get on my own, who helped open doors for me when I wasn't even in the room.

Who knows what resources, training, networks, or opportunities I missed because I lacked a sponsor? Who knows where I would be now professionally if I'd had a sponsor? As I reflect on my market research career, I see how at pivotal points a sponsor's help would have been so beneficial. I changed teams, geographic locations, and roles many times throughout my fifteen-year career, and at each transition point, I had to self-advocate to attain a new position.

Near the end of my career in my senior director role, I knew I had been doing the work and bearing the brunt of the burden of the team I led. It dawned on me that I would never be handed the vice president title I deserved and had more than earned. No, I had to fight for that too. My boss, the senior vice president of the team, was a woman, a white woman. She knew my strengths and knew how much I was managing. I was her right-hand person. She also knew how I had advocated for some of the young women in our group, fighting to get their salaries to the level that matched their contributions. But somehow she hadn't advocated for me.

I still remember the conversation that elevated me to the next level. I was frustrated and tired of proving my right to be promoted. We were having one of our weekly phone catch-up sessions, and in the middle of discussing the latest company crises, it occurred to me that I had to strike the iron while hot. She depended on me to make her role easy, and I knew at that moment that she knew she needed me. "You know Sarah, this situation is really frustrating and I'm tired of fighting this battle over and over. If I'm going to stay at the firm, it has to be worth my while. I need to get the benefits that come with being a vice president. If that doesn't happen in the next three months, I'm outta here," I said in a tone that communicated my resolve.

Quiet on the other end told me she'd heard me for real. Sure enough, in three months I was promoted. I'm proud of that achievement, and it was the promotion I needed to position me to resign a year or so later on a high note. But, holy heck, that accolade could have come much earlier without me having to fight for it if Sarah had been my sponsor. But she wasn't.

I didn't know back then that I even needed sponsoring. And even if I did, I'm not sure how successful I would have been in finding a sponsor in a company where people that looked like me were rare in upper management. That is the sad reality for many professional, high-achieving women of color.

This leads me to another truth. Sometimes you can get lucky and get a sponsor by the merit of your work and abilities alone. While this can happen, most of us will need to be intentional and even strategic about securing one. A big part of that process is being vulnerable and transparent enough to ask for their support. You need to show them why you're worth investing in.

Executive career coach and author Kathy Caprino shares that "women are so often 'in the wrong room' in their networking… they stay stuck associating with people at their same level but fail to reach higher and connect with people of influence who can make things happen to us that we can't achieve on our own."[4]

Here are a few tips for securing a sponsor.

1. **Intentionality is key.** Since sponsors ensure you have a greater shot at getting to that next rung on the ladder, developing a strategy to secure a sponsor and getting one is a process. It's not a "one and done" type of thing, so it might take some time. But get cracking at it. As you meet new people and build professional connections, consider who can help support your career goals as a mentor or sponsor. Consider the following questions:

   - Where do I need the most support?
   - Who do I need to build stronger ties with within my company, organization, or sphere?
   - Who has been a supporter that just needs an invitation to be a mentor or sponsor?

- What professional organizations do I need to join to broaden my network?
- Where do I need to improve in building these strategic relationships?

2. **Get on their radar.** If you're looking to get the attention of a potential sponsor, they have to know who you are. Part of being intentional is making yourself visible to them so you're cultivating your relationship. Follow them on LinkedIn. Like and comment on their posts. One of my clients made it a point to schedule monthly check-ins with her CEO so that he was up to date on her contributions. In your conversations, be prepared to ask questions, and make sure you showcase your strengths, expertise, and accomplishments—don't assume because they know you they know everything you bring to the table. At first, this may feel uncomfortable. That's because you're stretching yourself. Embrace the discomfort; it's just a cue that this person is qualified to fulfill the sponsorship role for you.

3. **Seek out someone you already have a relationship with.** This may seem like a no-brainer, but it's worth mentioning. We often take for granted the folks in our network, but this should be the first place you look. Look for folks who naturally motivate or inspire you, those who are many steps ahead of you career-wise. Folks who already have a sense of what you're bringing to the table. The more aware they are about your potential, the greater their chance of supporting and advocating for you. Mutual respect is important.

4. **Look for specific traits in your sponsor.** It's helpful to approach your sponsorship search with clarity about what you need and how a sponsor can help you. It's also important to have a sense of what you're looking for in a sponsor. Here are a few traits to keep in mind:

- Your respect for them is unquestionable.
- You trust them implicitly.
- You know that they want to support you in your career, and even more, are willing to fight for you and your success if needed.
- You're comfortable enough with them that you can make the request (if needed) for them to sponsor you and you can share your highest career aspirations with them.
- You have (or know you can develop) a great rapport with them and have (or can develop) an authentic connection with them.

- They are generous and not self-absorbed with their own career.
- They are intentional about keeping in touch with you so they know how to support you.
- They aren't attached to the outcomes of their advocacy for you as much as they're willing to do what they can to vouch for you.
- Their job/role is secure. This last one is tricky but important. If they're in a role at the same company where they are fighting to keep their own job, they're not able to be reliable or consistent with their advocacy. [5]

Be A Woman Who Champions Other Women

As women, we need to stick together. We need to collaborate, connect, and create together, because together we rise. "When your light shines brighter, others won't be harmed by the glare; they'll be encouraged to become a more luminescent version of themselves... Leaders hold up a light to show you the way... True leaders are just as excited for your success as they are for their own, because they know that when one of us does well, all of us come up. When one succeeds, all of us succeed." These words by Brooke Baldwin resonate deeply with me. [5]

I believe this to the core of my being. As a collective, as women supporting other women, we are an unstoppable, undeniable cadre of trailblazers, game-changers, and disruptors. We have the power, together, to change our society for the benefit of all.

Many of us have an inner fire, drive, call, or purpose we know is meant for us. But often we never see that vision to fruition because we tell ourselves we're not qualified, or we don't have the time or resources, or the dream has passed, or someone better than us can do it, or any number of self-limiting saboteurs.

These are the beliefs that keep us tethered to playing small and dimming our full brilliance. But I challenge you to consider: What if you're meant to be a first? What if the work you do, the thing you create, or the venture you launch is the very accomplishment someone behind you needs to see so they can step into their purpose? What if your purpose is not just for you but for those who come next as well?

It's not news that we live in a patriarchal society and many of the systems and structures in place benefit men more than women. Like the stats in this book reveal, women are still underrepresented in leadership roles in many sectors, spaces, and spheres. The way for us to move forward collectively is by supporting each other, pulling each other up the ladder we are climbing, and being advocates and allies for each other.

Shirley Chisholm, the first Black woman elected to the United States Congress (talk about a first!) said, "If they don't give you a seat at the table, bring a folding chair." One of my clients, a self-proclaimed disrupter, shared with me that she takes this quote a step further—if needed, she tells herself, she'll put her chair on the dang table! Or better yet, as Brooke Baldwin says, we should just build our own table. Baldwin writes, "With a bigger table and a new model for uplifting each other, we don't have to sharpen our elbows and push each other out of the way."[Ibid]

If you believe that every woman is meant to shine in her brilliance by bringing her unique gifts to the fore, also believe that you may be that first—the first to help her see what's possible for her.

One of my clients understands that being one of the few Black female VPs in the global Fortune 500 company she works for matters. She now gets to blaze the trail for the women of color who aspire to be like her. Moreover, she gets to climb a whole new mountain as she envisions herself being the first Black female SVP in the company. When (not if) she achieves this goal, imagine the possibilities she opens for the myriad of WOC not just in her company but those outside it too.

That's the heart and soul of impact.

Let's take a look at a woman who used her pain, passions, and platform to start a movement that liberated legions of women. Tarana Burke founded #MeToo in 2006. The hashtag encouraged victims of sexual assault and harassment to tell their stories without fear of stigmatization. This small feat grew into a movement that became a global phenomenon, creating a wave of women and men coming forth with accounts of sexual assault and naming their abusers.

Almost ten years later, in 2017, the movement peaked, with many high-profile celebrities being publicly accused and finally reaping the consequences of their actions—most notably, former Miramax founder and movie producer Harvey Weinstein, former NBC host Matt Lauer, former New York governor Andrew Cuomo, and more.

I recently had the honor of meeting Tarana Burke at a local book signing of her book *Unbound*. Burke always saw her advocacy as a collective one, with the potential for many voices to affect the change she had always envisioned.

One of my biggest takeaways from the two-hour event was her response to my question about what impact she wanted her memoir to have. She shared, "There is more freedom to access by telling yourself the truth." Until she started drafting the book, she wasn't aware that there were truths she'd been hiding from herself.

When those truths became known to her on a conscious level, she could address them and then heal from them. And with healing comes freedom!

Regarding advocacy, Burke said, "The best thing we can do is tell ourselves the truth," because until we can fully advocate for ourselves, we can't advocate for others.

One of the stories she shared was when she first saw Maya Angelou, her idol, on TV at fourteen years old. Because Maya had shared her story of sexual abuse at a young age in her groundbreaking book *I Know Why the Caged Bird Sings*, Burke assumed Maya *knew* her because they had a shared trauma. Her shock when she saw Maya's joy and presence reciting her poem "Phenomenal Woman" on TV set Burke on a path to discover and claim her own joy. Before that pivotal moment, she had not understood that joy and pain could coexist.

Maya opened up possibilities for Tarana Burke. And Burke has opened up freedom and possibility for millions of women across the world through her advocacy, the #MeToo movement, and now through sharing the truth of her journey in her book, *Unbound*.[6]

Burke had worked behind the scenes for years as an activist, advocating for change for marginalized girls and women who experienced sexual assault before the movement exploded into an international phenomenon. Her website states, "Tarana J. Burke asserts that 'me too.' is more than just a moment in time. As the founder of this vital and growing movement, and as someone who has been organizing within issues facing Black women and girls for more than three decades, Tarana has a commitment and vision that is bigger than any hashtag or viral moment."

Burke never sought the spotlight or demanded the credit for the seeds she'd sown and the work that birthed the movement. In an interview with Brooke Baldwin, Burke shared that when she started #MeToo, she wanted "to not only show the world how widespread and pervasive sexual violence is but also to let other survivors know they are not alone."[7]

By bringing women together and validating the experiences of each other with those two simple words, "me too," Burke paved the way for a new type of empowerment, one she calls "empowerment through empathy." #MeToo became a rallying cry for women who were victims of sexual harassment and a collective amplification of women raising their voices together to stand for themselves in new and powerful ways.

When we authentically tell our truths publicly, we open up a sacred space for others to experience transformation. This is how we curate legacy.

As an immigrant woman living in a country for decades that, in many ways, is still foreign to me, finding and forging community has been vital. I have had to find family outside my family. While this hasn't always been easy, cultivating community is an aspect of my life that has been a constant. When I look back on my life, I can see all the ways God's hand has brought people into my life at specific junctures for that moment, season, or long passage in my life's journey.

I've mostly found these life sojourners among women, for it is women God has used to encourage, support, guide, mentor, cheer, or sometimes carry my burdens with me.

Women empowering women is a mandate I have always believed in strongly, and the only way this happens is in community with each other. In the past few years, I have intentionally joined or formed communities of women because I believe God has shown me through my own needs how much we ALL need each other to thrive.

Burke used her pain and fueled it into a purpose that has set free millions of survivors of sexual abuse. She has changed the way the world thinks and talks "about sexual violence, consent, and body autonomy." She has used her platform to share her belief that "healing is not a destination but a journey."

This is just one example of the transformative impact of a woman empowering other women.

It's important to note that when we form our circles, communities, and collectives, they must include people who make us feel supported, seen, and safe.

In a video snippet Brené Brown shared on Instagram on April 19, 2022, she talked about "candle blower outers," a concept she and her hubby taught their kids around the age when their friendships got "dicey." This made-up phrase caught my attention! Here's what Brown said about "candle blower outers" in a nutshell (paraphrased):

> *You've got this flame, and this is your spirit, your soul, your light. Sometimes it will shine really, really bright. You want to surround yourself with people who, when it's shining really bright, they'll say, "Wow, what a beautiful light!"*
>
> *And you want to be the type of friend that when your friend's light is shining you say, "What a great light!" You want friends who protect your light.*
>
> *We don't want to surround ourselves with "candle blower outers." We want to be around people who have room in their life for our light because our light comes with us.*

We want to be in the company of Flame Igniters! We want to be around those who, because of their advocacy and championing, can help us rise higher *with* them. We want to surround ourselves with people that are FOR us, rooting for us all the way.

Yes, and Amen!

The Beauty of Having a Coach in Your Success Squad

I would be remiss if I didn't talk about the benefits of having a coach, specifically a leadership or career coach, as part of your Success Squad. Hiring a leadership coach is a smart choice as you explore your current goals and ambitions, leverage and mobilize your strengths, gain more self-awareness, and achieve new or higher objectives.

Many of my clients hired me during a career transition because that is my niche. Having the support, accountability, and perspective of a coaching relationship was important for them as they were thrust into a new, more visible position, thinking of leaping into a brand new one, or pivoting into their own business.

The reality is that the larger platform, impact, or influence of leadership can be overwhelming. Leadership involves change, and change can be uncomfortable or downright scary. For many women, the increased visibility of a leadership role often brings with it greater feelings of inadequacy, fear of failure, insecurity, or that pesky imposter, so it's important to have someone at your side who can realign your perspective with the truth when self-doubt occurs.

Having a champion, encourager, and co-visionary in a coach can be just what a new leader needs to adopt a more positive outlook and mindset as she acclimatizes to her new position. Coaching can also help identify and address issues, challenges, and blind spots before they become insurmountable.

When seasoned professionals reach a certain echelon of their career and start to truly recognize the expertise and unique value proposition they bring, exploring new career options is not just prudent but wise. In these instances, coaching can help widen a client's perspective, generate new awareness, hold them accountable to the best version of themselves, and help them articulate what type of role they are vying for in this mature stage of their career. For some, a career change may be forced upon them by a move, which may open new options for them to explore with a coach.

Transition can also look like deciding to leave a corporate career to pursue a long-held dream of entrepreneurship. In this scenario, hiring a business/career coach to help you craft a personal brand, define your target market, refine your offer, and make a seamless transition into entrepreneurship is an excellent investment to ensure you're set up for success.

At its core, coaching is about perspective-shifting, seeing possibilities, expanding awareness, creating a game plan, and taking consistent action toward change once key objectives are identified. The coach facilitates a dialogue grounded in curiosity, non-judgment, and possibility so that the client has space to process, internalize, and execute the agreed-upon actions.

Here are a few specific benefits high-achieving women can expect from career and leadership coaching.

1. **Identify, leverage, and mobilize strengths.** Women, especially high achievers, often downplay or underestimate their strengths because they tend to take them for granted. One of my program manager clients is especially gifted in seeing the flaws or weaknesses in ideas, concepts, or systems. But because this ability came so easily to her, she didn't value this talent or even see it as one of her differentiating strengths. From our work together, she started to see how much this "superpower" (as I like to call giftedness) had buoyed her in her career and been instrumental to her success. Now she can fully own and embrace her strength of "Restorative" (the CliftonStrengths definition of this talent) and use it more effectively and strategically to benefit her team.

2. **Improve your relational skills.** For many leaders, their technical or business expertise is what got them where they are, but as they rise to greater levels of leadership, they need more relational and people skills to be successful. Leadership is about empowering people to execute against a vision, so developing better people skills is critical. This is where a coach's support is beneficial in expanding your awareness and encouraging you to see things from different perspectives.

3. **See yourself more clearly and navigate blind spots.** Gaining honest self-awareness is a significant benefit of partnering with a good leadership coach. Throughout your coaching engagement, your coach will share their perceptions of you and challenge your mindset. Because of the new insights you gain from coaching, your ability to objectively examine yourself will improve. Your coach can also help you discover strengths and talents you may not have known existed, which builds your confidence as you grow in your position as a leader.

4. **Achieve what you want.** At the end of the day, a good leader cares about their impact. A career or leadership coach plays an integral role in clarifying your desired impact, the goals you aspire to achieve, and the actions and changes you need to make to achieve them. Your coach is your ally, a key player in your support system as a leader, your champion. A great coach keeps your vision for yourself as a leader alive, especially in those moments when doubt, insecurity, or fear creep in.

   This is a role I get particular fulfillment from—reminding my clients of their brilliance, their wins and success, what they've overcome, and how they've grown in the time we've worked together. These are the times when big paradigm shifts can occur with a client because they can finally grasp why they took on a leadership role to begin with. This realization redirects their focus to one of success rather than obsessing over what they may have done wrong or where they fall short.

   A client had this to say about her new leadership mandate after coaching with me:

   > "Having (an) understanding of my strengths and innate skills gives me a stronger sense of self and the freedom to stretch and take more risks. I know that I'm more than qualified and am no longer afraid to challenge myself. I used to think I didn't have what it took to command attention or have an impact and that I was better at leading from behind. Now I comprehend the special qualities I bring as a leader—a quiet leader, a more relational leader, a leader that puts people first. I've learned to embrace my gifts, trust my instincts, and leverage my skills to be a great, impactful leader. And I know that I can lead from the front."

5. **Help you feel heard and seen.** The coaching container created by a coach who has a similar lived experience has the power to support a leader to feel validated, understood, and heard—especially when she is a woman of color who needs an outlet to share her specific challenges. It helps leaders to have someone who is not attached to their decisions within their company or organization, who is not in the fire, and who helps them self-reflect, vent, or share their greatest anxieties. A good coach helps you articulate and process thoughts and experiences in a safe space and gives you an objective perspective to see things through a different lens. This can be especially beneficial in a chaotic environment where there is no playbook

to fall back on. Your coach can provide the support to remind you of what is most important, helping you stay focused on your long-term game.

6. **Ignite transformative change!** Coaching helps leaders become aware of and challenge ingrained habits, mindsets, and perspectives, and consider novel approaches. This alone may be worth finding a coach because the transformation that happens when your paradigm fundamentally shifts is life changing. A coach can support leaders in expanding the possibilities available to them and help them see that they can adopt a new posture that's more aligned with who they truly are. This was the case with my client Brenda, who came to me amid an incredibly stressful juncture in her career. She was torn between whether to stay or leave the company where she worked. She felt undervalued and underappreciated yet kept beating herself up because she told herself she just had to work harder. She was super qualified and a sought-after contributor, yet she was not getting the compensation and respect she deserved.

   One of the big mindset shifts we worked on was getting her to value herself enough to see what she wanted and deserved from her job. Only when her mindset shifted about her self-worth and her exceptional capabilities could she imagine a future in a role where she could excel and thrive and be valued for her brilliance. With that mindset shift came the clarity she needed to leave and find a new position.

   Another one of my clients articulated her change from our work together this way:

   > "Natalie encouraged me to think more positively. I'm a natural critic and hard on myself and being able to talk with someone about my fears—and having that person not give me a different perspective but put me on a path to see a better perspective myself—was game-changing. She was always drawing me back to a more balanced perspective. Now when I find myself wanting to berate myself, I hear her voice in my head saying, 'Give yourself grace!'"

7. **Become a more confident, effective leader.** This, in a nutshell, is why you hired a coach in the first place. Confidence comes with a more balanced, objective view of your strengths and special gifts, greater clarity on your "why" in leadership, and assurance that you have a champion along the way. Your growth as a leader is exponentially greater with a coach

because you have a safe space to process your feelings, behaviors, and thoughts; an accountability partner to ensure you take required action; a challenger who will help you see and course correct for your blind spots; and a partner to help you ideate, envision, plan, and strategize so you can be assured your vision for leadership is realized. For a small investment, these outcomes are huge gains. Honestly, there is no downside to hiring a leadership coach when you're prepared to do the work required to grow and change.

Surviving and thriving at work takes a village. Going it alone is no longer going to cut it. Your Success Squad can fill so many of your professional needs for guidance, support, feedback, perspective, a space to vent, championing and encouragement, knowledge, and advocacy. Some of these things you can get informally from podcasts, YouTube videos, conferences, or books. But there is nothing quite like that one-on-one personalized attention from folks who know and care about your success.

Your Success Squad is the backbone of your career success, elevation, and maintenance. Just as your wardrobe is incomplete without key backbone pieces, so is your career without your Success Squad.

Chapter 12

Rule the Runway:
Play Big!

*"Every woman's success should be an inspiration to another.
We're strongest when we cheer each other on."*

~ Serena Williams

WHEN I WAS THIRTEEN years old, I watched TV in awe with my family as Janelle "Penny" Commissiong confidently sashayed across the runway during a national beauty pageant contest. A body-conforming silver, shimmery evening gown hugged her curvy body in all the right places. She had it all and easily snagged the Miss Trinidad and Tobago beauty pageant title that ensured her entry into the international Miss Universe competition that year.

Penny, as she is affectionately known to Trinbagonians, commanded a poise, beauty, and confidence so undeniable that none of the other contestants (as beautiful as they were in their own right) really had a shot. There was something special about Penny from the start that made her stand out. Not just in her radiant beauty but in her nonchalant calm and mature self-control. Months later the country would learn that Penny was crowned Miss Universe in Santo Domingo, Dominican Republic, breaking a twenty-year color barrier. In 1977, Penny became not just the first Caribbean woman but the first Black woman ever to win the competition. This was a big deal!

We watched the pageant a couple of days later when it was locally broadcast, already knowing the result. As an awkward tween struggling to find beauty and acceptance in myself, I saw in Penny a vision of how things could be when a woman blessed with a bountiful mix of beauty, intelligence, self-possession, and charm possessed a light so stunning that her brilliance was unstoppable.

In every segment of the competition, Penny shone so brightly that she easily became a crowd favorite, making it glaringly evident how her improbable win materialized. As they announced the first runner-up, securing her victory, Penny allowed just a moment of surprise before she resumed her dignified stance, smiling radiantly for the cameras in full command of the moment that would forever be etched in international pageant history. I felt so proud of her, as a Trinidadian woman, a Caribbean woman, and a Black woman.

I was not alone. The twelve other Black contestants among the eighty or so that competed in the pageant huddled around her at the end of her ceremonial walk, sobbing with what I believe must have been a mix of joy, pride, and affirmation. Yes, Black women are beautiful; we knew that ourselves. But now the world seemed to have recognized it too.

Because of my statuesque height, slim figure, and pretty face, when I first came to the United States, folks would always ask me whether I was a model. I had done a couple of local shows, but because I was incredibly shy and so uncomfortable in my frame at that time, the modeling gigs never took off.

When I got into the fashion arena as an image consultant, I worked behind the scenes on several local DC metro area fashion shows and enjoyed accessorizing the models and giving them that confidence boost before they got to strut their stuff. A few years later, I had the opportunity to be a model in one of the shows, and I couldn't wait to get my chance to rule the runway.

I got to design my own dress, and I had chosen a knee-high, backless, deep V-neck, gold dress that I couldn't wait to wear. The kicker was that I also had these three-inch pewter-colored heels to pair with it. The runway would be the first time I'd strut anywhere in such high heels. Heels and I were not close friends, so much so that I had to practice walking in those shoes weeks before the event.

The night of the show, with my hair styled in an up-do I was not particularly fond of, with dark-hued, smokey eye shadow that made my eyes tear up, the dress fitting like a glove (but also feeling a bit too skimpy in hindsight), and my killer heels, I felt nervous. To make matters worse, I was picked to kick off the show. All my anxieties and insecurities about being in the spotlight flooded my brain, but before I had time to work it all through, my name was announced and I was on the runway.

To say it was a less-than-stellar moment would be an understatement. I didn't fall flat on my face or anything (thank God!), but I wasn't the confident, bold,

Flaunting It diva I had imagined I would be. The moment came and ended in mere minutes, and I was so disappointed.

Multiple factors contributed to my humdrum experience as a runway model that evening. I didn't feel confident about how I looked with the hair, makeup, and heels. I didn't have a posse of folks cheering for me to boost me up. But mostly, I didn't believe in my innate brilliance that night. I walked too fast. I didn't sashay. I played small. I didn't enjoy it at all. It was a pressure-filled experience that was so fleeting it almost felt like it didn't happen.

When I look back at the photos of the show, I see a model. I see a tall, beautiful, mature woman looking gorgeous in a really pretty dress. But I felt none of those things at the time. And that's so sad.

In hindsight, as much as I had worked for years empowering women to believe in their highest, finest vision of themselves, as much as I talked about Flaunting It in my book, I still had some work to do on my inner mind game.

I devoted many pages in this book to mindset because our mindsets are the foundation of truly Flaunting It. Our mastery of our inner game never ends. It's a continuous, evolving journey with ebbs and flows, like the rest of life.

I hope all the tips, tools, empowerment, and knowledge you've gained thus far underscores the importance of your mindset in how you show up. How we think of ourselves and the narratives we tell ourselves inform how big a trail we can blaze.

Our power, influence, and impact flow from inside of us. We all have inner work to do before we can show up fully empowered, confident, and fearless. This is how we stand solidly in our magnificence.

This chapter is my final rallying cry for you to step up and out to claim your brilliance. You have to Flaunt It to make the impact you're uniquely designed to make. I know I've said it dozens of times already, but I can't say it enough: for your leadership to be transformational, you must be confident in your unique brand of brilliance.

You are blessed with gifting and talents meant not just for yourself but to benefit others as well. You deserve to thrive doing work that plays to your strengths, energizes you, and allows you to bring your brilliance to the world every day, while positively impacting those you lead, mentor, guide, and influence.

Let's finish out this book with some final encouragement for you to play bigger, step out in your trailblazing brilliance, make your mark, and leave a legacy-building impact on your people. This is not a blueprint, because there isn't one. Consider these guiding signposts as you navigate your very own leadership journey.

Play Bigger

Most women grew up thinking that to be a "good" woman meant pleasing others. The unfortunate result of this thinking is that our worth got tied up with others' perception of us. In other words, other people got to determine how worthy we were.

The challenge is that we're often not even aware that we think like this. I have worked with women who stress themselves out, over-achieve, and unconsciously hustle for their worth from bosses, colleagues, and others, only to be let down when the validation doesn't come. Because their identity is so wrapped up in gaining approval from others, their confidence and self-esteem are married to how well they think others think they're doing.

This is a vicious cycle that can become highly toxic depending on the type of people a woman surrounds herself with. So many women struggle with anxiety and depression because they're not feeling seen or valued by others, unable to recognize their worth has to come from within.

Additionally, some women hold onto lies or limiting beliefs that originated from their childhood experiences that they carry into adulthood. Only when they are challenged to examine that long-held belief do they begin to see how it has shaped so much of their behavior. Often, I'll have a client struggling with limiting beliefs state the truths or facts around that limiting belief.

For example, if her lie is "Working hard is the only way I achieve anything," I challenge her to come up with at least seven truths about her qualifications and experiences. How did she do in school? What did she achieve? What has she been successful at? What are her innate strengths? What does she get most com-plimented on? And so on. These answers must be indisputable facts—hard data that cannot be challenged. Then I ask her to compare these truths with the lie (which she thinks is the truth). Often a new awareness emerges slowly but surely. The truth cannot lie. Facts are facts. And that lie she's holding onto, that limiting mindset, cannot stand strong against an arsenal of truths.

Depending on how deeply ingrained the lie is, this can be its own process taking weeks or months to eradicate, often with the help of a therapist. But there are times when just the acknowledgment of truth against the limiting belief is enough for a woman to start shifting her paradigm. And with that shift, so much opens for her.

After undergoing this process, one of my clients was excitedly sharing about all the doors that were magically opening for her. As I listened with awe at the amazing opportunities available to her, I asked her whether these were truly new opportuni-ties or whether she was only now ready to receive them. It gave her pause.

What I helped her see is that, as her mindset started to shift and her confidence grew, as she believed the truth about the strengths and skills she brought to the table, opportunities that were invisible to her before became unveiled. The opportunities had been there all along. She just hadn't been ready to claim them.

When we play bigger in our mind, when we believe in the infinite possibilities all around us, the veil is removed from our eyes, and we see the truth: our openness to the possibilities unveils the opportunities that connect us with our brilliance.

When we claim our gifts and talents and fully believe in our potential, we can stand tall and secure in our value and share our brilliance with the world, making our full impact.

One of my clients was vying for an elite fellowship in her state that would allow her to transition from her successful full-time career to building a consultancy practice. The transition was so scary for her that she almost sabotaged her ability to contend for the fellowship by nearly missing the deadline!

The days before our coaching session, I encouraged her not to get caught up in wanting everything to be perfect. I could see her confidence flailing. She was resorting to playing small, forgetting her vision to use her amazing expertise and skills in the public sector for greater impact. She waited until the final minute to submit her application.

For her to make the cut to garner one of the fellowship grants, she must grow into believing that she is deserving, qualified, and equipped to level up her career game. She must consider the cost of not following this new venture and denying the call of her heart, the cost of staying in the status quo when she knows she's gone as far as she can.

Often as women, we shrink our physical presence in prominent spaces when we feel out of place, inadequate, or insecure. We slouch, keep our heads down, draw in our arms and legs, or slump our shoulders. Or we move to the back of the room, speak softer or not at all. We're diminishing our presence by these behaviors, and when we do that, we're also telling ourselves that we're not enough.

As we talked about in chapter five, physically minimizing our presence communicates a lack of authority, influence, and power. It conveys doubt about our right to be present and take up space, to be seen fully, to be visible enough to be acknowledged.

So often because of the way we were raised as women to "be nice and not rock the boat," or because of our own insecurities and hang-ups, folks never get to experience the full magnificence of our brilliance.

Similarly, too many of us wait to be invited into rooms and spaces where we already have a seat because our playing small mindset can't comprehend that we truly belong.

In her book *Professional Troublemaker*, author and influencer Luvvie Ajayi Jones writes that many of us have "had so much practice shrinking ourselves and trying to make ourselves smaller that when it's time for us to take up space, we don't even know how. Even when we are called, we run. Even when we are celebrated, we tell people it's too much. Even when we're told to speak, we use a whisper."[1]

It's time to free ourselves from our protective defaults and show up as the largest version of ourselves.

Studies show that when a man is considering applying for a job, he'll apply if he feels he's at least 60 percent qualified. He will talk himself up and justify to himself that he'll make up the difference on the job.

Women, on the other hand, tend to overthink these things. These studies show that women typically feel they must be close to 100 percent qualified before they apply. Is this realistic? No. But so many of us act like it is. We need to give ourselves more grace and take a page out of men's playbooks. Sometimes we may need to fake it till we make it. And by fake it, I mean considering ourselves qualified even if we're just 60 percent there, like a man would, so we don't stop ourselves from pursuing opportunities we may be great at if only we gave ourselves a chance.

There could be something else at play too. The reason a lot of women won't become who they want to be is that they're too attached to who they've been. Let that sink in for a moment.

What are you so attached to that you're afraid to let go of? What's preventing you from becoming the highest version of yourself? So many of us live our lives in our comfort zone. We go through the motions and never really end up living our lives to the fullest. Is this what *you* want? I doubt that else you wouldn't have picked up this book.

Do you find yourself admiring other women who are flying, but you don't fly yourself because you're too afraid to jump? What is this fear costing you? Imagine for a moment that your fear wasn't part of the consideration. What would become available to you that wasn't before? And who would you become with this new access to parts of yourself and experiences that were invisible before?

Are you afraid of the backlash you'll get for operating in your brilliance? The naysayers will get louder, but why should you let that derail you? Jones says, "Standing unapologetically in how good you are and how worthy you are will have some people not liking you. Because sometimes we reflect other people's shortcomings. We are a mirror of their failures. And because of that, we will be the target of disdain because people want that confidence and resent it in us."[Ibid]

While this may be true for you, don't let that discourage you. Placating others doesn't get you where you need to be. If your actions are dictated by other peoples' responses, you'll never be able to shine your light.

Sister, you're meant to be more than ordinary. You're meant to be EXTRAOR-DINARY! Instead of focusing on the negative repercussions of basking in your brilliance, think of ALL the good that will come from it—for you, your sphere, your people, and the generations of women behind you.

Trailblazers Unite!

I got the name for my company, The Unveiled Way, about six years ago in what I often refer to as a Holy Spirit download. I finally understood how to brand my secret sauce. I'm the "Brilliance Unveiler"™ for high-achieving women navigating a career transition.

One of my clients recently reminded me that the word "unveiler" doesn't even exist in the dictionary. Every time I write it, I get the red squiggly line indicating a spelling error.

As the Brilliance Unveiler, I bring my superpowers of coaching, exhortation, branding, intuiting, championing, challenge, and deeper healing, all of which facilitate unveiling. That's a lot of stuff to capture and the word "unveiler" does it perfectly. But to get to that clarity, I had to own my brilliance boldly and get very clear on my Woo.

I've always been the outlier, the first, or "the only," which meant that existing structures, procedures, and cookie-cutter approaches never worked for me. Mind you, I never set out to be a disruptor or a rule-breaker, but over time I learned that for things to work for me, it usually meant I needed to color outside the lines a bit… or a lot. Try as I might to fit into norms, templates, and status-quo-ness, I could never quite conform to most norms.

I have now learned to embrace my uniqueness and to accept the way I function and thrive. But along the way, I've also discovered there are others out there like me. The innovators, trailblazers, visionaries, creatives, and change-makers. We march to the beat of our own drum, and we leave folks scratching their heads when we come up with fresh, creative, sometimes seemingly crazy ways of doing what has always been done the same way.

Our superpowers are the things that make us outliers. We bring inventiveness, paradigm-shifting thinking, and rule-changing perspectives to how life is lived, work is done, and systems are utilized. We may not be popular, but folks come to respect us and admire our distinct contributions.

Maybe you've always been told you're too sensitive, too different, too much to handle, or too "out there" with your thinking. Perhaps because of society's pressure and what it says one "should" and "shouldn't" do, you've resigned yourself to playing small and keeping your ideas to yourself to fit in, to belong. But is that truly working for you? Are you feeling truly seen and appreciated for who you are by dimming your lights?

Maybe you got tired of all the criticism because you couldn't fit in or live the way you were "supposed" to as a woman. So you held yourself back, muted yourself, and hid your superpowers to the point where you may have even forgotten what they are and how you feel when you permit your full self to shine.

I get it. We like to be liked. It's nice to go with the grain, not against it. But try as you might, you just can't. It's just not how you're wired. Some people in your past may have been threatened or intimidated by you, so they behaved in hostile ways that made you believe *you* were the problem.

Maybe your brilliance made other people feel "less than," so to compensate, you contorted yourself, shrunk yourself, diminished yourself so you wouldn't offend. Now this may have become your default and you tell yourself that's the way it has to be.

No it's not, sister!

The world needs your brand of brilliance whether it knows it or not. There are people out here yearning for someone just like you to say what's in your heart, to be who you're meant to be, to build and create the products, services, or experiences you have been uniquely shaped to birth.

You are magnificent!

But only when you're able to let go of your need to fit in, only when you break free from the lies that have stumped your growth, will you be able to truly experience the contentment and satisfaction that come from being in alignment with your truth.

I see you, friend. And I know that the road has been bumpy and windy, but you're here, and you're exactly where you need to be. I want to encourage you to honor the long-held desires of your heart.

From one trailblazer to another, I want you to know you're not alone. I want you to understand that you being fully yourself is enough. Your impact in your arena will be unstoppable and undeniable—if only you allow yourself to come out of hiding and shine like the bright star you are.

Often, operating in our brilliance gives us the authority and capacity to be a first, to carve a whole new path, and blaze a whole new trail so we can light the way for other people who need our specific light. When you are "in the zone" of your excellence, it's effortless, distinctive, and powerful.

This is exciting, ladies!! Do you feel the power of the possibilities when you walk in your purpose, operating in your brilliance boldly? Do you *FEEL* it?

However you're called to lead, we need you to step into your brilliance and walk out your purpose. Your people need you to create, inspire, build, innovate, and dream big. When you blaze a new trail, you have the authority and influence to turn around and light the way for those behind you, who found their purpose on your trail.

As a leader, trailblazer, influencer, or game-changer, there is a certain posture that helps you leverage your influence for the most transformative impact. Here are a few things that may differentiate you:

You See Possibility Over Problems

One of the characteristics of impactful leaders is that they see challenges as opportunities. It is the same with you. You're not intimidated or stressed out by problems. You don't throw your hands up in the air and give up in frustration. No, you are excited and motivated to resolve issues and challenges because you view problems as learning opportunities. You trust that you can figure it out, find a way, or source a solution, so you're not discouraged by problems at all. For some of you, resolving issues may be one of your superpowers.

One of my clients saw herself as a compass to help women-owned businesses find their way through crises. She thrived in crazy business situations that would overwhelm others. Her impact came from her ability to be calm in chaotic management situations that would level others to the ground. This enabled her to help her clients get back on their feet, resolve their business issues, get the systems back on track, and position the business to thrive again.

Hillary Clinton is someone who's stayed stoic and strong in the face of tremendous public hardships. She came on the scene as she campaigned for her husband Bill Clinton's 1992 presidential bid, playing a crucial role as one of his chief advisors. With her own thriving law practice in tow, and a career unequaled by any previous presidential candidate's wife, Clinton was severely scrutinized, especially by conservatives. This would be a throughline throughout her decades of public service. As first lady, and during her two runs for the US Presidency in 2008 and 2016, Hillary faced obstacle after obstacle, scandal after scandal, and failure after failure, losing both bids to become the first female President of the United States.

Nevertheless, she persisted, enjoyed a five-year run as secretary of state under President Obama, and used her experiences to inspire other women through her bestselling books, and a 2020 Netflix special *Hillary*, based on her life and legacy.[2] Always a fervent advocate for women, Clinton's posture can be summed up in her own words: "I have always believed that women are not victims. We are agents of change, we are drivers of progress, we are makers of peace—all we need is a fighting chance."

You see possibility, and that opens up your vision to a wider canvas where more is possible. Nelson Mandela famously said, "It's only impossible until it's done," and that is the mantra you live by.

You're a waymaker, sister. You have the presence, platform and privilege to make a way for others and carve a path where there wasn't one before. You bust boundaries, remove roadblocks, obliterate obstacles, and forge a new way ahead, one that is free and open so that ALL who need this path to get to their destination have access to it.

You Speak Truth to Power

You care about your impact, and you're not attached to what others say about you. You care more about who you serve rather than what your detractors say. You are not afraid to speak up and advocate for those who don't have a voice. In fact, you boldly say things that others dare not say because they are afraid of backlash. You care about the truth. You leverage your influence to speak unapologetically to advance the causes and issues you care about.

Amanda Gorman's poem "The Hill We Climb," which she read at President Biden's inauguration, speaks of unity and inclusion, themes near and dear to the young poet laureate's heart. Her work focuses on issues related to feminism and race and her impact comes from these ideals which she strongly advocates and stands for, inspiring young women across the country.

In 2019, Gorman filmed a video for NowThis News in which she shared eight reasons why Americans should "stand against" abortion bans and efforts to limit women's reproductive rights. She spoke boldly and strongly in the video, now circulating again in 2022 because of the tension created by the overturn of Roe v. Wade by the US Supreme Court.

Her words eloquently echo the truths that those who support women's reproductive rights stand for: "When the penalty for rape is less than the penalty for abortion after the rape, you know this isn't about caring for women and girls. It's about controlling them... Through forcing them into motherhood before they're ready, these bans steadily sustain the patriarchy, but also chain families in poverty and maintain economic inequality."[3]

Wielding the power of her voice via her spoken word poetry makes this young woman with visions of becoming a future President of the United States a prime example of the power in all our voices.

Your voice matters and you know it. So you write, speak, and advocate, using your influence and platform to say what needs to be heard. It's the power you wield with your words that empowers you to be a leader for others.

You Bring Your Passion to Your Purpose

It's your passion that fires you up and keeps you resilient. It drives you to see your vision fulfilled. You are focused and determined to see it through. This fire helps you endure and rallies others to your cause. You don't back down or give up. You keep pressing forward even when things look discouraging. You draw on your passion and vision. You "keep hope alive" just like Martin Luther King Jr., who rallied fiercely and persistently in his fight for racial justice, which was his single mission until his untimely death.

Brené Brown taught us why leaning into vulnerability is the fastest path to authentic connection in her viral TEDx talk over a decade ago. Now, after six number-one New York Times bestselling books, two podcasts, and a Netflix special later, she has used her passion as a researcher on the topics shame, empathy, vulnerability, and courage to help us reimagine what leading, loving, and living healthily could be like.

Brown is not afraid to share her humanity and shortcomings as she drops her latest research findings in her down-home, often salty, authentic manner. Her passion for this work has turned her into a sought-after expert in topics that were not part of the narrative before she appeared on the scene. Now the head of her own media empire and a leadership expert who routinely consults with companies like Google and Disney, Brown's latest book, *Atlas of the Heart*, is a map for all of us to connect and communicate more deeply by learning how to articulate what we're feeling.[4]

Brown's passion fueled her purpose. It made her stay the course, even when the going felt hard. As a leader and trailblazer, she understood the importance of her work, and doubled down when others may have quit.

If this resonates, this is you too. You are passionate about your purpose and that passion will fuel you to endure. That passion will also help ignite that spark in those who need *your* leadership influence.

You Believe in Your Impact

You know it just takes one person to start a ripple effect of change, and you've answered your call with a resounding "yes!" You're ready to impact your sphere in transformative ways. You know in your heart that your legacy matters. The way you live your life to benefit others is an inspiration. You're strong, courageous, and unstoppable. You know you can have influence, and that conviction changes the way you lead. You draw people to you with the power of your passion and your fearless approach to getting things done. Your confidence helps people believe in themselves too.

Just look at what producer Shonda Rhimes has accomplished with her production company Shondaland. Her body of work over the past decades is impressive and unprecedented—not just for a Black woman, or a woman, but overall. She has almost single-handedly changed the way storytelling is done in Hollywood so that it's inclusive, entertaining, and provocative enough to communicate narratives around people of color that never get told or seen.

In her Netflix *Bridgerton* series, she reimagines the world of nineteenth century England where racism doesn't seem to exist and gives us a glimpse of what's possible when we remove the things that racism, colorism, and a lack of representation and diversity inhibits, limits, and shuts down. A whole new world opens in this realm of "the ton" where those issues are not even part of the conversation. With *Bridgerton*, Rhimes gives us a cultural reset. A perspective reboot. A mindset reconfiguration. And that changes the whole game.[5]

In discussing the series, Rhimes says, "We're just not interested in erasing anybody from the story, ever. In Shondaland, that is how we do; that's just how we tell stories. While it's important for *Bridgerton*, it's important for every story being told. When you're watching television, you should get to see people who look like you."[6]

In *Time Magazine*'s 2021 feature of the "100 Most Influential People," writer Amma Asante says about Rhimes, "As she marches to the beat of her own drum with the power of her pen and her might as a producer, she continues to challenge and dilute the strength of stereotypes that have confined Black women."[7]

As an impact-minded woman, a woman who brings her fresh perspectives to her arena, you open doors of opportunity for others that had been previously shut. You create windows of possibility that didn't even exist. Your leadership is game changing, inspirational, and necessary.

Rising Up

At the beginning of 2021, I had a vision for women, particularly Black women. I saw this invisible energy of Black women rising as a collective, claiming their leadership, breaking free from systemic shackles, and taking courageous leaps forward.

The headlines bore this vision out. Kamala Harris got elected as the first female Vice President of the United States. Stacy Abrams orchestrated turning Georgia blue in a highly competitive state election. Amanda Gorman was named the youngest poet laureate (and a few more firsts after that!).

Later in 2021, Rosalind Brewer and Thasunda Brown Duckett, both Black women, became the CEOs of Walgreens Boots Alliance and TIAA respectively, currently the only two Black women CEOs of Fortune 500 companies—of which there have only been four EVER! To top that, Ngozi Okonjo-Iweala became the first woman to lead the World Trade Organization, a 164-member group of nations that oversees trade across the world.

And Rihanna, the beloved Barbadian singer, Grammy winner, actress, and fashion icon became a self-made billionaire late last year. Much of her wealth comes from her wildly popular Fenty Beauty cosmetics line. Her Savage by Fenty lingerie also helped her cross that billionaire mark. Forbes estimates she's worth $1.7 billion, making her the wealthiest female musician in the world and second to Oprah as richest entertainer. She's only thirty-four years old!

2022 is bringing the same energy.

In April, another trailblazing Black woman headlined the news. Judge Ketanji Brown-Jackson became the first Black woman to become a Supreme Court Justice in its 232-year history! A woman didn't reach the Supreme Court bench until 1981 with Justice Ruth Bader Ginsburg, and the first woman of color, Sonia Sotomayor, only took her seat in 2009. Moreover, there have only been two Black justices in the Court's history: Thurgood Marshall and Clarence Thomas.

Now Justice Ketanji Brown-Jackson is the third, bringing a new, necessary, and fresh perspective to the court. Her confirmation is an inspiration to Black women and girls everywhere.

In June, Opal Lee, the Grandmother of Juneteenth, was nominated for the 2022 Nobel Peace Prize.

In the September issue of *Vogue*, Serena Williams announced her plans to retire from tennis—a career she's had her entire life, and a career that has made her a legend, a GOAT, a household name, and a global icon. The announcement created its own headlines from other women, who identified with the difficulty of her choice to move on from a career she dominated, to focus on motherhood and her new venture capitalist firm, Serena Ventures. Williams' retirement announcement itself started a new, much needed, more open discourse about women, career, and motherhood—women all over needed to hear someone like *her*—a Black mother, champion, overcomer, and trailblazer say those things so that they too can feel free to pivot if that was their call.

These women and others showed us the power of tenacity, perseverance, courage, faith, and, most importantly, the confidence to pursue their respective dreams. They played big, shattered glass ceilings, and broke ladder rungs to get to the pinnacles of their career, realizing their vision for their unique impact on the world.

I am a champion for all women, but as a Black woman who knows the particular challenges we face, I am especially encouraged when I see Black girl magic shining brightly for all to see.

Black women are rising! Rising even in some of the most challenging years in our lives.

But guess what? When Black women rise, ALL women rise.

The truth is that all women are rising in these uncertain times. We are rising as a collective, lifting each other higher in the process.

I see this with my clients. Women stepping out and owning their brilliance to harness their influence and positively help those they serve.

The time is now. No more waiting for:

- Everything to align perfectly
- Feeling comfortable instead of scared
- More expertise or knowledge
- A specified sum of money saved up
- The "right" time
- Permission from others

You, sister, are meant to rise too, so rise in your arena, in the way you are specially shaped to impact your sphere.

Shine On, Girl!

We live in a society where women need to work twice as hard to get half the respect and less than three-quarters of the same pay as men, so if it feels like hiking uphill in mud just to get to the top of your career mountain because it *is* tough.

But you're resilient, strong, fierce, and brilliant. You've overcome and achieved SO much despite the obstacles and systemic inequities. Don't stop now.

If you've been tracking with me you know I believe with every fiber of my being that we are each designed and shaped to fulfill a unique purpose on this planet that our Creator ordained for us. Our makeup, experiences, culture, upbringing, expertise, strengths, and personality all work together to make us unique, awesome creations with a specific mandate and mission to fulfill.

If you believe and embrace that, you should have the courage to step forward on the path that is yours and yours alone.

Sometimes our vision of ourselves is so small. When we dare to think of ourselves in the most brilliant light, we may see only a tiny glimmer at first, not the full, spectacular glow. It is ultimately fear that holds us back—fear to be seen as amazing as we are, fear of scrutiny, fear that we might not measure up to our true magnificence.

The cynics, pessimists, and critics are both inside and outside us—in our minds and all around us. It can be hard to turn down the volume so you can hear the call of your heart.

But until you own your spotlight, you are depriving the world of your unique magnificence. You can use many excuses to justify why you are not worthy. But you are. I hope this book has shown you that.

If you think your dreams are big and bold now, know that there is room for a bigger, brighter, bolder vision still. Often our vision is too small to fully conceive of what's possible. We must push beyond the confines of our own limited thinking and dare to see that SO much can be ours, there for the claiming.

As leaders, trailblazers, and disruptors, we must walk by faith and not sight. What is not known can look impossible or crazy. But it takes faith and belief in one's vision and God's call upon you to build that new product, launch that "crazy" initiative, or start that business.

As a first, you likely won't have a blueprint or a template. There's no manual or map. But you're shaped and designed to do the thing that hasn't been done before. The thing that may seem crazy to everyone else. You may be the person meant to build that blueprint so those behind you can follow.

You, sister, are created to build and innovate so that others will be able to see what's possible from the trail you blaze. Let Barack Obama's words motivate you: "Change will not come if we wait for some other person or if we wait for some other time. We are the ones we've been waiting for. We are the change that we seek."

Turn down the outside noise and turn up the volume to what your heart and spirit know to be true.

Don't be bound by your logic. Trust your inner wisdom and knowing to guide you on your purposeful path.

Because you, my friend, have your version of the "It factor" and with it your creativity, resourcefulness, savvy, or troubleshooting will have a distinct flair only you can execute. Your creating, building, serving, impacting is YOURS to own, girl!

It's your time.

For all the times you've been silenced, bulldozed, or interrupted, it's your time.

For the times you played small because you were terrified of putting yourself out there, it's your time.

For the times when you felt dismissed and didn't dare speak your truth, it's your time.

For all the times you downplayed your achievements and dimmed your light, it's your time.

For all the times you cared so much about being liked that you didn't stand solidly in your values, it's your time.

It's your time to shine!

I'm starting to get glimpses of God's bigger plan. I see this vision of women rising, and as we rise, we lift each other up. It's about a rising collective of women shaking off the shackles that have kept us small and insignificant, pushing forward courageously and boldly, and impacting the world in unfathomable ways.

As the saying goes, a rising tide lifts all boats. We can't do it alone. But together? Together we're unstoppable.

I feel this deep down. There is energy percolating. It's happening, sister! Now is our "for such a time as this" moment.

I hope after reading this book you're ready to stand tall and strong and be part of the army of female leaders changing the world.

You're made for this moment. Take it from me, you're as ready as you'll ever be.

The time is NOW—it's your time to shine, girl!

Notes

Preface

1. Natalie Jobity, *Frumpy to Fabulous: Flaunting It, Your Ultimate Guide to Effortless Style.* (Maryland, Elan Image Management, LLC, 2010).
2. McKinsey and Company, "Women in the Workplace 2021," report, https://www.mckinsey.com/featured-insights/diversity-and-inclusion/women-in-the-workplace.

Introduction

1. Brené Brown, Dare to Lead: *Brave Work. Tough Conversations. Whole Hearts.* (New York, Random House, 2018).
2. Natalie Jobity, ibid.

Chapter 1

1. Natalie Jobity, ibid.
2. Os Guinness, *The Call: Finding and Fulfilling the Central Purpose of Your Life.* (W Publishing Group, 1998).
3. Natalie Jobity, ibid.
4. Amy McLaren, *Passion to Purpose: A Seven-Step Journey to Shed Self-Doubt, Find Inspiration, and Change Your Life (and the World) for the Better.* (Hay House, Inc, 2021).
5. Kevin Lawrence, *Your Oxygen Mask Workbook.* (Lioncrest Publishing, 2018).
6. Amy Mackelden, Harper's Bazaar, "Duchess Meghan Pays Tribute to 'Justice of Courage' Ruth Bader Ginsburg in a Statement," Sep 19, 2020, https://www.harpersbazaar.com/celebrity/latest/a34083157/meghan-markle-ruth-bader-ginsburg-tribute-statement/.

7. Ernest Hemingway, *For Whom the Bell Tolls.* (Charles Scribner's Sons, 1940).

8. Our Daily Bread, "A Life of Integrity," March 22, 2022.

9. Natalie Jobity, "Clarity for Your Calling Guide," https://www.theunveiledway.com/clarity-for-your-calling-subscribe.

10. "The Three Trees," Bible.org, February 2009, https://bible.org/illustration/story-three-trees.

Chapter 2

1. Katty Kay & Claire Shipman, *The Confidence Code: The Science and Art of Self-Assurance—What Women Should Know.* (New York, Harper Collins, 2014).

2. Brittney Cobb @ABlackFemaleTherapist, Instagram, December 22, 2021.

3. Deborah Smith Pegues, *Lead Like a Woman: Gain Confidence, Navigate Obstacles, Empower Others.* (Oregon, Harvest House Publishers, 2020).

4. Brené Brown, *Atlas of the Heart: Mapping Meaningful Connection and the Language of Human Experience.* (New York, Random House, 2021).

5. Brittney Cobb, Instagram, December 2021.

6. McKinsey and Company, "Women in the Workplace 2021," report, https://www.mckinsey.com/featured-insights/diversity-and-inclusion/women-in-the-workplace.

7. KPMG LLP, KPMG, "Women's Leadership Study: Moving Women Forward into Leadership Roles," 2015, https://www.readkong.com/page/kpmg-women-s-leadership-study-moving-women-forward-into-3880315.

8. Reshma Saujani, *Brave, Not Perfect: Fear Less, Fail More, and Live Bolder.* (New York, Currency, 2019).

9. Brené Brown, *The Gifts of Imperfection, Let Go of Who You Think You're Supposed to Be and Embrace Who You Are.* (Minnesota, Hazelden Publishing, 2010).

10. Carol Dweck, *Mindset: The New Psychology of Success.* (New York, Ballantine Books, 2016).

11. Katrina M. Adams, *Own the Arena: Getting Ahead, Making a Difference, and Succeeding as the Only One.* (New York, Amistad, an imprint of Harper Collins, 2021).

12. David Biello, "Inside the debate about power posing: a Q & A with Amy Cuddy," February 22, 2017, https://ideas.ted.com/inside-the-debate-about-power-posing-a-q-a-with-amy-cuddy/.

13. Nedra Glover Tawwab, *Set Boundaries, Find Peace: A Guide to Reclaiming Yourself.* (TarcherPerigee, an imprint of Penguin Random House, 2021).

Chapter 3

1. *Molly's Game.* (SXT Entertainment, 2017).
2. Matthew 25: 14-30, NLT, the Bible.
3. Natalie Jobity, *Frumpy to Fabulous: Flaunting It, Your Ultimate Guide to Effortless Style.* (Maryland, Elan Image Management, LLC, 2010).
4. Craig Groeschel, *Craig Groeschel Leadership Podcast.* "Q&A with Christine Caine: Leading Through Insecurity," November 18, 2021.
5. Camille Preston, Ph.D. *Psychology Today.* "3 Reasons to Go With Your Gut: A rationale for leading with your head, heart, and body," June 19, 2022, https://www.psychologytoday.com/us/blog/mental-health-in-the-workplace/202206/3-reasons-go-your-gut.
6. Lissa Rankin, M.D., mbgminfulness, "18 Ways To Develop & Strengthen Your Intuition," March 1, 2021, https://www.mindbodygreen.com/articles/how-to-strengthen-your-intuition.
7. Kathy Caprino, *The Most Powerful You: 7 Bravery-Boosting Paths to Career Bliss.* (Harper Collins Leadership, 2020).
8. *Encanto.* (Walt Disney Studios, 2021).

Chapter 4

1. Natalie Jobity, ibid.
2. Carol Dweck, *Mindset: The New Psychology of Success.* (New York, Ballantine Books, 2016).
3. Danielle Page, "How imposter syndrome is holding you back at work," *NBC News Magazine.* Oct. 25, 2017, https://www.nbcnews.com/better/health/how-impostor-syndrome-holding-you-back-work-ncna814231.
4. Valerie Young, *The Secret Thoughts of Successful Women: Why Capable People Suffer from the Impostor Syndrome and How to Thrive in Spite of It.* (New York, Crown Publishing Group, A Division of Random House, 2011).
5. Danielle Page, ibid.
6. Sheryl Nance-Nash, "Why imposter syndrome hits women and women of color harder," BBC, July 27, 2020, https://www.bbc.com/worklife/article/20200724-why-imposter-syndrome-hits-women-and-women-of-colour-harder.
7. Dr. Lisa Orbe-Austin and Dr. Richard Orbe-Austin, *Own Your Greatness: Overcome Impostor Syndrome, Beat Self-Doubt, and Succeed in Life.* (California, Ulysses Press, 2020).

8. "Advancing the Future of Women in Business: A KPMG Women's Leadership Summit Report," KPMG, Oct 7, 2020, https://womensleadership.kpmg.us/summit/kpmg-womens-leadership-report-2020.html.

9. Melody Wilding, "5 Ways to Overcome Imposter Syndrome," *Business Insider*, Feb 19, 2020, https://www.businessinsider.com/5-ways-to-overcome-imposter-syndrome-in-the-workplace-2020-2#early-warning-signs-of-imposter-syndrome-2.

10. Michelle Obama, "'Unity With Purpose.' Amanda Gorman and Michelle Obama Discuss Art, Identity and Optimism," *Time Magazine*, February 4, 2021, https://time.com/5933596/amanda-gorman-michelle-obama-interview/.

11. Lisa Orbe-Austin, Institute of Coaching, "Beyond Imposter Syndrome: Coach Clients to Defeat the Internalized Negative Voice and Live in Their Greatness," https://instituteofcoaching.org/resources/webinar-beyond-imposter-syndrome-coach-clients-defeat-internalized-negative-voice-and-live.

12. Valerie Young, ibid.

13. Brené Brown, *Dare to Lead: Brave Work. Tough Conversations. Whole Hearts.* (New York, Random House, 2018).

14. Michael Bungay Stanier, *The Advice Trap. Be humble, Stay Curious & Change the Way You Lead Forever.* (Toronto Canada, Box of Crayons Press, 2020).

Chapter 5

1. Natalie Jobity, *Frumpy to Fabulous: Flaunting It, Your Ultimate Guide to Effortless Style.* (Maryland, Elan Image Management, LLC, 2010).

2. Jo Saxton, *Ready to Rise: Own Your Voice, Gather Your Community, Step into Your Influence.* (Waterbrook, 2020).

3. (C) Becky Hemsley, "Breathe," (Talking to the Wild, 2021). Becky Hemsley, *Talking to the Wild: The bedtime stories we never knew we needed.* (Wildmark Publishing, 2021).

4. Brooke Baldwin, *Huddle, How Women Unlock Their Collective Power.* (Harper Business, 2021).

5. Jo Miller, *Woman of Influence: 9 Steps to Build Your Brand, Establish Your Legacy, and Thrive.* (McGraw Hill, 2019).

6. Deborah Smith Pegues, *Lead Like a Woman: Gain Confidence, Navigate Obstacles, Empower Others.* (Oregon, Harvest House Publishers, 2020).

7. Priya Fielding-Singh, Devon Magliozzi, and Swethaa Ballakrishnen, "Why Women Stay Out of The Spotlight at Work," *Harvard Business Review*, 2018, https://hbr.org/2018/08/sgc-8-28-why-women-stay-out-of-the-spotlight-at-work.

8. Sally Helgesen and Marshall Goldsmith, *How Women Rise, Break the 12 Habits Holding You Back from Your Next Raise, Promotion, or Job.* (New York, Hachette Books, 2018).

9. Alizah Salario, *Chief*, "Multitasking Is a Lie: Women Aren't Doing More in Less Time, They're Just Doing More," June 29, 2022, https://chief.com/articles/women-multitasking?utm_campaign=2022-06-30-editorial.

10. Jo Miller, ibid.

11. Kathy Caprino, *The Most Powerful You: 7 Bravery-Boosting Paths to Career Bliss.* (Harper Collins Leadership, 2020).

12. Katrina M. Adams, *Own the Arena: Getting Ahead, Making a Difference, and Succeeding as the Only One.* (New York, Amistad, an imprint of Harper Collins, 2021).

13. Reshma Saujani, *Brave, Not Perfect: Fear Less, Fail More, and Live Bolder.* (New York, Currency, 2019).

Chapter 6

1. Sylvia Ann Hewlett, *Executive Presence: The Missing Link Between Merit and Success.* (New York, Harper Collins, 2014).

2. *The Kings Speech*, Paramount Pictures Studios, 2010.

3. Brené Brown, *Daring Greatly: How the Courage to Be Vulnerable Transforms the Way We Live, Love, Parent, and Lead.* (New York, Avery, 2014).

4. Natalie Jobity, *Frumpy to Fabulous: Flaunting It, Your Ultimate Guide to Effortless Style.* (Maryland, Elan Image Management, LLC, 2010).

Chapter 7

1. Chioma Nnadi, *Vogue*, "Oh, Baby! Rihanna's Plus One," April 12, 2022, https://www.vogue.com/article/rihanna-cover-may-2022.

2. Brené Brown, *Atlas of The Heart: Mapping Meaningful Connection and the Language of Human Experience.* (New York, Penguin Random House, 2021).

3. Gallup, *Now, Discover Your Strengths: The revolutionary Gallup program that shows you how to develop your unique talents and strengths.* (Gallup Press, 2020, 20th anniversary edition).

4. Brené Brown, ibid.

5. Institute of Coaching, "Leading with Humanity the Future of Leadership and Coaching," 2021, https://instituteofcoaching.org/ioc-report-leading-with-humanity-the-future-of-leadership-coaching.

6. Shuck B, Alagaraja M, Immekus J, Cumberland D, Honeycutt Elliott M., *Human Resource Development Quarterly.* "Does compassion matter in leadership?" December 2019, http://dx.doi.org/10.1002/hrdq.21369.

7. Brené Brown, ibid.

8. Tracy Brower, *Forbes,* "Empathy Is The Most Important Leadership Skill According To Research," September 19, 2021, https://www.forbes.com/sites/tracybrower/2021/09/19/empathy-is-the-most-important-leadership-skill-according-to-research/.

9. Brené Brown, ibid.

10. Jo Saxton, *Ready to Rise: Own Your Voice, Gather Your Community, Step into Your Influence.* (Waterbrook, 2020).

11. Henry Cloud & John Townsend, *Boundaries: When to Say Yes, How to Say No to Take Control of Your Life.* (Zondervan, 1992).

12. Nina Burrowes, *The Guardian,* "Think authenticity is about being honest and open? Think again." April 11, 2014, https://www.theguardian.com/women-in-leadership/2014/apr/11/real-meaning-authenticity-leadership.

13. Natalia Karelaia, *Insead,* "The Advantages of Being (Seen as) Authentic," July 20, 2020, https://knowledge.insead.edu/leadership-organisations/the-advantages-of-being-seen-as-authentic-14741.

14. Jo Miller, *Woman of Influence: 9 Steps to Build Your Brand, Establish Your Legacy, and Thrive.* (McGraw Hill, 2019).

Chapter 8

1. Sally Helgesen and Marshall Goldsmith, *How Women Rise, Break the 12 Habits Holding You Back from Your Next Raise, Promotion, or Job.* (New York, Hachette Books, 2018).

Chapter 9

1. Brittney Cobb, @ablackfemaletherapist, Instagram, July 13, 2022.

2. Sally Helgesen and Marshall Goldsmith, ibid.

3. Kathy Caprino, *The Most Powerful You: 7 Bravery-Boosting Paths to Career Bliss.* (Harper Collins Leadership, 2020).

4. Lindsey Galloway, *Chief*, "Too Intense, Too Loud, Too Aggressive: How to Navigate the Double Standard of Being 'Too Much,'" July 13, 2022, https://chief.com/articles/double-standard-too-much-as-a-leader?utm_campaign=2022-07-14-editorial.

5. Brené Brown, *The Gifts of Imperfection, Let Go of Who You Think You're Supposed to Be and Embrace Who You Are*. (Minnesota, Hazelden Publishing, 2010).

6. McKinsey Global Institute's Forward Thinking podcast, January 2022, https://www.mckinsey.com/~/media/McKinsey/Email/Intersection/2022/01/27/2022-01-27b.htm.

7. Deepa Purushothaman, Deborah M. Kolb, Hannah Riley Bowles, and Valerie Purdie-Greenaway, *Harvard Business Review*, "Negotiating as a Woman of Color," January 14, 2022, https://hbr.org/2022/01/negotiating-as-a-woman-of-color.

8. Deepa Purushothaman, *Fortune*, "Women of color can no longer buy into the 'inclusion delusion,'" March 28, 2022, https://fortune-com.cdn.ampproject.org/c/s/fortune.com/2022/03/28/women-careers-color-inclusion-delusion-kbj-supreme-court-gender-power-business-corporate-culture-deepa-purushothaman/amp/.

9. Georgene Huang, *Forbes*, "New Research Reveals 1/3 Women Of Color Are Ready To Leave The Workplace By Next Year," April 7, 2021, https://www.forbes.com/sites/georgenehuang/2021/04/07/new-research-reveals-13-women-of-color-are-ready-to-leave-the-workplace-by-next-year.

10. Carla Mathis & Helen Villa Connor, *The Triumph of Individual Style: A Guide to Dressing Your Body, Your Beauty, Your Self*. (Fairchild Pubns, 2002).

Chapter 10

1. Natalie Jobity, *Frumpy to Fabulous: Flaunting It, Your Ultimate Guide to Effortless Style*. (Maryland, Elan Image Management, LLC, 2010).

2. NPR, "Meet America's Newest Chess Master, 10-Year-Old Tanitoluwa Adewumi," May 11, 2021, https://www.npr.org/2021/05/11/995936257/meet-americas-newest-chess-master-10-year-old-tanitoluwa-adewumi.

3. American Psychological Association, "Stress in America™ 2021: Pandemic impedes basic decision-making ability," October 25, 2021, https://www.apa.org/news/press/releases/2021/10/stress-pandemic-decision-making.

4. Deloitte, "Well-Being and Resilience in Senior Leaders," 2021, https://www2.deloitte.com/ca/en/pages/consulting/articles/well-being-and-resilience-of-senior-leaders.html.

5. Reshma Saujani, *Brave, Not Perfect: Fear Less, Fail More, and Live Bolder*. (New York, Currency, 2019).

6. Alizah Salario, *Chief*, "Multitasking Is a Lie: Women Aren't Doing More in Less Time, They're Just Doing More," June 29, 2022, https://chief.com/articles/women-multitasking?utm_campaign=2022-06-30-editorial.

7. Morgan Smith, CNBC, "1 in 3 women are considering leaving the workforce or changing jobs—here's why," September 27, 2021, https://www.cnbc.com/2021/09/27/1-in-3-women-are-considering-leaving-the-workforce-or-changing-jobs.html.

8. Mayo Clinic, "Job burnout: How to spot it and take action," https://www.mayoclinic.org/healthy-lifestyle/adult-health/in-depth/burnout/art-20046642.

9. Dr. Jacinta M. Jiménez, Institute of Coaching, "Buffering Against Burnout," https://instituteofcoaching.org/resources/webinar-buffering-against-burnout.

10. Dr. Jacinta M. Jimenez, *The Burnout Fix: Overcome Overwhelm, Beat Busy, and Sustain Success in the New World of Work*. (McGraw Hill, 2021).

11. Reshma Saujani, *Brave, Not Perfect: Fear Less, Fail More, and Live Bolder*. (New York, Currency, 2019).

Chapter 11

1. McKinsey and Company, "Women in the Workplace 2021," report, https://www.mckinsey.com/featured-insights/diversity-and-inclusion/women-in-the-workplace.

2. Heather Foust-Cummings Sarah Dinolfo Jennifer Kohler, *Catalyst*, "Sponsoring Women to Success," 2011, https://www.catalyst.org/wp-content/uploads/2019/01/sponsoring_women_to_success.pdf.

3. McKinsey and Company, "Women in the Workplace 2021," report, ibid.

4. Kathy Caprino, *The Most Powerful You: 7 Bravery-Boosting Paths to Career Bliss*. (Harper Collins Leadership, 2020).

5. Brooke Baldwin, *Huddle. How women unlock their collective power*. (New York, HarperCollins, 2021).

6. Tarana Burke, *Unbound: My Story of Liberation and the Birth of the Me Too Movement*. (Flatiron Books: An Oprah Book, 2021).

7. Brooke Baldwin, *Huddle. How women unlock their collective power*. (New York, HarperCollins, 2021).

Chapter 12

1. Luvvie Ajayi Jones, *Professional Troublemaker: The Fear-Fighter Manual*. (Penguin Life, 2021).
2. 2020 Netflix special *Hillary*.
3. Amanda Gorman, NOWTHIS NEWS video, 2019.
4. Brené Brown, *Atlas of The Heart: Mapping Meaningful Connection and the Language of Human Experience*. (New York, Penguin Random House, 2021).
5. Bridgerton, Netflix, Shonda Rhimes.
6. Netflix, "Shonda Rhimes Shares How 'Bridgerton' Season 2 Promotes Representation On and Off Screen," March 21, 2022, https://about.netflix.com/en/news/shonda-rhimes-bridgerton-season-2-representation%E2%81%B8.
7. Amma Asante, *Time Magazine*, "100 Most Influential People," 2021, https://time.com/collection/100-most-influential-people-2021/.

Acknowledgments

FIRST, I WANT TO THANK you, dear reader. If you're reading these words, it means you've finished the book and you're committed to living your purpose out loud and letting your light shine for all to see. If this book impacted, ignited, or empowered you to own and leverage your brilliance, please share it in your circles. I can't wait to see how you'll become the trailblazing, game-changing, and change-making leader you're meant to be!

This book would not have taken the shape it did if I hadn't enrolled in Christian Book Academy led by Shelley and CJ Hitz. Your self-paced book learning platform, videos, and virtual writing retreats helped me write and publish my book in invaluable ways. But most important to me was the ideation challenge in one of the first videos, where I literally reworked my table of contents to include my image/style perspectives that I write about in the Author's Note. THAT was God, but your group was the vessel. Thank you.

My special thanks to my friends and family who were as excited about this book coming to fruition as I was. Too many to list out but thank you because your excitement is contagious!

Lisa Moving, your restorative strengths are so awesome! Thank you for talking me off the ledge when I wanted to bail on "you know what" and for all the tweaks you helped me make in the design process that made the book cover perfectly on brand for me.

Dale Morrissey, you know how much I value your visual skills. Thank you for your patience and guidance as I showed you iteration after iteration of my cover mock-ups.

A special thank you to Jo Miller, author of *Woman of Influence* and Sally Helgesen, author of *How Women Rise*. Your books were part of my research, and I quote both several times in my book. It is such an honor that you would agree to read my book and endorse it. I am humbly grateful.

I so appreciate ALL my endorsers—my colleagues, fellow authors, and dear friends who agreed to read my book ahead of publishing: Beatrice, Lisa, Sackeena, Coretta, Nicole, Carmen, Eugina, Patti, Melissa—you ladies are the best!! Thank you for your support, believing in me, and this book!

It takes a village to put a book together. I am grateful to you Carmen Riot Smith for how well you understood the power of my voice and kept it intact and your awesome championing throughout the editing process. Nadene Seiters, your enthusiasm to support this project from the beginning was undeniable, and I'm so glad I could lean on your proofreading strengths. Hitch of booknookbiz, I love your dedication to your book formatting work and your frequent and clear communications about this huge part of the process—you're amazing! Zvonimir, my fellow uber nitpicker—you are the best and I was so lucky that you formatted my book. We made a great team!

To my book cover designer Immaculate Studios—this was challenging at times; let's be real. But what we created in the end is perfect! Thank you for your professionalism and patience with my many tweaks.

My special thanks to Kathy Caprino, career and leadership coach, author, educator, and speaker dedicated to the advancement of women in business for granting me permission to reprint multiple paragraphs from page 23 of her book, *The Most Powerful You: 7 Bravery-Boosting Paths to Career Bliss.* Learn more at https://kathycaprino.com.

And to Talking to the Wild Poetess, Becky Hemsley, for allowing me to reprint the full text of her poem *Breathe,* a phenomenal piece of work that I know resonates with all my readers! Thank you so much, Becky. You can see more of her amazing work on IG @talkingtothewild and in her book of the same name, *Talking to The Wild.*

I couldn't have written this book without my clients who help me see who I am in my brilliance and whose stories help illustrate so many points in this book. I am honored, privileged, and so grateful I get to work with you. It gives me no greater gratification than to see each of you own your amazing brilliance and rule your very own runways!

Finally, my Creator, the one and only Jesus Christ, whose special anointing on my life has given me a heart for sharing my knowledge and wisdom through my writing. How many times did you speak to me in the middle of the night to help guide what I wrote in these pages! Your reshaping of this book before my very eyes humbles me and makes me know that I'm now in alignment with your desires for me. This book is the fruit of my obedience, and I pray, Lord, that it blesses the lives of everyone who reads it.

About the Author

*N*ATALIE JOBITY's experiences as a market researcher, entrepreneur, image consultant, and business consultant have all positioned her to become the Brilliance Unveiler™. In her women's leadership company, The Unveiled Way, she empowers high-achieving purpose-driven women at career crossroads to unveil their distinctive brilliance, see the possibilities in their purpose, and have ripple-making impact in their leadership arena.

Natalie left her successful 15-year career as a market researcher and founded Elan Image Management, her image consulting firm, building a nationally recognized business and brand in a few years. Natalie worked individually with hundreds of women, helping them understand how to dress intentionally and authentically using her "Presence with A Purpose" framework. She also facilitated workshops and led seminars on professional presence and personal branding for women-focused organizations, companies, and ministries and wrote for a variety of national and local publications.

In 2011, Natalie wrote and self-published an image empowerment book, *Frumpy to Fabulous: Flaunting It*, that quickly became a #1 Amazon best-seller in the self-esteem and beauty categories.

In her 15 years empowering women as an image consultant and now as a Leadership & Career Coach and Personal Brand Strategist, Natalie brings an authentic, customized, intuitive approach to help purpose-driven women unveil their brilliance, so it becomes potent, powerful, and purposeful with ripple-making effects for years to come. If you need empowering encouragement, challenging coaching, authentic accountability, or a passionate co-creator, consider her your vitamin B12 shot that propels you forward!

Natalie is a certified coach with the International Coaching Federation (ICF) at the ACC level. She is also a Certified Professional Life Coach (CPLC) by the esteemed Professional Christian Coaching Institute and a certified Strengths Champion Coach (Gallup CliftonStrengths). Her formal education includes an MBA in Marketing from Baruch College, CUNY; a Masters in Finance from Cambridge University; and a magna cum laude B.S. in Accounting & Economics from Rutgers University.

Natalie was born and raised in Trinidad and Tobago and resides in Howard County, Maryland with her cat Trinity. She loves going on long walks outdoors jamming to her favorite tunes, eschewing norms against singing out loud in public.

Contact Information

For media inquiries contact
itsyourtimetoshinegirl@gmail.com

For more information on Natalie's services, visit
www.theunveiledway.com

Connect with the author on Instagram @theunveiledway
#itsyourtimetoshinegirl #theunveiledway
#brillianceunveiler

Subscribe to my email list:
https://www.theunveiledway.com/clarity-for-your-calling-
subscribe

Complete "What is Your Leadership Brand" assessment
at: https://www.theunveiledway.com/what-is-your-
leadership-brand

Thank you for reading!
If you loved this book, please take a moment
to post a review on Amazon.

www.ingramcontent.com/pod-product-compliance
Lightning Source LLC
Chambersburg PA
CBHW062037090426

42740CB00016B/2936